TOWARD UNDERSTANDING THE NIGERIA-BIAFRA WAR AND LINGERING QUESTIONS

An Igbo Perspective

JOSEPH NNODIM

Copyright © 2022 Joseph Nnodim
All rights reserved
First Edition

PAGE PUBLISHING
Conneaut Lake, PA

First originally published by Page Publishing 2022

ISBN 978-1-6624-7660-0 (pbk)
ISBN 978-1-6624-7662-4 (hc)
ISBN 978-1-6624-7661-7 (digital)

Printed in the United States of America

To my father, Maxwell Ogbonna,
and my mother, Joy Onyegecha.

Contents

Preface vii
Acknowledgments xiii
Prologue xv
Part 1: Before the Coups 1
    Chapter 1: Colonial Origins—the South 3
    Chapter 2: Colonial Origins—the North 13
    Chapter 3: Amalgamation 19
    Chapter 4: Constitutional Politics, Political Parties,
                    and Independence 22
Part 2: The Coups 49
    Chapter 5: The Nigerian Army Officer Corps 51
    Chapter 6: January 15, 1966 57
    Chapter 7: Uneasy Interlude 75
    Chapter 8: July 29, 1966 81
Part 3: After the Coups 97
Part 4: Biafra and the Nigeria-Biafra War 113
    Chapter 9: Economic Crisis 117
    Chapter 10: Diplomatic Crisis 123
    Chapter 11: Military Crisis 133
    Chapter 12: The Mid-West Campaign and its Politics 164
    Chapter 13: The Plot to Overthrow the Government
                     of the Republic 179
    Chapter 14: Enugu Falls—the End 194

Part 5: Mass Starvation—Nigeria and the International
 Community 197
Part 6: Assessment 211
 Chapter 15: The Leadership 213
 Chapter 16: The Followership 227
Epilogue..241
Appendix : Biosketches of Principal Characters 255
Bibliography..267
Index..273

PREFACE

Coming of age is a critical stage in the lives of young persons. They are immersed in the precarious waters of adolescence, uncertainly navigating from youngster to youth. It is a very impressionable time at which experiences tend to loom large as well as etch indelibly. For me, it began during the hostilities in Nigeria in the late 1960s, which ended catastrophically for my ethnic group, the Igbo, and scarred the lives of my generation. The Igbo are one of the three largest ethnic nationalities in Nigeria (the other two are Yoruba and Fulani-Hausa), and dating back to colonial times, often toxic rivalries characterized the relationship among them. These rivalries generated crises that waxed and waned over decades before reaching a climax in the brutal civil war of 1967–1970. By every account, at least one million Igbo children perished through starvation. Several hundred thousand lives were lost in the shooting war and the series of pogroms that preceded it. Since most of the fighting took place in Igboland, the physical devastation there was equally epic. Why and how did this happen? How come the Igbo, arguably one of the most resourceful ethnic groups in the world, succumbed to so tragic a fate?

My teenage mind could by no means have wrapped itself adequately around the momentous events as they unfolded. As the years passed and my interest in conflicts around the world, both historical and contemporary, grew, the urge to revisit those events became irresistible. It is my expectation that, viewed now with mature eyes, they will be better appreciated and a fuller understanding gained. That understanding, I believe, is worth sharing.

As I reflected on the road traveled by Nigeria, it struck me with clarity that it was paved with error after error and so could lead to nowhere but a disastrous destination. It also became apparent that derelictions in the exercise of leadership held the answer to why that was the case. I have therefore tried to find and examine the subjective accounts of those at the helm of affairs during that most traumatic era to ascertain what they had to say for themselves.

Some key actors were painfully ahistorical and left no written records, which is a crying shame. According to historian Max Siollun, Gen. Murtala Muhammed, who led the coup d'état of July 29, 1966, and his fellow conspirators vowed they would never discuss in public what they did. For many years, Gen. Chukwuemeka Odumegwu-Ojukwu, the Biafran head of state, would deflect questions with the promise of denouement in a magnum opus that was in the making. It did not materialize before his demise on November 26, 2011. Himself a student of history, I have since wondered whether there is a manuscript somewhere awaiting posthumous publication. Gen. Yakubu Gowon, the Nigerian head of state, to the best of my knowledge, has written nothing. Mercifully, there are other routes to historical reconstruction than the self-reports and recollections of the principal actors.

Many lesser military and political leaders of the era have published their experiences. The story of war, however, is like that of the hunt—it is usually told by the party that prevailed, and they spin it to extol their exploits. Not surprisingly, most of the "winner" first-person accounts are self-serving, chest-thumping, even cringeworthy drivel. Nevertheless, they add value to the discourse when consumed with discernment—reading the lines and then between them—to get closer to useful information. The "losers" are often too preoccupied with picking up the pieces of their lives to bother, but a few have produced outstanding testimonies.

The story of the hunt, when told by the quarry, undoubtedly departs substantially from the version of the hunter. In this narration, I will approach the subject from that perspective—that of the harassed and harried. By a curious twist of fate, the Igbo who had produced a disproportionately large number of the crusaders for Nigerian independence from colonial domination quickly became the favorite whipping boy of the bullies in the country. Time and again, the Fulani-Hausa would fly into mass-murderous rage and

TOWARD UNDERSTANDING THE NIGERIA-BIAFRA WAR AND LINGERING QUESTIONS

slaughter the Igbo living among them with no rational explanation and sometimes to the surprise of some of their leaders. An incident that took place in Kano in May 1953 will be described. I have tried to grapple with this and other similar questions in the context of the Igbo ethos, experience, and errancy.

In the effort to fathom the Igbo, a very salient opening point to make is that in their dense rain-forest environment, they saw no need for large-scale centralized sociopolitical organizations, and such systems did not evolve. Instead, precolonial Igboland comprised autonomous villages (*Ama*) held together by kinship, commercial travel, and shared religious belief systems (Anene 1966; Isichei 1973). This contrasts sharply with other major players in the "Nigerian supranational state" (Ejiogu 2004), who had histories of empire and similar polities. So, in the collective existence of the Igbo, individual and small-group dynamics, for better or for worse, predominated and still do.

Traditional Igbo society is overwhelmingly republican and egalitarian, with important decision-making pursued through a process of direct democracy (Anene 1966; Nzimiro 1972; Afigbo 1973). Very few Igbo groups operate as monarchies, and the evidence is that they were borrowed from their non-Igbo neighbors (Nzimiro 1972; Afigbo 1973). Regardless, there are authority patterns and asymmetric relationships among members in the sociopolitical unit, with superordinate and subordinate actors in the dynamic process of governance (Ejiogu 2004).

The precolonial Igbo were a profoundly religious people, and as has been mentioned above, shared religious beliefs and nationwide oracular systems were one of the bonds that united the nation. Like other institutions of the Igbo, traditional religion was nimble, eclectic, and loosely structured (Thomas 1914). Although there was a priesthood, all adults were qualified to officiate in rituals, and they did. Also, the authority super actors exercised in the sociopolitical space was believed to be derived from ancestors and deities.

The other bequest of Igbo traditional religion is the concept of "*chi*." Ilogu (1974) described "*chi*" as the "divine particle" with which every sentient being is endowed, enabling him/her to share in the Supreme Being and is the basis of his/her immortality and communion with the ancestors. It is the "guardian angel" (Metu 1981) on whose nature and potency the fate and fortunes of the individual hang. Operationally though, it is the individual who must take the initiative, whereupon his/her "*chi*" consents and provides leverage, as captured in the saying "*onye kwe, chi ya ekwe*"—when one affirms, his/her chi reaffirms (Chukwukere 1971; Ejiogu 2004). Sociologically, an Igbo individual's "*chi*" empowers him/her to seek out, embrace, and adapt to change and innovation without prejudice to his/her core Igbo identity. According to Isichei (1969), the Igbo "*chi*" concept explains the legendary proclivity of the Igbo to pick up on external stimuli, evaluate, and respond rapidly to them. We are, however, all too familiar with individuals who, to all intents and purposes, work very hard yet have little to show for their labors. It is believed to be due to dissonance between such individuals and their "*chi.*" It is absolvent for the mortal, as indicated by the saying "*Omemara chi ya ekwe nu ya, onye uta atana ya*" (S/he shall be blameless if failure is due to "*chi*" not getting behind a project). It may well be that such a project might not have been in his/her best interest ultimately, although s/he might not know it.

The above unique distinguishing attributes of precolonial Igbo society and politics (village-scale democratic organization) and traditional religion ("*chi*" doctrine) have fostered a distinctive worldview. Perhaps for this reason, the Igbo failed (and still fail) to appreciate, if not understand, the motive forces which animate the other groups which are differently organized, chief of which is the existential threat these groups often begin to feel in the course of sustained interaction with the Igbo. The story of Nigeria, going back to the preindependence era as we shall see, is replete with manifestations of this dynamic. It is therefore profoundly intriguing that the Igbo, often led by impeccably educated people who had studied history at some of the world's preeminent institutions, were seemingly oblivious of one of its most cogent lessons pertinent to their circumstance, namely that success in transactions at the geopolitical marketplace demands sound counterpart awareness, astute calculation, and shrewd timing because, almost invariably, they have complex ramifi-

TOWARD UNDERSTANDING THE NIGERIA-BIAFRA WAR AND LINGERING QUESTIONS

cations and entail more than ordinarily meets the eye. I argue that in large measure, it was miscalculation and wrong timing that led to the debacle of the Nigeria-Biafra War.

The conflict did end with the mellifluous slogan "No victor, no vanquished," which was coined by the federal government to reassure an apprehensive world that there would be no reprise of the pogroms that triggered the secession of the East. Thank goodness the bloodbath did not resume, but it was indeed a theater of the absurd where saints were canonized—not for the good works they did but for the hideous atrocities they did not continue to commit. The fact of the matter is that there was a "victor" and there was a "vanquished." That fact has consistently informed the realities of the reconstituted country since 1970, and to lose sight of it would be utterly reckless and irresponsible.

Alongside the Igbo in the then East were other ethnic groups—Ibibio, Annang, Efik, Ogoni, Ijaw, Ekoi *et al.*—and their contributions to the fabled Glory of the East and to Nigeria as a whole were legion. Sight must not be lost of them, and they deserve to be celebrated. However, when presented with options, loyalties naturally, perhaps understandably, became divided. The federal government was fully cognizant of this chink in Eastern solidarity and exploited it to the hilt. Nevertheless, these other ethnic groups filled their quota for heroes, for the most part, during the strife. As the reader will find out, the Igbo were not monolithic either. It was layered and complex. All the groups of the then East suffered much tribulation during the conflict, but the Igbo bore the brunt of it. Therefore, it is for the Igbo that it is most especially imperative to understand the historical events of that era as best they can so as to make the best possible sense of their present and enable future generations to avoid the missteps that led to the vulnerabilities and vicissitudes of their forebears.

The present exploration of the Nigeria-Biafra War spans the period beginning from the engagement of Britain with the people in the geographical area that would eventually become Nigeria in the mid-nineteenth century to the collapse of the secession effort by the East. The two military coups that took place in 1966 stand out as watershed events which divide the period of interest into two—before and after.

I decided to end the combat narrative with the fall of Enugu, the Biafran capital. It was never recaptured by Biafran forces. A nation's identity is embodied and symbolized by its capital. In diplomatic circles, the ability of a nation to defend its capital city is considered evidence of its mettle and fitness to exist. The undisputed occupation of a nation's capital by its enemy in war is invariably tantamount to loss of the conflict. It is therefore logical to conclude that the Biafran cause, to all practical intents and purposes, was effectively lost with the fall of Enugu in October 1967.

The shooting war continued for twenty-seven more months, but during that time, the spectacle was behind the lines. Surrounded and territorially squeezed, Biafra was hit very hard in the later months as the deprivative policies of the Federal Government of Nigeria reached fruition. Children died from starvation at a rate never before seen in modern times. The story of the Nigeria-Biafra War is as much a story of armed conflict as it is of the use of starvation as a weapon.

Acknowledgments

The inspiration for this work was the need I felt to put down on paper and weave into a narrative the answers I have been giving to the countless questions of my children—Ijeoma, Kelechi, Ahamefula, and Ebubechukwu—about their ethnic origins and the often brow-raising tales they hear or read about the land of their birth. Their children—Ugochinyere, Oruebubechi, Chimamanda, Oluwamuyiwa, Oluwarotimi and Oluwatobi—are proving to be even more curious, and so I decided I really needed to write things down to help keep my stories consistent. I am ever so grateful to them because the immense joy they have brought to my life came with intellectual challenges.

In the event, what was intended to be an internal memo kept feeding on itself and burgeoned into a major writing project of sorts. Every once in a while, my other children—Kemjika, Olukunle, Crystal, and Nafisa—would demand to know how far along I had gone with the writing and how soon it would be before they'd have something to read. Their thinly disguised prodding was very effective at keeping me on task, and I am very grateful to them for it.

When I thought I was done with the manuscript, I sent it to a brilliant childhood friend, Dr. Noel Ihebuzor, UNICEF consultant and a keen scholar of contemporary Nigerian politics. He told me he liked it then took a "mean" pencil to it and sent me back to my writing desk, at which I struggled with his editorial comments for several months. I have forgiven him because the final product is so much better with his intervention.

I had hoped to be able to spend a working vacation in London so as to use the British Library on Euston Road for primary materials sourcing and fact-checking. Then the COVID-19 pandemic hit, bringing with it travel restrictions. Even if one could travel, workplace exigencies of the medical crisis banished vacation time from the calendar. Into the breach stepped the staff of the University of Michigan Library. Our librarians, even though they were working from home, would respond with amazing alacrity to my unending requests for material, quickly obtaining for me through the interlibrary loan system those not in our ample holdings. I owe them a debt of gratitude.

We live in the age of computers, but I admit with some embarrassment that physical books never lost their appeal to me. When I begin to toil away, they pile up very quickly all around me. My work space is usually a controlled-chaos domain that the ordinary observer may be forgiven for describing as a mess. It is often not confined to my study, and my wife, Ngozi, has had to put up with this for a very long time. Also, as I was agonizing over a title, she scanned the contents page, read a couple of chapters, and told me what it should be. I am grateful for her astuteness, love, and forbearance.

It is difficult, if not impossible, to remember everybody who made a contribution to the realization of this project. Although many will go unnamed, I hereby acknowledge their input and offer them my very sincere thanks.

Prologue

It was a cool late January evening in 1970, with a trace of harmattan haze still in the air. I was sitting in a chair outside our home in Owerri, savoring the cacophony of chirping insects and bird calls. We lived on Wetheral Road, which, at the time, was the edge of town. The other side of the street was farmland and brush. It was idyllic in its own way.

Soon, the background noise was punctuated by shouts of "Hey!" coming from up the street to my right. I looked in that direction but could not quite make out the source in the gathering gloom of dusk, and I resumed contemplating the vegetation in front of me. Successive yells sounded closer, and then, all of a sudden, there was a soldier of the Nigerian Army looming over me. "You no hear say I dey call you?" he hollered and swung the cane, presumably a swagger stick, he was carrying at me. I tilted to one side to evade the strike but not nearly enough. It caught me a glancing blow at the side of the head. I slowly rose to my feet, sizing him up from the boots on his feet to the field service cap on his head. He was at least three inches taller, more muscular, and about two decades older than me. I had been physically assaulted for no just cause as far as I could tell. What to do? Lunge for the stick and try to wrest it from him? Or throw the hardest punch I could muster at his chin? Either move would be foolhardy. What if he was carrying some other weapon, say, a firearm? What if he had friends coming up right behind him? With a swagger stick, he was likely a senior noncommissioned officer and might have company. Would it make sense for me to call for help, and if I did, who would show up? These ruminations flashed through my mind, and I did not fancy my chances if I had a go at him. What I did was stare at him in the eyeballs for what might have been five, maybe ten, seconds then avert my gaze to look over his shoulder in a nonverbal "I don't blame you." I then sat back down in my chair, and a few seconds later, my assailant turned around and strutted back into the street.

When my anger had simmered down, I reflected on the encounter. In the event, the soldier did not tell me why he was trying to get my attention, but my best conjecture was that he had lost his way trying to get back to his barracks, a common occurrence at the time. Unfortunately, he lacked the proper skill to obtain the information he needed. Instead, he opted for a ham-handed approach that woefully failed to impress in the anticipated manner and condemned him to further prolonged pointless perambulation. The occupying force in the town, to which he likely belonged, was billeted at the secondary school actually only about a couple of miles away.

About a fortnight before, the officer administering the Republic of Biafra and head of government Gen. Philip Efiong had ordered a "disengagement of troops," bringing the Nigeria-Biafra War to a close. Biafra had lost the thirty-month struggle. With loss came indignities big and small, I thought.

PART 1

BEFORE THE COUPS

Nigeria is named for the River Niger, the third longest on the African continent (approximately 2,600 miles, behind the Nile [at 4,132 miles, the world's longest] and the Congo [2,900 miles]). It was created on January 01, 1914, by the amalgamation of the Northern and Southern Protectorates hitherto administered separately by Britain. The name was coined by Ms. Flora Shaw, a so-called "expert in colonial affairs," in an article she published in the January 08, 1897, issue of the *Times* of London. She would later become Lady Lugard, wife of the first governor-general of the country.

CHAPTER 1

COLONIAL ORIGINS—THE SOUTH

On the Atlantic coast, Lagos had been plying a flourishing trade in slaves, beginning with Portuguese merchants in 1730. With the transactions still occurring over a decade after abolition, the British consul Mr. John Beecroft ordered a naval expedition to attack the city in November 1851. Its ruler, Oba Kosoko, was deposed, and the following year, a vice-consul, Mr. Louis Fraser, was appointed. On March 05, 1862, Lagos was declared a crown colony, with Mr. William McCoskry as acting governor. Four years later, it was administratively merged with the Sierra Leone for eight years and then with the Gold Coast (present-day Ghana) until January 13, 1886, when it regained its "autonomy" as a separate crown colony.

Eastward were communities that inhabited villages at the estuaries of the distributaries of the River Niger (Itsekiri, Ijo [anglicized as *Ijaw*], Ibeno) and the Cross River (Efik). They, too, participated in the transatlantic slave trade for as long as it lasted. As Britain became more secure in its transition from an agrarian and manual production economy to one dominated by machine manufacturing, it abolished the slave trade (Slave Trade Act of 1807) and later freed the 800,000 slaves owned by its 46,000 slave-holding citizens (Slavery Abolition Act of 1833). It is worth mentioning though that these "worthy but now-deprived citizens," among them Sir John Gladstone, whose son, William, would become prime minister (1868–1894), were handsomely compensated for their loss of "property" to the tune of 40 percent of total British government expenditure for 1834 (twenty million pounds, estimated at sixteen to seventeen billion in 2016 pounds). Sir John alone received 106,769 pounds (approximately eighty million 2016 pounds) for his 2,508 slaves on nine plantations in the West Indies. The "freed" slaves were also required to perform forty-five hours per week of uncompensated service for their former owners for four years.

At any rate, forest products, especially palm oil, replaced slaves as the prime commodity. Not only was it a raw material for soap and margarine, it was also processed into lubricant for the machines that powered the industrial revolution. The oil palm grew in the hinterland inhabited by the Igbo and Ibibi (anglicized as *Ibibio*). The coastal traders traveled there, purchased the palm oil, and brought it to the coast where British and other European mercantile interests had set up trading outposts. Sadly, the oil was often exchanged unfairly for worthless items such as "old soldiers' jackets and cocked hats" (Dike 1956) since there was no agreed currency or purloined outright without compensation. Still, the Europeans were vexed that they had to deal with the coastal natives at all.

By the mid-nineteenth century, British sailors and their mercantile sponsors had begun to explore the lower stretches of River Niger north of the delta. In July 1857, an expedition cosponsored by Mr. MacGregor Laird of the Scottish Birkenhead shipbuilding family and the British government, comprising traders and agents of the Church Missionary Society (CMS), set up a trading post and missionary station at Onitsha. This afforded the traders the greater proximity to the vast wealth of the hinterland they had only dreamed about when they operated from their coastal establishments. For the missionaries, the opportunity to evangelize and promote Christian civilization was greatly enhanced. This convergence of commercial and religious intentions, pursued under the protective umbrella of the British government, was to be the dominant theme of the colonial experience.

At Onitsha, the indigenous merchants settled into an apparently stable and profitable "middleman" position, buying palm produce, shea, and ivory from the interior and then selling them to

TOWARD UNDERSTANDING THE NIGERIA-BIAFRA WAR AND LINGERING QUESTIONS

British traders, who, in return, sold to them such products as textiles, spirits, cowries, and firearms. This relationship however was not to last. When in the 1870s commodity prices slumped in Europe, the British traders drastically slashed the prices they were willing to pay. Their indigenous partners took umbrage and retaliated with disruptive practices, the most notable of which was the embargo, which shut down trade from December 1877 to March 1878. The agent-general of one of the trading companies called for "something to be done" to the people of Onitsha, and in October 1879, the acting consul, Mr. S. F. Easton, obliged. With the HMS *Pioneer* firing from the river and marauding troops loose on land, they laid waste to the town.

The British were by no means the only Europeans scrambling for territory in Africa. Other key players were France, Belgium, Portugal, Spain, and the Netherlands. These countries were bitter rivals, with shifting alliances and a long checkered history punctuated by wars. Inevitably, they squabbled as they grabbed territory—the British and French in West Africa, the British and Ottomans in Egypt, the French and Belgians in Central Africa. Imperial Germany was a latecomer to the scene, but with characteristic Prussian penchant for regimentation, Kanzler Otto von Bismarck proposed and then convened the Berlin Conference of November 15, 1884–February 26, 1885, in the hope that the acquisition of territory in Africa would be conducted in an orderly manner. It was attended by the thirteen European imperial powers of the day and the United States of America. They carved up the continent into "spheres of influence," which they shared among themselves and established protocols for their occupation. No Africans, not even representatives of those with whom the Europeans had signed trade "treaties," were invited to attend.

At Berlin, the British government secured for itself controlling influence over the Niger and Benue Rivers as well as the hinterland to their south and north. It was, however, not particularly interested in the trading activities in the lower Niger because at that stage, they amounted to relatively little in the overall context of the imperial economy. According to Robinson et al. (1981), 1.3 million pounds in exports and 1.5 million pounds in imports from all of tropical Africa during 1880–1884 was approximately 4 percent of the trade with

India alone during the same period. Whitehall therefore considered it sufficient to merely ensure that the territory was open to all British traders, only weighing in when brute force was needed to suppress local dissent. From experience, however, Mr. George Goldie-Taubman (later Sir George Goldie, after knighthood in 1887) thought differently. He had been one of the advisors to the British delegation to Berlin (the others were John Holt and Alfred Jones). He arrived in the Niger Delta in 1877 at the head of a trading firm, the Central African Trading (CAT) company. There were several other companies, some British and some French, also doing business along the coast, and he came to the conclusion that the competition among them was counterproductive. The other inefficiency he identified was the reliance of European traders on indigenous middlemen. He dealt with the competition among British firms by having CAT buy up interests in its competitors. His strategy was so successful that by 1879, CAT had controlling shares in all the major British companies, and he proceeded to consolidate them into the United African Company (UAC). The competition between British and French companies, however, was a different kind of problem. To bolster his bargaining position, he needed more proverbial muscle—more capital and/or more involvement, direct or indirect, by Whitehall. Only the first option was open to Mr. Goldie-Taubman since the British government would remain largely uninterested until July 14, 1884, when Imperial Germany declared a protectorate over the Cameroons. On July 08, 1882, Mr. Goldie-Taubman incorporated a new company, the National African Company (NAC) Limited, which purchased the assets of the UAC with an increase in nominal capital to one million pounds. He then challenged the French companies to a trade war by hiking up the prices of produce by as much as 25 percent. Toward the end of 1884, the French firms succumbed and agreed to sell their interests on the Niger and Benue. The NAC had prevailed and become the regional mercantile hegemon. There remained the matter of the middlemen, though.

Clearly, Mr. Goldie-Taubman was no disciple of free trade. He sent NAC agents to all the major communities in the lower Niger to "negotiate" lopsided treaties in which the local people were documented as having ceded "the whole of [their] territory to the

National African Company (Limited), and their administrators, for ever." Along with the territory came, not only access to trade but also control of its dynamics. Not surprisingly, they proceeded to craft administrative structures and instruments designed to maximize their profits, including bypassing the indigenous traders as much as they could. By the end of 1884, thirty-seven communities south of Asaba had been coerced into such agreements.

These machinations and chicanery did not go unchallenged. In 1876, the Nembe people of the delta petitioned the British Foreign Office regarding the encroachments on their middleman roles, stating "what we want is, that the markets we have made between the river and Onitsha should be left to ourselves." The following year, the British consul Mr. Henry C. Tait rammed a treaty down the throats of Obi Anazonwu of Onitsha and his chiefs, requiring them to cede land in perpetuity to British traders and the CMS. The Obi and his chiefs made it clear they would not abide by its terms. A couple of years later, the acting consul ordered the HMS *Pioneer* to sail up the Niger to Onitsha "to investigate the outrages against British traders." The people of Patani attacked the NAC stations at Ase and Asaba in 1882, and predictably, the British consul Edward H. Hewitt inflicted a punitive expedition on them.

When agents of the NAC came up against a local trade titan they could not easily bypass, as was the case with Jubo Jubogha, better known as King Jaja of Opobo, they offered a monopsonistic arrangement. Jubo Jubogha, born Mbanaso Ozurumba in Umuduru, Amaigbo, was a freed Igbo slave who had risen to headship of the Anna Pepple Trading House. The language of the typical treaty the NAC was offering ran thus:

> We bind ourselves not to have any intercourse with any strangers or foreigners except through the said National African Company (Limited), and we give the said National African Company (Limited) full power to exclude all other strangers or foreigners from their territory at their discretion. (Riaz 2019)

Clearly no incentive there for the Anna Pepple Trading House to transact exclusively with the NAC.

In 1869, conflict erupted among the trading houses in Bonny over kingship. Jaja and his followers opted to leave, migrating to a new location about twenty-five miles to the east, where they set up the Opobo city-state with him as sovereign. King Jaja was an astute merchant with a vast trading network of his own, and soon, Opobo eclipsed Bonny in economic and political importance. He and his agents had effective control over the source market in the hinterland. In addition, he was able to reach agreements with MacGregor Laird's shipping line to export palm produce directly to Liverpool in their vessels. That he could outmaneuver the NAC and independent European traders in the marketplace, finding ways around them when they couldn't around him riled them no end. Soon, there was tussling, and in 1884, the king negotiated a treaty with the British consul Mr. Edward Hewitt, placing the Opobo city-state under the protection of the British government. As was consistent with protectorate treaties at the time, it did include a clause recognizing the king's privileges over the hinterland oil palm produce trade.

Pursuant to the Berlin Agreement of February 26, 1885, the British Foreign Office declared a protectorate over the Oil Rivers territories on June 05, 1885. The Oil Rivers Protectorate extended from the Niger Delta eastward to Calabar, which thereafter replaced Fernando Po as the seat of the British consulate general. King Jaja sought clarification from the British vice consul Mr. Henry Johnston and received a written assurance that

> the Queen (Victoria [sic]) does not want to take your country or your markets, but at the same time she is anxious that no other nations should take them. She undertakes to extend her gracious power and protection, which will leave your country still under your government: she has no wish to disturb your rule. (Crowder 1962)

TOWARD UNDERSTANDING THE NIGERIA-BIAFRA WAR AND LINGERING QUESTIONS

A pragmatist, King Jaja had his men set up a blockade of the Opobo River estuary to prevent any incursion. His relationship with the British would not recover thereafter.

In March 1886, the British Foreign Office granted administrative rights over the new protectorate to the NAC "under powers vested in them by the native Chiefs and under the supervision and control of Her Majesty's Government." The petition of the NAC for a royal charter was finally ratified on July 12, 1886, and the following month, it changed its name to the Royal Niger Company (RNC), with George Goldie at its helm. Although a private enterprise, a royal charter conferred on the RNC the status of a quasi-sovereign "company-state" vested with "all rights, interests, authorities and powers for the purposes of government, preservation of public order, protection of the said territories or otherwise of what nature or kind soever." It did not establish its own constabulary until 1888, but there was such convergence of interests that the services of the forces of Her Majesty's government were always freely available to the company in dealing with local recalcitrance.

Understandably, the legal situation became confusing, resulting in disruptive disputes over the terms of trade. King Jaja addressed a letter dated August 12, 1887, to the British prime minister Robert Gascoyne-Cecil (Third Marquis of Salisbury) seeking further clarification regarding the status of his protectorate treaty with the British Crown. As reproduced by Mulligan (2009), it read in part that "he (Consul Johnston) made me understand that the Protectorate treaty is nullifed, and as such I do not know upon what treaty, then, is he acting; his law here is, 'Do what I say, or I hand matter to the senior naval officer, that you and your country be dealt with.'" He followed up by dispatching a deputation comprising Mr. Cookey Gam, Mr. Shoe Peterside, Mr. Albert Jaja, and Mr. Sunday Jaja to London to convey his concerns to the undersecretary of State Sir James Ferguson on September 13, 1887.

On a personal level, Vice-Consul Johnston, who had been on station for only two months, had it in for the king. In official dispatches, he had described him at various times as "a grasping, unscrupulous, overbearing mushroom king," "a swaggering bully," "a grasping, ruthless, overbearing ex-slave." In mid-September 1887, reportedly without consultation with the British government, Consul Johnston decided to topple and deport him. He sailed to Opobo on the HMS *Goshawk* and invited King Jaja to a meeting at the Harrison Factory on the waterfront. Rightly fearing for his safety, the king demanded that the vice-consul hand over a white man to his people for the duration of his absence meeting with him. The vice-consul opted instead to provide a written guarantee of safe conduct on September 18, 1887, which the king accepted. However, when he and his party arrived at the venue, the guns of the *Goshawk* were trained on them, and the vice-consul proceeded to read him an ultimatum to either surrender and be taken to Accra in the Gold Coast for trial or refuse to do so and "be warred upon." The vice-consul, officer of the British Crown, had lied. In effect, he had entrapped and kidnapped the King. As pointed out by Geary (1965), safe conduct is not to be converted into a snare under military and international law; the safety of the bearer is guaranteed. King Jaja was taken aboard the *Goshawk* to Bonny where he was transhipped for Accra. On September 21, 1887, the vice-consul cabled London to report that "Ja surrendered. Am now taking him on mail steamer to Accra. Opobo quiet, no fighting. Peaceful settlement. Trade reopened." The Foreign Office replied, demanding that he "report by telegraph precise circumstances under which you thought arrest necessary." Vice-Consul Henry Johnston lied again, writing on September 23, 1887, that "Ja preparing escape, strong place interior, where he built houses and stored supplies; able there throttle all Bonny and Opobo trade and European building at markets unsafe." On November 29, 1887, they put King Jaja on trial in Accra, with characteristic colonial hypocrisy and lack of a sense of irony, for obstructing free trade. Admiral Sir Walter Hunt-Grubbe found him guilty on December 01, 1887, and sentenced him to exile to St. Vincent in the West Indies. He died at Santa Cruz, Tenerife, on July 08, 1891.

In 1892, British forces moved against the Ijebu Kingdom, and within one year, it and the rest of Yorubaland, already enfeebled by nearly two decades of internecine strife, were subdued. Treaties of Protection were signed with the Alafin of Oyo on February 03, 1893, and the Olubadan of Ibadan on August 15, 1893. The Oil Rivers Protectorate was extended westwards in 1893 to include the hinterland north of the Lagos Crown Colony and renamed the Niger Coast Protectorate. In 1896, a contingent of the Protectorate Force led by Consul General James R. Phillips forayed into Benin City with the intention of provoking conflict hence an excuse to depose the Oba and annex his kingdom. The force was soundly defeated, with only two of its number escaping with their lives. The following year, a punitive expedition of over a thousand men under the command of Sir Harry Rawson marched on the city, which they thoroughly devastated but not before carefully crating and carting away its inestimable treasures in bronze art, many of which remain on exhibit to this day in the British Museum, London. The Oba of Benin, Ovonranmwen Nogbaisi, surrendered on August 05, 1897, and was exiled to Calabar, where he died seven years later. As the nineteenth century drew to a close, the British Colonial Office and the RNC had gained control of territory extending from Lagos to Calabar on the Atlantic Coast and to Lokoja at the confluence of the Rivers Niger and Benue.

The RNC, however, continued to squabble with rival French and Germans mercantile interests over domain and their boundary disputes kept the relationship between the British and the other European colonial powers beleaguered. Internally, it fared no better. Although clause 14 of the Charter forbade it from establishing any sort of monopoly, its trade practices had precisely that effect. Its licensing scheme and schedule of customs and tariffs effectively inhibited competition. The indigenous middlemen were devastated, as were the small independent coastal traders such as Messrs Moore and Company and Messrs Stuart and Douglas, with whom they had forged a mutually profitable collaboration over the decades. In January 1887, these Liverpool merchants persuaded their member of parliament (MP), William F. Lawrence, to take up their case. The MP addressed a letter to the secretary of state, drawing attention to the inherent contradictions of the RNC's policies and conflicts of interest as both a trading company and a regulator of trade. In 1894, the Nembe people protested violently, attacking several RNC stations at Akassa. Sir John Kirk was dispatched by the British Government in May 1895 to investigate. He elicited from the protesters that "for some time after the Charter was granted they [the RNC (*sic*)] drove us away from our markets in which we and our forefathers had traded for generations." The new colonial secretary Mr. Joseph Chamberlain was not as enamored of the RNC as his predecessors had been. By 1897, questions were being raised about the role the RNC was playing literally as a proxy of the British government. In 1898, the Anglo-French Convention resolved the boundary disputes between the two countries, and the following year, the British government and the RNC began negotiations on decoupling the administrative outfit of the company from its commercial operations. The government paid the RNC the sum of 865,000 pounds sterling for its administrative arm and revoked its charter. On January 01, 1900, the territories hitherto administered by the RNC were merged with the Niger Coast Protectorate to form the Southern Protectorate. In 1906, the Southern Protectorate was divided into three provinces, the Eastern, Central, and Western, which were administered from Calabar, Warri, and Lagos respectively.

CHAPTER 2

COLONIAL ORIGINS—THE NORTH

To the north of Rivers Niger and Benue were the Sokoto Caliphate and remnants of the Kanem-Borno empire. The Sokoto Caliphate was founded by Usman dan Fodio during his Fulani *Jihad* (1804–1808). Usman dan Fodio was born in December 1754 at Maratta, Gobir sultanate in the Hausaland of present-day northwestern Nigeria. His forebears belonged to the Toronkawa clan and had emigrated from Futa-Toro in present-day Senegal to settle there in the fifteenth century. He began life as an itinerant Islamic preacher at about 1775 and purveyed a redemptive message which resonated with aggrieved Hausa peasantry, the so-called *talakawa*. They flocked to him, and soon, he had a sizable followership based in the town of Degel. For many years, the Sultan of Gobir was very tolerant toward Shaykh Usman and his followers. In the 1790s, however, he noticed that the community had begun to conduct themselves *ultra vires* and were even acquiring weaponry. He moved to reassert his authority, limiting proselytization and imposing sartorial restrictions. In February 1804, Shaykh Usman and his followers felt seriously threatened and left Degel, migrating northwest to Gudu. They proclaimed a caliphate with him as imam. The *jihad* was on, with the overthrow of the Gobir ruling dynasty as its primary objective.

After initial military reversals, a string of successes followed as the Hausa states (both Hausa Bakwai and Banza Bakwai) were overrun. Kebbi was taken in the early months of 1805, and soon afterward, Daura, Katsina, and Zamfara succumbed to caliphal authority. Kano fell to the imam's forces in 1807, and in October 1808, the capital of Gobir was finally taken. Although the Shaykh remained formally Caliph, administrative powers were in the hands of his two viziers, his son Muhammad Bello and his brother Abdullah dan Fodio. In 1809, Muhammad Bello moved the Caliphate's headquarters from Gwandu to Sokoto. The Shaykh took up residence in nearby Sifawa, where he continued to teach and write. He, however, moved to Sokoto in 1815 and died there two years later.

After the death of the Shaykh, his son and brother embarked on a successful expansion of the caliphate such that at its height in the mid-1830s, it abutted present-day Burkina Faso in the west and stretched into present-day Cameroons in the east. It also made inroads to the land of the Yoruba, reaching as far south below the Niger as Ilorin, which had been a part of the Oyo empire. In 1817, Kakanfo Afonja, a rebellious regional military commander of the Alafin, had successfully pulled Ilorin out of the empire with assistance from the Fulani. Six years later, his Fulani allies killed him, proclaimed Ilorin an emirate, and pledged allegiance to the Sokoto caliphate. In all, the caliphate comprised about thirty-one emirates, with an estimated population of about ten million. The Emirs were appointed by the vizier in Sokoto, and they swore allegiance to him.

The Borno Empire and its predecessor, the Kanem Empire, date back to the eighth century, peaking under the rule of Mai Idris Alooma in the sixteenth century. By the late eighteenth century, it was centered around Lake Chad, and its western reaches extended well into the land of the Hausa. During the Fulani Jihad, Borno lost its Hausa territories but otherwise continued to resist the incursions of the Sokoto Caliphate until the intervention of the British.

In 1822, the British colonial secretary at the time, Lord Bathurst, appointed a Scottish physician, Walter Oudney, consul and dispatched him to Kuka, the capital of the Borno Empire. Dr. Oudney was accompanied by Capt. Hugh Clapperton, and they reached their destination on February 17, 1823. They were reportedly well-received by the sultan, Shaykh al-Kaneimi. In December, they decided to travel west. Dr. Oudney was soon stricken by illness and died en route to Kano. Captain Clapperton pressed on and became the first European to visit Sokoto in 1824. He went back to Kuka and then returned to England via Tripoli, arriving to acclaim on June 01, 1825. Later that year, he set out with another expedition that sought to reach the Caliphate from the south and explore the trading opportunities the Caliph had made known he was interested in. They reached Badagry on the Atlantic coast and headed north across Yorubaland, entering the Caliphate and crossing the River Niger at Bussa in January 1826. By July 1826, they reached Kano and shortly afterward arrived in Sokoto. Unfortunately, war was raging between the Caliphate and the Bornu Empire at the time. As the Europeans waited for hostilities to cease, fatal tropical illnesses swept through their number with disastrous results. Only one member of the party, Mr. Richard Lander, survived. Mr. Lander was Commander Clapperton's servant. He headed back to the coast and returned to England in July 1828.

Two years later, Mr. Lander and his brother John led an expedition commissioned by the British government to explore the lower Niger. They arrived at Badagry on March 22, 1830, and retraced their path of four years before to Bussa, where they took to the river and sailed east then south to the delta and sea. They also explored the River Benue, the largest tributary of the River Niger, before returning to England in 1831.

With the River Niger now established as a viable route to the interior, Mr. MacGregor Laird and several other businessmen incorporated the African Inland Commercial Company in 1831 for the purpose of engaging in "direct commercial intercourse with the inhabitants of central Africa." The following year, they put together another expedition, again led by Mr. Richard Lander, with the objective of setting up a trading station at Lokoja, the confluence of the Rivers Niger and Benue. Unfortunately, it ended disastrously with the loss of thirty-nine of the forty-eight voyagers on the expedition to tropical illnesses. Mr. Laird was one of the survivors, and he returned to England after convalescing at Fernando Po.

Success came in 1854 when, with quinine now available for the treatment of malaria, a joint expedition comprising traders, government officials, and African functionaries of the CMS sailed upstream in a small steamer, *The Pleiad*, commanded by William Baikie, and returned to the coast after 118 days with no mortality. Confidence grew, and the commercial interests began to move upriver, setting up trading stations. As has been described, Mr. Goldie-Taubman arrived on the scene in the last quarter of the century, and his company, the NAC, progressively bought out the majority of its British competitors. Its French rival, Compagnie Francaise de l'Afrique Equatoriale (CFAE), was also doing brisk business, which did not escape Mr. Goldie-Taubman's attention. In 1882, the NAC pressured the emir of Nupe to abrogate his trade agreements with the CFAE. They were, however, reinstated the following year when the agent-general of the CFAE arrived at the emir's palace with 201 rifles, 200 barrels of gunpowder, and 200 pieces of cloth and departed without them.

On the River Benue, the CFAE was dominant, and an early attempt by the NAC to challenge it was stymied by indiscretion. Its senior agent, Mr. William Wallace, had visited the emir of Sanda in 1883 and was able to secure trading privileges. Unfortunately, the representative he left behind at the Yola station got caught in a relationship with one of the ladies of the palace and drew the Emir's ire.

The NAC pursued the same aggressive territorial treaty policy in the North as it did in the South. Although the language evolved over time to reflect the growth and changing roles of the company, the following four elements were always embodied, according to Riaz (2019): cessation of territory by the locals to the company in perpetuity, the right of the company to deny foreigners trading rights in the territory, protection of private property, and the maintenance of local custom. By the spring of 1886, as the NAC was angling for a royal charter, it had locked down territory in as many as 195 treaties, which guaranteed for them exclusive wealth extraction privileges. The local chieftains suffered no real loss of sovereignty since all their powers outside the marketplace were left intact. Some treaties even stipulated payments to be made to them by the NAC—three thousand and two thousand bags of cowries annually to the sultan of Sokoto and emir of Gwandu respectively. Mr. Goldie-Taubman boasted that his company's approach which did "not seek to interfere with the authority of Mohammedan Princes over their own subjects" was superior to the French strategy of "imposing direct European rule."

Caliphate economy was based on large-scale plantation farming to provide the raw materials (cotton, shea, groundnuts) for the European export market. It relied heavily on the slave labor of non-Muslim prisoners taken during the waves of *jihad*. Since slavery was abolished throughout the British Empire in 1833, the NAC (the RNC after July 12, 1886) faced a conundrum. However, the language of its treaties afforded it a fig leaf, enabling it to speciously argue that it had no legal or moral liability since it was not directly involved in the production of commodities or the management of the locals utilized for that purpose.

In 1894, the RNC engaged the services of Mr. Frederick Dealtry Lugard, an inveterate imperial adventurer. For one year, he led their treaty-making effort in the territory of the Borgu that was hotly contested with the French. The colonial secretary Mr. Joseph Chamberlain called him back in August 1897 and commissioned him to establish a military outfit to deter the French. The result was the two-battalion West African Frontier Force (WAFF) comprising indigenous soldiers led by British officers. The following year, the differences between the British and French were resolved at the Anglo-French Convention, and with the revocation of the charter of the RNC on January 01, 1900, its trade area was constituted into the Northern Protectorate, with headquarters first at Lokoja, the confluence of the rivers Niger and Benue, then later at Zungeru, which was to be the birthplace of Dr. Benjamin Nnamdi Azikiwe and Gen. Chukwuemeka Odumegwu-Ojukwu. Mr. Frederick Lugard was appointed high commissioner of the Northern Protectorate and knighted in 1901.

It goes without saying that the Sokoto Caliphate could not have the same kind of relationship with the protectorate as the one that had existed between it and the RNC. The literature is sparse on the contentions between the caliphate and the protectorate, but the matter of slavery would undoubtedly have been a sore point. Regardless, Sir Lugard soon sought to assert British military authority in the new protectorate. In 1902, the Northern Regiment of WAFF subdued the senescent and enfeebled Borno Empire and, the following year, turned on the Sokoto Caliphate. The Kano-Sokoto Expedition was launched from Zaria in January 1903, led by Col. Thomas Morland. Kano was taken in February, and Sokoto was brought to heel the following month. The caliph fled the city, and on March 21, 1903, Frederick Lugard appointed Muhammadu Attahiru II, a great-grandson of Usman Dan Fodio, sultan of Sokoto but with practically all powers of the office stripped away. Frederick Lugard resigned as high commissioner of the Northern Protectorate in September 1906 and was appointed governor of Hong Kong the following year. He returned to West Africa in September 1912 as governor of the Northern and Southern Protectorates.

Chapter 3

Amalgamation

Administratively, the Northern and Southern Protectorates could not be more different. In the North, preexisting structures at the service of emirs and local chieftains were incorporated into the colonial apparatus as "Native Authorities." Unfortunately, they were not economically viable and needed to be supported directly from London. According to Carland (1985), the British taxpayer grant-funded the Northern Protectorate to the tune of at least a quarter of a million pounds annually. In contrast, the Southern Protectorate was totally self-sufficient fiscally, its revenues increasing from 361,815 pounds in 1901 to 1,933,235 pounds in 1910. Soon enough, talks began about merging the protectorates in the expectation that the North could be weaned off the British treasury and custom revenues from the South used by a central administration to pay for programs in the North. The colonial secretary at the time, Lord Lewis Harcourt, subsequently wrote with perverted graphic casuistry that he had issued a "special license" for Frederick Lugard to "effect the alliance" between a "promising and well-conducted youth" and a "Southern lady of means." He closed with the prayer that the "union be fruitful and the couple constant." His choice of a nuptial metaphor with extractive intent was very premeditative. He had himself married into the moneyed J. P. Morgan family. He also had the reputation of a lothario in London society. On January 01, 1914, the Northern and Southern Protectorates and the Colony of Lagos were amalgamated to create the Colony and Protectorate of Nigeria (figure 1). The North must have said a resounding "amen" to the colonial secretary's prayer and have since then taken the words "fruitful" and "constant" to heart. Sir Frederick Lugard served as Nigeria's governor-general until August 08, 1919.

The amalgamation was by no means an exercise in nation building. According to Odogwu (1985), Sir Lugard insisted that he was tasked to "unify administrations, not peoples." After all, unifying subject peoples would be antithetical to the imperial ethos. Accordingly, enormous amounts of energy were expended in creating and promoting policies that divide, about which more will be said in due course. The colonial administrators became so enamored of the North that they would often take leave of their thinking faculties when formulating comparisons between the North and South. Mr. Walter R. Crocker, who was quoted extensively by Odogwu (1985), in one breath extolled the "supreme merit" of the Koranic Studies of the North and in another bemoaned the fact that "ninety percent (in some cases more) of the government artisans and motor drivers and clerks and Railway servants and Post-and-Telegraph men employed throughout the Northern provinces are foreigners from the unpopular South." He seemed oblivious of the etiologic relationship between the two and actually went on to write that "any man who had had the experience of both the Northern and Southern native would not hesitate for a moment in his general preference for the former over the latter." Sadly, it was probably on the basis of views like those espoused by poor Walter that British colonial policies were being made.

Even after Britain created Nigeria, the Fulani continued to entertain hegemonistic aspirations. They made no secret of the fact that their objective remained to propagate their religiopolitical agenda not just from west to east across the lower Sahel but also from the arid north to the Atlantic Coast. Hear the sainted Sir Abubakar Balewa addressing the Legislative Council in 1947: "I should like to make clear to you that if the British quit Nigeria now at this stage, the Northern people would continue their interrupted conquest to the sea." Agreed amalgamation was imposed in 1914, but come 1957,

TOWARD UNDERSTANDING THE NIGERIA-BIAFRA WAR AND LINGERING QUESTIONS

self-government was offered to the regions, and the North balked. One wonders why the South failed to recognize it as a branch point at which to start making the case that there was really too little in common with the North to justify continuing to travel the same path. Three years later, a congenitally anomalous country was born with all the ingredients for trouble *in situ*. The context of the constitutional milestones along that path provides telling insights into the country's turbulent gestation.

CHAPTER 4

Constitutional Politics, Political Parties, and Independence

Sir Hugh Clifford (knighted 1901) succeeded Sir Frederick Lugard as governor-general in 1919. Unlike his predecessor, he believed that the benefits of European political experience should be introduced as quickly as possible to the colony and resented indirect rule. In the Clifford Constitution of 1922 based on his recommendations, the elective principle was adopted for the first time. A forty-six-seat legislative council, four of which were to be occupied by elected members, was proposed for the South. The Colonial Office, however, opted to preserve indirect rule in the North.

The Clifford Constitution gave the nod to organized political activity. On June 23, 1924, Mr. Herbert Olayinka Badmus Macaulay, whose maternal grandfather was Bishop Samuel Ajayi Crowther, founded the first Nigerian political party, the Nigerian National Democratic Party (NNDP). For over a decade, it dominated the Lagos Town Council, which was the seat of all the political activity of any significance in the country at the time. In due course, the NNDP apparently became rather too cozy with the colonial authorities and was strongly challenged by the more radical Nigerian Youth Movement (NYM) formed in 1934 by Professor Eyo Ita (East, present-day Akwa-Ibom, alumnus Columbia University) along with Samuel Akinsanya (West, trade unionist) and Ernest Ikoli (East, present-day Bayelsa, first editor of the *Daily Times*). On a platform rejecting the system of indirect rule through traditional rulers, they contested the election of 1938 and upset the NNDP, taking control of Lagos Town Council. In due course, most of the leading lights (including Nnamdi Azikiwe, Hezekiah Davies, Obafemi Awolowo, and Samuel Ladoke Akintola) were to become members of the NYM, at least for a time.

In 1938, the NYM protested the so-called "pool" arrangements among British cocoa merchants whereby they agreed not to bid against one another at the marketplace. They sought audience with Sir Bernard Bourdillon, who became governor-general in 1935, and were successful in enlisting him in their cause. These merchants were engaged in a similar practice in the Gold Coast, and when Sir Bourdillon took up the case with the Colonial Office, the Nowell Commission on the Marketing of West African Cocoa was empaneled. The commission found that "the legitimate interests of sellers were prejudiced by the suppression of competitive buying" and recommended that "the Agreement should be finally withdrawn." Sir Bourdillon maintained warm relationships with the growing Nigerian elite until his retirement in 1943. It was during his tenure that the South was divided into East and West (1939; figure 2).

As the political awareness of Nigerians burgeoned, they elevated their sights. In 1944, Mr. Herbert Macaulay formed the National Council of Nigeria and the Cameroons (NCNC). It was conceived as a broad-based ("big tent") movement whose goal was to wrest independence, no less, from the British. Within its fold were nationalist political organizations, ethnic and cultural groups, and trade unions. Notable exceptions were the ethnocultural organization, Egbe Omo Oduduwa (founded by Chief Obafemi Awolowo), and the Nigerian Union of Teachers. The first president of the NCNC was Sir Herbert Macaulay himself, and Dr. Nnamdi Azikiwe was national secretary. Two years later, Sir Herbert Macaulay died and was succeeded as president by Dr. Nnamdi Azikiwe, with Professor Eyo Ita as national deputy president. That year, Westminster served up the Richards Constitution.

Sir Arthur Richards (knighted 1942) was appointed governor-general after Sir Bourdillon's retirement. The constitution named after him went into effect on January 01, 1947. Notably, it established regional legislative Houses of Assembly. Although credited with acknowledging the diversity of the colony, it undoubtedly set in motion the machinery that drove its political division. The governor-general and his executive council retained ultimate power and could overrule any laws passed by the regional houses. The input of the increasingly vocal local elite and opinion leaders was not sought as the constitution was being created. Predictably, the NCNC opposed and protested vigorously against it. In a countrywide campaign, it obtained endorsements from 153 communities and dispatched a delegation of seven (Ms. Fumilayo Ransome-Kuti, Mr. Peter M. Kale, Dr. Abubakar Olorun-Nimbe, Mallam Zana Bukar Dipcharima, Prince Adeleke Adedoyin, Chief Nyang Essien, and Dr. Nnamdi Azikiwe) to London for a meeting with the colonial secretary, Mr. Arthur Creech Jones. The delegation was received in audience on August 13, 1947, but their demand for revisions to the constitution was declined. The Richards Constitution was, however, eventually suspended after four years.

Lessons learned, the new governor-general Sir John Stuart Macpherson (knighted 1945), who assumed office on February 05, 1948, began broad consultations on a replacement constitution in March 1949. They culminated in a general conference in Ibadan in 1950, attended by delegates from all over the country, the overwhelming majority (50 of 53) of whom were Nigerian. The Macpherson Constitution was finally promulgated on June 29, 1951. It created a central legislature, a single-chamber House of Representatives, and the three regions into which Nigeria had been divided largely for administrative convenience initially became federating units. At the Ibadan Conference, the emirs of Zaria and Katsina had threatened that unless the North was assigned at least half the number of seats in the proposed central legislature, it would cease to associate with the South. The conniving colonial administrators acquiesced, allocating half of the elected seats in the House of Representatives (68 of 136) to the North and claiming it was based on population, even though the census of 1950–1953 was still ongoing. In the regions, there was an elected House of Assembly and an executive council comprising elected and appointed members. It is noteworthy that at the outset, only the North and the West had a house of chiefs consisting of hereditary rulers of which most of the East had no tradition. Many years later, a case would be made for creating such a chamber to seat "natural rulers" in the East. Ministers had no control over their departments, and all executive decisions were taken by the full executive council. This was another concession made to the North, who had opposed the ministerial system out of concern that at the center, their ministers would not measure up to the standards of their southern counterparts and, in the region, might encroach on the powers and privileges of the Emirs.

The Macpherson Constitution further nurtured the sense of regional autonomy in many politicians. This caused them to refocus their outlook from national to regional as they sought to lay the foundation of their political power on an ethnic base. In June 1949, soon after consultations for the constitution began, the northern cultural organization, Jamiyya Mutanem Arewa, metamorphosed into the Northern People's Congress (NPC). It was led by Alhaji Ahmadu Bello, with Alhaji Abubakar Tafawa Balewa as his deputy. Alhaji Ahmadu Bello was a great-great-grandson of Shaykh Usman dan Fodio, founder of the Sokoto Caliphate. He received his early education at Katsina Training (now Barewa) College and taught English at Sokoto Middle School from 1931 until 1934 when he succeeded his brother (and father before him) as head of his home district, Rabah (as Sarkin Rabah). In 1938, he made an unsuccessful bid for the sultanate but became crown prince (Sardauna) instead. His bureaucratic responsibilities in the emirate grew tremendously, and he was sent to England to study local government administration in 1948. Under the Richards Constitution, Ahmadu Bello represented Sokoto in the regional House of Assembly. He promptly gained recognition in the Jamiyya and quickly rose to its leadership. In the election of 1951–1952, he was reelected to the regional house and became minister as well as member of the executive council.

Although the backgrounds of Alhaji Ahmadu Bello and his deputy, Alhaji Abubakar Tafawa Balewa, could not be more different, their early career trajectories were remarkably similar. Tafawa Balewa had a plebeian upbringing, but he, too, attended Katsina Training College and went on to teach English at his hometown middle school in Bauchi. He became headmaster in 1941, and four years later, was sent for further studies to the Institute of Education of the University of London. In 1946, he was elected to the regional House of Assembly and the following year was sent to Lagos as one of its representatives in the Central Legislative Council. He was reelected in the polls of 1951–1952 that ushered in the Macpherson Constitution and was appointed minister.

The third major political party of the pre-Independence era was the Action Group. It was founded in Ibadan on March 21, 1951, by Chief Obafemi Awolowo, with the Egbe Omo Oduduwa (Yoruba for "Society for the Descendants of Oduduwa") as its nucleus. Jeremiah Oyeniyi Obafemi Awolowo attended Wesley College, Ibadan and in 1927 enrolled for correspondence courses, which earned him a bachelor's degree of the University of London. He eventually traveled to England in 1944 to study law and was called to the bar two years later. Obafemi Awolowo returned to Nigeria in 1947 and started a law practice at Ibadan. The Egbe, which he had founded during his stay in London, was reconstituted in 1948, preparatory to its transformation into a political party. Chief Awolowo's political philosophy at the time was federalism. He advocated for a central government which would guarantee the separate interests of the various ethnic groups in the country.

The Action Group and the Northern People's Congress made no secret of their parochialism from their inception. They were both content with their exclusively regional footprints. In contrast, the NCNC pursued a broad nationalistic agenda and struggled to discourage the debasement of the debate to regionalism and ethnic dominance, which clearly served the purposes of the colonial master. The goals of the Action Group and NCNC did converge in the desire of both parties for rapid progress to self-government. The preference of the NPC, however, was for a much more sedate approach, lest the British depart before the North felt ready to hold their own against the South. Whereas the Action Group and NPC were receptive to the Macpherson Constitution, the NCNC was harshly critical of it. They argued that the colonial masters merely went through the motions of consultation while indeed valorizing the input of rural traditionalists whom they could influence over that of urban nationalists who had more sophisticated points of view. They also took issue with the incorporation of Lagos, the colonial capital, into the West. At its third annual convention in Kano, August and September 1951, the NCNC adopted a unitary form of government as its constitutional goal to counteract the Macpherson Constitution's emphasis on regionalism.

The Action Group was heavily invested in curbing the activities of the NCNC in the West, and the showdown came in the elections of 1951–1952. The NCNC won all the seats in Lagos. When counting was completed, the Action Group had won only twenty-nine of the eighty seats. It lost all six seats in Ibadan to the Ibadan People's Party (IPP) led by Chief Augustus Akinloye. There were other much smaller parties involved, e.g., the Ondo Improvement League and Otu Edo as well as Independents. Vigorous horse-trading ensued, and when the dust settled, Egbe Omo Oduduwa had succeeded in persuading a total of twenty candidates who had won seats under other banners to decamp to the Action Group. The national secretary of the NCNC Chief Kola Balogun had thought he had a dependable collaborative understanding with the IPP. In the event, only one member of that party—Chief Adegoke Adelabu (who rejoiced in the alias "Penkelemesi," for Peculiar Mess)—sided with the NCNC. The Action Group prevailed, and Chief Awolowo became head of the regional government. The Ibadan electorate was none too pleased about the defection to the Action Group of the representatives they elected on the platform of the IPP and would proceed to punish them in the federal election of 1954 at which the Action Group won only one of the five seats in Ibadan.

Under the Macpherson Constitution, election to the central legislature was indirect—by an electoral college comprised of members of the regional houses of assembly. Dr. Azikiwe had won his seat in Lagos, which was now a part of the West in whose legislature the Action Group had garnered a majority. Needless to say, he was not elected to the House of Representatives and was faced with the prospect of relative obscurity in the position of leader of opposition in a regional House of Assembly.

Dr. Azikiwe was a colossus of early Nigerian politics and even had tremendous credibility on the continental stage. On the faculty of Lincoln University, Oxford, Pennsylvania, during 1932–1934, he had designed and taught a course on African history. Returning to Ghana in 1934, he edited the *African Morning Post* newspaper in Accra, Gold Coast. When he finally came home to Lagos in 1937, he founded the *West African Pilot*, an important mouthpiece of fiery nationalist propaganda which he grew into a stable of six daily newspapers published all around the country in urban centers including Lagos, Ibadan, Onitsha, Kano, and Calabar. Also in 1937, he published *Renascent Africa*, a treatise in which he laid out his pan-African vision. Clearly, sitting in a regional assembly and altercating in opposition to a government with a primarily ethnic agenda was not an attractive proposition. In 1952, he headed east to Enugu.

The NCNC was the party in government in the East. The arrival of its national president was problematic, and the party struggled with accommodating him. A very troubling succession of events followed as ministers who were asked to resign for cabinet reshuffling to take place refused to do so. The recalcitrant so-called "sit-tight" ministers were expelled from the party, and a vote of no confidence was passed on the cabinet. The head of government and national deputy president of the party Professor Eyo Ita founded the National Independence Party (NIP) on February 23, 1953. A crisis quickly developed and paralyzed the house, causing the lieutenant-governor to dissolve it on May 06, 1953. Fresh regional elections were held, and predictably, Dr. Azikiwe won a seat and was selected as chief minister.

Another incident which shook confidence in the Macpherson Constitution ignited in Lagos and later exploded in Kano. On March 31, 1953, an Action Group member of the House of Representatives, Mr. Anthony Enahoro, had moved a motion for self-government "in the year 1956." Members of the NPC were opposed to it, expressing preference for the vagueness of "as soon as practicable." When another NPC member tried to end the debate by tabling a motion for adjournment, Action Group and NCNC members walked out. According to reports, the NPC members were taunted and ridiculed by crowds in Lagos, to their intense displeasure. The North began to drop hints that it might secede. In a speech on May 12, 1953, Dr. Azikiwe shared his views on the subject and counseled leaders of the North "to weigh the advantages and disadvantages of secession before embarking upon this dangerous course."

On May 16, 1953, Chief Samuel Ladoke Akintola, the deputy leader of the Action Group, arrived in Kano to address a meeting of his party at the Colonial Hotel. He was greeted by a hostile, stone-throwing crowd of local people that had assembled outside the hotel. The following day, matters escalated as irate Fulani-Hausa mobs invaded the area of the city inhabited by non-indigenes, predominantly Igbo, killing and destroying property in what would become a recurrent scenario. On May 18, 1953, the colonial authorities declared a state of emergency and deployed armed troops to Kano. The turn of events must have struck the Sardauna of Sokoto, Alhaji Ahmadu Bello, as strange. What had begun as a disagreement between the Fulani-Hausa and the predominantly Yoruba Action Group ended up claiming dozens of Igbo lives. He remarked that "the Yoruba were oddly out of it." The casualties stood at 43 dead and 204 wounded (36 and 272 respectively by some accounts). In the British House of Commons, the Right Honorable Fenner Brockway demanded that the minister of State for Colonial Affairs Mr. Henry Hopkinson conduct a "very thorough, penetrating inquiry" into the circumstances of the riot because he "had very definite information" that five days before the mayhem, the lieutenant-governor was warned that indigenous members of the administrative staff had been given "special leave so that they might attack a meeting which was being held." While the political parties framed the riot as wrangling between those who wanted self-government in 1956 and those who did not, the colonial authorities concluded it was interethnic and an ominous portent. The secretary of state for the colonies Sir Oliver Lyttleton decided it was time for a new constitution.

Consultative constitutional conferences were held in London in July and August 1953. The NCNC and Action Group collaborated in ensuring that the National Independence Party that had broken away from the former was not invited to participate. On the subject of internal self-government in 1957, it was agreed that the decision should be individualized, allowing any region that felt ready to proceed to so do. To the chagrin of the Action Group, the colonial secretary sided with the NCNC and NPC that Lagos should cease to be a part of the West.

In October 1954, the Lyttelton Constitution was promulgated. It created a fully federal system, comprising the three geographic regions of Nigeria, the Southern Cameroons, and Lagos as federal capital territory once again separate from the Western Region. Each region had a governor, premier, cabinet, legislature, and civil service, with the significantly weaker federal government represented in Lagos by a governor-general, bureaucracy, and house of representatives. Regional autonomy was further entrenched, and the competencies of the federal and regional legislatures were more clearly defined. Ministers now had control over their ministries.

As regional self-government approached and subsequent national independence was being contemplated, preparations for a successor constitution to the Lyttleton document soon got underway. However, plans for a conference in London in 1956 were shelved when yet another crisis erupted in the East surrounding the relationship between the premier Dr. Nnamdi Azikiwe and the African Continental Bank (ACB), which he had founded in 1947. Addressing the British House of Commons on July 24, 1956, the colonial secretary Mr. Alan Lennox-Boyd reported that although Dr. Azikiwe had informed the governor that he had resigned his directorship of the bank on becoming premier, enterprises associated with him were still large shareholders in it. Also, the sum of 877,000 pounds of public money and other large sums from Marketing Board reserves had been deposited with the bank in 1955. The chief whip of the Eastern House of Assembly Mr. Effiong Okon Eyo called for an independent commission of inquiry. In reaction, the premier filed a libel action against Mr. Eyo. After an unproductive exchange of letters between the colonial secretary and the premier on the subject, the former decided to appoint a commission of inquiry with Sir Stafford

TOWARD UNDERSTANDING THE NIGERIA-BIAFRA WAR AND LINGERING QUESTIONS

Foster-Sutton, chief justice of the Federation of Nigeria, as chair. The Rt. Hon. Fenner Brockway immediately came to the defense of the premier, hinting that it was the governor of the region himself who actually recommended that the government invest large sums of money in the bank. Nevertheless, the final report of the commission was critical of the premier's conduct but accepted his defense that his primary motive was innocuous enough—to ensure that there was an indigenous bank whose objective was to liberalize the availability of credit to the people.

The Constitutional Conference finally began in London in May 1957. The demand for independence in 1959 was rejected. Instead, the Colonial Office agreed to internal self-government for the East and West in 1957 and for the North in 1959. Before it adjourned in June 1957, special commissions were set up to study specific issues of crucial importance (e.g., revenue allocation, electoral constituency delimitation, and state creation) and prepare reports for consideration when the conference reconvened the following year. The report of the Commission on Minority Groups in Nigeria, headed by Sir Henry Willink, was probably the most eagerly awaited. These groups, especially those inhabiting the Middle Belt in the North, the Benin and Warri provinces in the West, and the Calabar, Ogoja, and Rivers provinces in the East, had for many years expressed concerns about domination and marginalization by the majority ethnic group in their regions, namely the Fulani-Hausa, the Yoruba, and the Igbo respectively. Their fears escalated as independence approached, and they demanded that structural rearrangements be undertaken to assuage their apprehensions, proposing either the creation of new separate states for them or redrawing the map in some other way to eliminate their minority status and its associated disadvantages.

The Willink Commission, in its wisdom, acknowledged the fears agitating the minds of minority groups but decided that their demand for state creation was not an effective solution. Among the reasons cited was that state creation had a "generational character" and would unleash a fissiparous dynamic, with an unending demand for more and more states. Also, the commission was not convinced that splintering up the country further would necessarily address marginalization and distributive injustice, which were at the core of their angst. The commission recommended instead that a bill of rights be incorporated in the Independence Constitution to guarantee the rights of minority groups and promote national integration.

When the Constitutional Conference reconvened in Lagos in September 1958, the report of the Willink Commission was hotly debated. The NCNC and NPC accepted the recommendations of the commission, while the Action Group initially opposed them. When, however, it became clear that a deadlock would drag out the proceedings and possibly result in the postponement of independence, the Action Group relented.

The Independence Constitution was enacted by an order-in-council to go into effect on October 01, 1960. It established a federal democratic system of government on the Westminster model. The Queen of England, represented by an indigenous governor-general, would be the ceremonial head of state. An elected prime minister would be head of government. An upper House of Senate was created at the center, and finally, a house of chiefs in the East. Legislative powers were divided into three lists: exclusive (central government), concurrent (central and regional governments), and residual (local government). A Supreme Court was appointed, but ultimate judicial power remained with the Privy Council in London.

Pursuant to the recommendations of the Willink Commission, the Independence Constitution embodied elaborate provisions for the protection of fundamental human rights aligned with the United Nations Universal Declaration of Human Rights (1948) and European Convention for the Protection of Human Rights and Fundamental Freedoms (1953). Among them were the rights to life, personal liberty, fair hearing and family life, freedom from inhumane treatment, slavery or forced labor, freedom of conscience and religion, freedom of movement and residence, freedom of peaceful assembly and association, freedom from discrimination, and freedom of expression. It is worth mentioning that the NCNC proposed a constitutional bill of rights, modeled on the first ten amendments of the United States Constitution, in its Freedom Charter, which was adopted by the People's National Assembly at Kaduna in April 1948—all of eight months before the adoption of the Universal Declaration of Human Rights by the United Nations General Assembly. The Independence Constitution also addressed the question of the creation of new regions, specifying that, in each case, a referendum would proceed to hold if supported by two-thirds majority in the Federal House of Representatives and House of Senate as well as a majority in two-thirds of the regions. The new region would be created if votes in favor in the referendum were in excess of 60 percent.

Preindependence federal elections were held on December 12, 1959, and the NCNC received the most votes (2,594,577; 34 percent). However, thanks to the alchemy of the British colonial master, these votes translated into only 26 percent of the seats in the House of Representatives (81 of 312). The NPC got the most seats—134 with only 1,922,179 of the popular vote, which was even fewer than that of the Action Group (1,992,346, but for 73 seats). Since no party had won a majority of seats, a coalition government was inevitable. Perhaps still rankled by the bitter aftertaste of the 1951 experience in the West, the NCNC and its Northern Elements Progressive Union ally (founded August 08, 1950, with Mallam Aminu Kano as Chair) opted to reach accommodations with the NPC. The Action Group became the opposition.

For a long time and perhaps to the present day, the misfortune of the NCNC in Western House of Assembly in 1951 has been a point of very sore contention between the East and the West, more specifically, many Igbo and the Yoruba, the former readily pointing to it as evidence that the Yoruba could and should never the trusted. In my opinion, the analysis is somewhat unrealistic, the conclusion unsound and the generalization unwarranted.

For one thing, the Action Group of 1951, with its Egbe Omo Oduduwa origins, left no one in any doubt as to its ethnic coloration and prioritization of regional preoccupations. Nationalistic pretensions were an afterthought. It could almost persuasively argue to its electorate that a party like the NCNC with a broad agenda was unlikely to bring the same intensity to the pursuit of narrow local interests as would the Action Group. For better or for worse, it is hard to fault a local party for zealously, if jealously, guarding local turf.

For another, the NCNC at the time was not an Eastern, let alone Igbo party, by any rational stretch of the imagination. An Igbo was national president in 1951, but he had succeeded a Yoruba founding president. The national deputy president was from the East, but he was Efik. The national secretary of the party was Yoruba, as were many of the stalwarts who made the party tick—Ms. Frances Olufunmilayo Ransome-Kuti, Chief Adeniran Ogunsanya, Chief Theophilus Owolabi "TOS" Benson, Chief Joseph Odeleye Fadahunsi, and many others. Understandably, the other parties kept projecting their own ethnocentrism on the NCNC, and this was music to the ears of the colonial master since it would rather not deal with a movement incontrovertibly perceived as pan-Nigerian. On some level, however, many Igbo began to buy into the mischaracterization and came to regard the NCNC-Action Group debacle in the West as maliciously interethnic in its entirety. The "carpet-crossing" politicians who were successfully persuaded to jettison their presumably principled stance solely by appeals to their ethnic sentiments were, in all probability, pathetic scoundrels. Nevertheless, playing politics that way does not infringe on any rules and is arguably par for the course. Persuasion is the name of the game, and allowance is made for some players being more pitifully vacuous and tractable than others. No credible accounts of money changing hands or other similar overtly illegal activity are available.

Soon after independence, the Southern Cameroons left to join their Francophone neighbors to the east, and NCNC became the National Council of Nigerian Citizens. Some historical perspective is needed to put the relationship between Nigeria and the Cameroons in proper context. Small pastoral groups of the Fulani entered the northern part of present-day Cameroon in the eighteenth century. They were welcomed by the native population and granted settlement. However, in what was to become an enduring familiar pattern, they soon rebelled against their hosts and, propelled by the teachings and *jihad* of Shaykh Uthman dan Fodio, began to conquer territory

TOWARD UNDERSTANDING THE NIGERIA-BIAFRA WAR AND LINGERING QUESTIONS

and expand southward until checked by the Mfon Mbuembue of the Kingdom of Bamum.

In 1472, the Portuguese explorer Fernao do Po (also known as Fernando Po) reached the Atlantic coast, and in his wake came merchants, many of whom became very active in the transatlantic slave trade. However, Portuguese maritime supremacy eventually waned, and the slave trade fell into disfavor. British and German interests and trade in forest products (oil palm, rubber) took over.

Imperial Germany claimed the region as the Kamerun on July 14, 1884. After she was defeated in the First World War, the territory was mandated by the League of Nations to the victorious British and French. British Cameroon was a strip of land oriented north-south along the eastern border of Nigeria and bisected by the River Benue (figure 2). On January 01, 1960, the French granted independence to its Cameroonian territory, with Alhaji Ahmadou Ahidjo as president. Britain, however, refused to do the same, giving the Cameroonians the option of either remaining with Nigeria or joining La République de Cameroun. In a plebiscite held on February 11, 1961, under United Nations auspices, parts of British Cameroon administered with the Adamawa and Borno Provinces voted by a majority of 60 percent to integrate into Nigeria while the rest of the territory to the south voted to amalgamate with La République by 70.5 percent (figure 3).

Meanwhile back west, Chief Obafemi Awolowo had migrated to Lagos as leader of the opposition in the Federal House of Representatives after the 1959 elections. As premier of the Western Region, he had been very effective. The revenue from cocoa made the region very rich, and his government plowed the resources into highly popular programs and projects like free primary education, first television service in Nigeria (in partnership with British firm Overseas Rediffusion, maiden broadcast on October 31, 1959), the twenty-five-thousand-seat capacity Liberty Stadium, and the twenty-six-story Cocoa House (completed 1965). However, when it came to coalition-building outside his ethnic base, his track record was at best mixed and the best he often could do was court the so-called minorities in the other regions. His deputy, Chief Samuel Ladoke Akintola, who took over as Premier, was of a different mindset. Chief Akintola was more inclined to be conservative at a time the leader of the party was beginning to flirt with "democratic socialism." Further, Chief Akintola saw merit in rapprochement with the NPC, which, it had begun to appear, had a lock on power at the center. Chief Awolowo, in contrast, seemed to entertain the unrealistic aspiration that somehow someday he and the Action Group, with a little help from the minorities, would gain national power electorally. The two chiefs drifted apart with separate followerships in tow. The first open clash came on February 01, 1962, at the party congress in Jos when the Awolowo faction succeeded in disestablishing the position of deputy leader held by Chief Akintola. The party executive subsequently met on May 19, 1962, and demanded his resignation as premier. Needless to say, Chief Akintola refused, and a crippling political crisis developed in the region. The next day, he asked the governor Oba Adesoji Aderemi, the Ooni of Ife, to exercise his powers under Section 31 of the Regional Constitution and dissolve the House of Assembly in view of the impasse. His request was denied, and he then turned to the Speaker of the House, demanding he convene the house on May 23, 1962, to consider and pass a vote of confidence in his government. The Speaker also declined the premier's request.

The next day, May 21, 1962, the crisis escalated. The Awolowo faction of the House, who slightly outnumbered their Akintola counterparts, prepared and submitted to the governor a petition demanding the ouster of the premier. Apparently satisfied that it was sufficient evidence that the premier no longer had the confidence of the House to continue in office, the governor fired and replaced him with Alhaji Dauda Soroye Adegbenro, the minister of local government. Chief Akintola promptly challenged the legitimacy of his removal in the High Court, Ibadan, and the case came before the chief justice of the Western region, Justice Samuel Quarshie-Idun. He referred the question of whether the governor could remove a premier from office on the basis of a petition signed by House members rather than the loss of a vote of confidence on the floor of the House to the Supreme Court. He, however, ruled that Chief Samuel Akintola should remain in office during pendency of the adjudication by the higher court. In the event, the Supreme Court, on a three-to-one (Chief Justice Adetokunbo Adegboyega Ademola and Justices John Idowu Taylor and Vahe Robert Bairamian versus Justice Lionel Brett) vote decided that Governor Adesoji Aderemi had erred in the exercise of his powers.

The House of Assembly eventually convened on May 25, 1962. Although several versions of what transpired are available, they all agree that matters quickly got out of hand. Below is the account documented by a British University of Ibadan don at the time:

> After prayers, as Chief Odebiyi rose to move the first motion, Mr. E. O. Oke, a supporter of Chief Akintola, jumped on the table shouting, "There is fire on the mountain." He proceeded to fling chairs about the chamber. Mr. E. Ebubedike, also a supporter of Chief Akintola, seized the mace, attempted to club the Speaker with it, but missed and broke the mace on the table. The supporters of Alhaji Adegbenro sat quiet as they had been instructed to do, with the exception of one member who was hit with a chair and retaliated. Mr. Akinyemi (NCNC) and Messrs Adigun and Adeniya (pro-Akintola) continued to throw chairs; the opposition joined in and there was such disorder that the Nigeria Police released tear gas and cleared the House. (Nigerian Government and Politics; Mackintosh 1966)

A few hours later, another attempt was made to resume House proceedings. Unfortunately, it was no more successful than the first as, again, mayhem quickly broke out and fast-traveling pieces of broken furniture filled the airspace. The Speaker felt compelled to adjourn the meeting.

Chief Awolowo, who was present at the session, sought to minimize the debacle, remarking that when he left the chamber, those outside "did not even know that anything was happening inside."

However, newspaper reports at the time told a different story. The images of legislators bleeding from gashes on their scalps on the front pages of the national dailies horrified the nation. One memorable shot showed Chief Anthony Enahoro making his undignified escape horizontally between the concrete louvers of a window. The prime minister tendered a motion at the House of Representatives for the declaration of a state of emergency in the Western Region under Section 65 of the Constitution, seconded by Chief Festus Okotie-Eboh, the federal minister of Finance, and it passed with a vote of 232 to 44 (32 to 7 with 2 abstentions in the Senate). The regional government was vacated, and Dr. Moses Adekoyejo Majekodunmi, federal minister of Health, was appointed sole administrator.

More misfortune was to befall the Action Group in 1962. Within the first month of his tenure, the Sole Administrator set up a Commission of Inquiry headed by Justice George Baptist Coker of the Lagos High Court to probe the affairs of six statutory corporations in the West during October 01, 1954–June 16, 1962. The Coker Commission exposed financial malfeasance on a colossal scale. Chief Awolowo was found to have misappropriated and diverted huge amounts of public corporation funds for the purposes of the Action Group. Chief Akintola was exonerated of wrongdoing.

On September 22, 1962, the prime minister announced that a plot to overthrow the federal government had been uncovered. It turned out that British Intelligence (MI-6) had been monitoring the activities of certain Nigerians, some of whom had gone to Ghana and received paramilitary training while others were engaged in the importation and stockpiling of arms and ammunition. The information was duly passed on to the Nigeria Police. On investigation, all the persons involved were found to be affiliated with the Action Group. Chief Awolowo and thirty others were arrested. Formal charges were filed on November 02, 1962, and they were arraigned in Lagos High Court before Justice George Sodeinde Sowemimo. The riveting trial began on November 12, 1962, and ran until June 27, 1963, with ninety-five witnesses called and 383 exhibits examined. However, judgment was reserved *sine die*, and in the interim, unfortunately, the Awolowo family suffered a tremendous tragedy.

TOWARD UNDERSTANDING THE NIGERIA-BIAFRA WAR AND LINGERING QUESTIONS

Mr. Olusegun Awolowo, the chief's first son, who was a lawyer and one of his defense attorneys, was killed in a motor vehicle accident on July 10, 1963. The ruling was finally delivered on September 11, 1963, and Chief Awolowo was found guilty on three counts—treasonable felony under Section 41(b) of the Criminal Code for which he was sentenced to ten years imprisonment with hard labor, conspiracy to commit a felony under Section 516 of the Criminal Code for which he got five years, and conspiracy to effect an unlawful purpose under Section 518(6) of the Criminal Code, which earned him two years. All sentences were to run concurrently. Seventeen others were also found guilty and sentenced to various terms of imprisonment ranging from two to fifteen years. The stiffest penalty of fifteen years jail time was reserved for Chief Anthony Eronsele Enahoro, who had fled to the United Kingdom in September 1962 but was apprehended and extradited in May 1963. Mr. Samuel Gomnso Ikoku (Igbo, from Arochukwu in present-day Abia State), general secretary of the Action Group and leader of the opposition in the Eastern House of Assembly, evaded arrest and trial by escaping to Ghana.

Much was made at the time of the statement attributed to the presiding judge, Justice George Sowemimo, that his "hands are tied," taken to imply that he was under extrajudicial pressure to find Chief Awolowo guilty and sentence him to a jail term. The ligature under reference was actually the decision he had already made "to sentence the other accused persons who I find were tools in the hands of others." He therefore felt obliged to ensure that "a punishment by me in my court is such that others would see that there is no preferential treatment." Justice Sowemimo also said he was bound by the evidence, and there were about eight hundred pages of it. Chief Awolowo and others appealed their sentences to the Supreme Court (Chief Justice Adetokunbo Ademola, Justices Louis Mbanefo, John Taylor, Lionel Brett and Vahe Bairamian), but the cases were unanimously dismissed for lack of merit.

In June 1993, Mr. Samuel Ikoku, an upper-echelon party stalwart at the time, freely admitted in a public forum that there had indeed been a plot by the Action Group to topple the federal government of Nigeria, as charged. Unbeknownst to them, the Special

Branch of the Nigeria Police, led by Mr. John O'Sullivan, had planted informants in their midst "so the police knew every move we were making." The trial of Chief Awolowo and his coconspirators in 1962–1963 was therefore not a baseless persecutory "show trial," as his sympathizers sought to portray it. Instead, it was the justified judicial response to the first plot of a coup d'état in the history of the country.

The national census of 1962 was conducted while the treason trial of members of the Action Group was in progress. The public was always wary about enumeration exercises, considering them data acquisition activities for taxation and other similar extractive purposes for which they saw no benefit to themselves. In 1950–1953, the colonial administration had justified the very biased distribution of electoral seats among the regions, which inordinately favored the North, on the basis of census figures even as the exercise was in progress and the data were not exactly available. In 1962, the political class in the South was ready. The headcount was conducted simultaneously nationwide in the month of May. The results were never published. The prime minister reportedly took one look at the preliminary figures and rejected them outright. They apparently showed that the population of the North had fallen below that of the South, having increased by only about 30 percent whereas that of the South grew by at least 70 percent in the interval between 1950–1953 and 1962. According to Alao (2001), the prime minister declared that virtually everyone was a "willing liar of the first magnitude" and ordered a new census to be conducted the following year under the direction of Dr. Kofoworola Adekunle Abayomi. Dr. Abayomi was actually a founding member of the Nigeria Youth Movement, Egbe Omo Oduduwa, and the Action Group. The 1963 census was hastily conducted, and not surprisingly, the initial figures reinstated the numerical superiority of the North. Equally unsurprisingly, they were fiercely contested by Southern politicians. Then they decided to negotiate! The North accepted 29,177,986; the East 12,388,646; the West 10,278,500; the Mid-West 2,533,337; and Lagos 675,352.

The state of emergency in the West ended on December 31, 1962. Meanwhile, Chief Akintola had formed a new party, the United

People's Party (UPP). Due at least in part to the Coker Commission of Inquiry, which had found his stewardship during 1959–1962 above board, he was reinstated as premier on January 01, 1963. He quickly reached an understanding with the NCNC, the erstwhile opposition party, and together, the UPP and NCNC consigned the Action Group to opposition status in the regional House.

The disarray in the Western region and the Action Group played nicely into the hands of the Midwest State Movement (MSM), which had been lobbying for the creation of the Mid-West region from the Benin and Delta provinces. The MSM also profited immensely from the rapprochement at the center between the NCNC and the NPC. The Action Group had resigned itself to the inevitability of a Mid-West region but would not agree with the MSM regarding its composition. At the Willink Commission (1957–1958) for instance, Mr. Victor Remilekun Fani-Kayode, counsel for the Action Group, had argued that Warri division and Akoko-Edo belonged with Ondo province and that the Igbo and Ijaw should join their kith and kin in the Eastern region, leaving the contemplated Mid-West region very emaciated. By 1959, Mr. Fani-Kayode had joined the NCNC and would become Chief Samuel Akintola's deputy-premier in the NCNC-UPP compact of 1963. One of the commitments he extracted from the premier was that the government would not oppose the unfolding Midwest region creation process. The NPC was very hostile to state creation, but such was the amity among Chief Festus Okotie-Eboh, Alhaji Muhammadu Ribadu, and Alhaji Ahmadu Bello that an exception was made. On July 01, 1963, Dr. Michael Okpara himself came on tour to urge the people to vote in favor of the creation of the region. The referendum was held on July 13, 1963, and the votes in favor were 89.07 percent. The Mid-West region came into existence on August 09, 1963.

The constitutional change that ushered in the First Republic was made in 1963. In July of that year, all the political parties met and agreed to replace the Independence Constitution with one that dispensed with the British monarch as head of state represented by an indigenous governor-general. Instead, the head of state would be a president elected by the House of Representatives. However, executive governmental powers would remain with the prime minister. Another significant change embodied in the new constitution was the establishment of the Supreme Court as the court of last resort in the land, replacing the Privy Council, London. On October 01, 1963, Dr. Nnamdi Azikiwe became the first president of the Federal Republic of Nigeria. Alhaji Abubakar Tafawa Balewa remained prime minister.

Ahead of the federal elections of December 30, 1964, the first since independence, wide-ranging realignments occurred across the political landscape. Chief Akintola's UPP renamed itself the Nigerian National Democratic Party, invoking the name of Sir Herbert Macaulay's defunct party. It divorced the NCNC and tied the knot with the NPC to form the Nigerian National Alliance (NNA). The NCNC, Action Group, NEPU and the United Middle Belt Congress (UMBC) coalesced into the United Peoples Grand Alliance (UPGA). Much was at stake, both for the alliances individually and the nation as a whole. In the middle of October, UPGA published its manifesto, asserting that it represented "progress, democracy, and socialism" while the rival alliance stood for "reaction, feudalism, and neocolonialism." The NNA accused the UPGA of purveying an ideology "based on hatred, selfishness, and ambition." Beyond these atmospherics, there were few stated differences of principle. Both alliances condemned tribalism, poverty, disease, ignorance, lawlessness, tribalism, corruption, and the abuse of power.

Soon enough, matters began to overheat on the campaign trail. As the language of the politicians became increasingly incendiary, the so-called "youth wings" of the parties ramped up their militancy, physically assaulting their opponents and committing acts of arson and other kinds of damage to property. Although these allegations were traded bidirectionally between the alliances, the worst of them were leveled by the UPGA at the NNA. Charges were made that in the North, government officials were denying opposition politicians permission to hold meetings and rallies as well as detaining them under fabricated pretexts. The leadership of the NNA dismissed these complaints as "groundless" and countered that the UPGA was "spreading invented lies about imaginary bad treatment." Further, huge discrepancies were found between the voter rolls and the 1963 census returns, which was hardly surprising since the latter were a concocted compromise. The situation became so fraught that the leader of the UPGA and premier of Eastern Nigeria Dr. Michael Okpara sought audience with the president, Dr. Nnamdi Azikiwe, on December 24, 1964, to warn that if the irregularities were not rectified, the UPGA would boycott the elections. By this time, however, the president had already received official reports from the chairman of the Federal Electoral Commission and the police that led him to the conclusion that, under prevailing circumstances, the elections could neither be free nor fair. On December 28, 1964, the president conveyed his concerns to the prime minister with the recommendation that the elections be postponed for six months, and United Nations assistance solicited as was done for the British Cameroons plebiscite of February 11, 1961. The prime minister rejected the president's recommendation and opted instead to convene a meeting of regional premiers and governors on the eve of polling day. The representatives of the North and West, which were regions held by the NNA, did not attend. In protest, half of the members of the Federal Electoral Commission resigned. The Joint Action Committee of the Nigeria Trades Union called for a strike. The UPGA proceeded to order its supporters to boycott the elections.

In the East and in all but one constituency in Lagos, the UPGA boycott was total. In the Mid-West, the alliance changed its mind at about noon and called off the boycott. Turnout in the West was low. The election results were quickly released, and they showed that the NNA had won 199 seats to the UPGA's 58 (Anglin 1965). For the prime minister, this was as clear a victory for the NNA as there ever could be, and he waited for the president to call upon him to form the next government. On January 01, 1965, the president told the prime minister that the elections were "unsatisfactory in view of the violations of freedom of recent weeks" as a result of which he could not, in good conscience, ask him or anyone else to form a government. He concluded with a threat to resign, and the prime minister urged him to do so if he was unwilling to carry out his duty as dictated by the results of the election that had been "lawfully and constitutionally conducted."

The prime minister shared his thoughts with the chief justice of the federation Sir Adetokunbo Ademola, with whom he had a close personal relationship. Such was their closeness that the prime minister had passed over Justice Samuel Olumuyiwa Jibowu, the first indigenous High Court judge, and chosen Sir Ademola in 1958 to replace the retiring Sir Stafford Foster-Sutton as chief justice. This time, he told his friend that he was going to appoint Sir Kofoworola Abayomi president if Dr. Azikiwe made good on his threat. The chief justice, however, assured him that Dr. Azikiwe was not going to resign. It would appear that he and his colleague, the chief justice of Eastern Nigeria Sir Louis Nwachukwu Mbanefo, had already begun to brainstorm the brewing constitution crisis.

Meanwhile, the president had come under pressure from various political parties and civic groups to assume executive powers and call fresh elections. He was, however, unsure that he had constitutional legs to stand on if he played that hand. He also needed legal clarification regarding the loyalty of the armed forces and the chain of command. On the question of assuming executive authority, the attorney-general of the federation Dr. Taslim Olawale Elias advised that the president had "no power to form an interim or provisional government or to assume powers of the Parliament or of the Cabinet." The president met with the general officer commanding the Nigerian Army Maj. Gen. Christopher Welby-Everard, the chief of naval staff Cmdr. Joseph Edet Akinwale Wey, and the inspector general of the police Mr. Louis Orok Edet. It transpired that the general had himself already sought legal counsel on the matter from Professor Laurence Gower of the Law Faculty of the University of Lagos. He learned that operational control of the armed forces was a prerogative of the prime minister and informed the president as such. Effectively therefore, the president and head of state was outside the chain of command of the armed forces and merely a figurehead. This was corroborated by Justice Lionel Brett of the Supreme Court, who explained that the Army council and Navy board, which were estab-

TOWARD UNDERSTANDING THE NIGERIA-BIAFRA WAR AND LINGERING QUESTIONS

lished by the Army and Navy Acts respectively, answered to the minister of Defense, who was an appointee of the prime minister.

Chief Justice Ademola and Justice Mbanefo arrived at a proposal for the resolution of the crisis, which they presented to the president and prime minister on January 03, 1965. Its recommendations included the acceptance of the declared election results and the formation of a broad-based government predicated on those results, a rerun of elections only in constituencies where the process had been an "obvious mockery," the deferment of the determination of the detailed legality of the elections to the justice system, the formation of a commission to review the constitution, and the electoral machinery and the dissolution of the government of Western Nigeria "to allow a free expression of electoral will." The president and prime minister accepted the recommendations, and the next day, the former invited the latter to form a government. Disaster was averted—rather, postponed. The reruns happened on March 18, 1965. The seat count of the UPGA increased from 58 to 115. The haul of NNA remained unchanged at 199. Attention then turned to the Western Regional election scheduled for October 11, 1965.

The nation held its breath as the campaign unfolded along the same rancorous lines as the one ten months before. Over a dozen UPGA candidates could not file their nomination papers because the electoral officers were no longer showing up at their places of work or were just rejecting them. On polling day, the NNA literally outdid itself, perpetrating fraudulence on an unprecedented and harrowing scale. Hundreds of thousands of ballot papers were found on unauthorized persons, secreted within voluminous traditional clothing or disguised as pregnancies, and many party operatives were apprehended as they tried to stuff them into ballot boxes. Some returning officers held onto the results, refusing to send them to headquarters, even as the government-run radio was announcing results when counting was still going on. The police reportedly recovered copies of these fictitious results that were, in all likelihood, prepared well before polling day.

The eminent writer and Nobel laureate Professor Akinwande Oluwole Babatunde Soyinka was an active participant in the resistance to the miscarriage of the electoral process playing out at the time. In his memoir, he recalled that a team of radio journalists from the Eastern Nigeria Broadcasting Corporation (ENBC), led by Mazi Anyaogu Elekwachi Ukonu, came to cover the elections. They brought with them a transmitter which they set up in the home of Chief Awolowo in Ikenne. After polls closed, the UPGA received authentic results directly from constituencies all across the region and made them available to the studios of the ENBC at Enugu from which they were broadcast. Those results showed that the UPGA had won 68 seats while the NNA won 26. The UPGA duly claimed victory and declared that Alhaji Dauda Adegbenro was going to form the next government. The Western Nigeria Electoral Commission, for its part, went on air to announce that it was the NNA that had prevailed, with 82 seats to the UPGA's 11. The governor Sir Joseph Odeleye Fadahunsi invited Chief Akintola to form a government, and Alhaji Adegbenro was ordered arrested. This was more than the populace could stand. Supporters of the Action Group and the NNDP poured into the streets and began to go after each other. Soon enough, law and order broke down region-wide. In what came to be known as Operation Wet-ie, party thugs would douse their opponents in gasoline and set them ablaze, a killing method of comparable gruesomeness to "necklacing" that would happen in South Africa two decades later. There was such widespread wanton destruction of life, limb, and property that the region became known as the Wild, Wild West. Curfews were imposed by the beleaguered Akintola government, and the police struggled to no avail. The Balewa government in Lagos stood by and did not intervene. It had either been stunned into bewildered inaction or, as some analysts have suggested, was biding its time and had plans to unleash the armed forces. As it turned out, the crisis in the West was the death rattle of the First Republic.

Through all this, the East was calm. At the center, the NCNC was in relatively peaceful, albeit uninspired, workaday coalition with the NPC. Although Professor Eyo Ita had decamped in the crisis during the Macpherson Constitution and formed his own party to agitate for a Calabar-Ogoja-Rivers state, he rejoined the NCNC in 1956. Mr. Isaac Jasper Adaka Boro would not stir things up for another year. Until 1965, he was an undergraduate in chemistry at the University of Nigeria, reportedly supported by an NCNC scholarship. As president of the student union, he and a coeval, Mr. Jude Emezie, had actually sued the federal government after the December 1964 election, praying the court to nullify the results of the election and order the Federal Electoral Commission to conduct fresh polls. All in all, neither the Igbo nor the East as a whole was causing Nigeria any trouble.

PART 2

THE COUPS

Meanwhile, disenchantment with the political climate continued to grow, fueled by the mayhem in the West, rampant corruption among politicians, and the realization that existing constitutional mechanisms could not be used to dislodge the status quo and effect rectification. Outside the political class, the only other institution capable of acting on a national scale in coordinated fashion was the military.

CHAPTER 5

THE NIGERIAN ARMY OFFICER CORPS

In 1964, the Nigerian Armed Forces numbered about 10,500 officers and men. The oldest and largest branch was the Army, with about 9,000 soldiers. Its origins go back to the Northern Nigeria Regiment of the West African Frontier Force established by the British Colonial Office in 1900 under the command of the self-same Colonel Frederick Lugard and charged with checking French expansionist tendencies in the territories around the Northern Protectorate. The Nigerian Navy (900 officers and men in 1964) traces its roots to the Nigerian Marine formed in 1914 but, like the Nigerian Air Force (700 officers and men in 1964), was formally established in 1964 by the Navy and Air Force Acts respectively.

Shortly after the Second World War, the British decided to cultivate a Nigerian officer corps, drawing from the pool of serving senior noncommissioned officers. They would be sent to officer cadet schools in the United Kingdom for training and then granted short-service commissions. The first such officer was Louis Victor Ugboma (East, Igbo) who was commissioned in 1948. He was followed by Wellington Umoh ("Duke") Bassey (East, Efik), Johnson Thomas Umunnakwe Aguiyi-Ironsi (East, Igbo), and Samuel Adesujo Ademulegun (West, Yoruba) in 1949. Ralph Sodeinde (West, Yoruba) was commissioned in 1950, and three years later came Abubakar Zakaria Maimalari (North, Kanuri), Babafemi Olatunde Ogundipe (West, Yoruba), and Robert Adeyinka Adebayo (West, Yoruba), completing the early thin uppermost crust of the indigenous officer corps. Zakaria Maimalari stood out because he had enlisted after attending Government (now Barewa) College Zaria and was sent to the Royal Military Academy Sandhurst in Berkshire, England.

As independence approached, efforts to "nigerianize" the officer corps accelerated. Initially, recruitment was based on performance in entrance examinations and Igbo candidates excelled. As a result, by 1960, over 60 percent of army officers were Igbo, to the alarm of Northern politicians. According to the historian Max Siollun, the prime minister Alhaji Balewa once remarked, "We are surrounded by Igbo officers, if anything happens, they are going to kill us." The remedy they devised was a quota system which guaranteed 50 percent of officer cadet admissions to the North and 25 percent each to the East and West. The fact that the North did not have the number of suitably qualified candidates to fill their quota was no object—they lowered the admission standards. Needless to say, this did not go down well with Southern officers.

Army recruiters combed the North looking for prospects. They targeted secondary schools and sometimes took along young Northern army officers whom they showed off as models worthy of emulation. One such officer was the Sandhurst-trained Yakubu Dan-Yumma Gowon. Meanwhile, in the South, university graduates had begun to opt for careers in the military, and by the midsixties, there were seven of them with combatant commissions. The first was Chukwuemeka Odumegwu-Ojukwu, who had an Oxford University degree in history. The others were Emmanuel Arinze Ifeajuna, Emmanuel Udeaja, Adewale Ademoyega, Victor Adebukunola Banjo, Olufemi Olutoye, and Oluwole Rotimi. The first three were Igbo, and the rest were Yoruba. Not only were they highly educated, they were also politically astute, and the Northern establishment saw them as yet another level of threat. The leader of the NPC and premier of the Northern Region Alhaji Ahmadu Bello reportedly instructed the minister of Defense to halt the recruitment of Southern graduates into the armed forces. Political considerations had become a crucial element in military decision-making.

TOWARD UNDERSTANDING THE NIGERIA-BIAFRA WAR AND LINGERING QUESTIONS

In 1960, Maj. Gen. Norman Forster succeeded Maj. Gen. Robert Exham as general officer commanding (GOC) the Nigerian Army. He, in turn, handed over to Maj. Gen. Christopher Welby-Everard in 1962, on whom it fell to recommend an indigenous successor when his tour ended in February 1965. He had before him a slate of four brigadier generals: Johnson Aguiyi-Ironsi, Samuel Ademulegun, Babafemi Ogundipe, and Zakaria Maimalari. Max Siollun got access to the brief he wrote on these candidates and submitted to the permanent secretary of the Ministry of Defense on September 14, 1964. In a nutshell, the GOC quickly dropped Brigadier General Maimalari from consideration as "too young" and "not sufficiently mature." Brigadier General Ogundipe was his apparent top choice because he had "the military ability, leadership qualities, and the personal characteristics to make a good GOC." It is worth mentioning that Brigadier General Ogundipe had served in the British Army during World War II in the India-Burma theater, and among his stated characteristics was an easy-going personality which can be relied upon to score well with a colonial master. General Welby-Everard thought Brigadier General Ademulegun would be a divisive figure if appointed GOC. He commented that the brigadier had "a good many critics, not to say enemies, in the army." When it came to Brigadier General Aguiyi-Ironsi, he explained that it would be difficult for him to provide an accurate assessment since the brigadier general had never served under him. During Major General Welby-Everard's tour, Brigadier General Aguiyi-Ironsi had been away either as military attaché in London; in training at the Imperial Defence College, London; or as commander of the United Nations Force in the Congo (in the rank of major general). He, however, allowed that some accommodation should be made for Brigadier General Aguiyi-Ironsi in the form of either a new chief of defense staff position within the army but superior to that of GOC or otherwise employment outside the military.

After Major General Welby-Everard left on February 11, 1965, it was time for politicians to evaluate his recommendations in the context of their own reality. The NPC and NCNC were in coalition in Lagos. Brigadier General Maimalari was the NPC's candidate for

GOC, but support for him was not unanimous. Some senior members of the party seemed to be of the opinion that more than enough had been done for him already, and it wasn't clear that he deserved all, if any, of it. He and Umar Lawam were the first Nigerian cadets to be sent for officer training at the Royal Military Academy Sandhurst. He received his commission in 1953 and had attained the rank of major by 1961. Thereafter, he shot like a meteor to brigadier general in just two years (December 1962, according to Gen. Hilary Njoku). In contrast with Brigadier Generals Aguiyi-Ironsi and Ogundipe, who personally did not really care for the job, Brigadier General Ademulegun craved it passionately and had Alhaji Ahmadu Bello in his corner. Unfortunately, he wore his political sympathies on his sleeves for all to see, and that did not endear him to many of his colleagues. For some reason, he never saw eye to eye with Brigadier General Maimalari, and they were known to brawl and bicker in full view of junior officers, which was exceedingly unseemly. Brigadier General Aguiyi-Ironsi had the backing of the NCNC. The prime minister Alhaji Tafawa Balewa and the minister of Defense Alhaji Inua Wada of the NPC knew they had a coalition to keep together in Lagos and so threw their weight behind him to the displeasure of their boss in Kaduna. Brigadier General Aguiyi-Ironsi was, after all, the most senior, the most decorated, and the most distinguished. He had been aide-de-camp to Governor-General James Robertson and equerry to Queen Elizabeth II during her visit to Nigeria in 1956. Also to his credit was fluency in the languages of the three largest ethnic groups—Igbo, Yoruba, and Hausa. On May 23, 1965, he was promoted major general and appointed GOC of the Nigerian Army. Brigadier Generals Ademulegun and Maimalari were given commands of 1 Brigade (Kaduna) and 2 Brigade (Ikeja) respectively. Brigadier General Ogundipe was sent to London as military attaché to the Nigerian High Commission.

At this time, several subcultures were discernible in the Nigerian Army officer corps. The cleavages were multiple and complex—North vs. South, Christian vs. Muslim, graduate vs. nongraduate, elite military academy training vs. short-service commission. Max Siollun described it as "an unofficial 'caste' system." There was almost a loathing across the divides. The nongraduates, for instance, considered the graduates as ulteriorly motivated in seeking careers in the military, while the graduates thought of the nongraduates as unsophisticated and incapable of nuanced appreciation of the potential role of the military in an emerging nation. The southern officers considered most of their northern counterparts as unqualified, featherbedded beneficiaries of an unjust quota system whose careers were lubricated by political patrons. Gen. Philip Efiong remembered Lt. Col. Arthur Unegbe with whom he served in 1 Brigade, Kaduna, as one of those who thought the Sandhurst-trained officers like himself were the crème-de-la-crème of the Nigerian Army. He was commanding officer, Fourth Battalion, but had no compunction clashing with his Eaton Hall-trained brigade commander Brigadier General Ademulegun. When he was relieved of his command and transferred back to Army Headquarters, he protested vigorously to Sandhurst-trained Brigadier General Maimalari and other alumni of that Berkshire institution. During the tour of duty of the Fifth Battalion in the Congo in 1960, officer commanding "B" Company then-Major Maimalari felt sufficiently self-assured to disagree with his commanding officer, then-Colonel Aguiyi-Ironsi over rules of engagement at Kindu. Of course, the commanding officer promptly relieved him of his command and sent him back to Nigeria. There were officers who, somehow, straddled the boundaries, and this gave them unique appeal under many circumstances. A notable example was Yakubu Gowon, who was a Sandhurst-trained Northern Christian.

Such was the state of the Nigerian Army as the political situation deteriorated in the West in 1965, by which time seeds of the thought that something had to be done had germinated in many minds. However, it is possible that coup ideation in the Nigerian military might be as old as the country itself. According to General Hilary Njoku, commander of the Biafran Army during the first six weeks of the civil war, Lt. Col. Victor Banjo, director of the Corps of Electrical and Mechanical Engineers, "was known to be hatching a coup since 1960." Nevertheless, it was the imminent collapse in 1965 that galvanized efforts on at least two levels. On January

12, 1966, at the Second Battalion officers' mess, Ikeja, an inebriated Brig. Gen. Zakaria Maimalari unwittingly disclosed that senior officers sympathetic to the Nigerian National Alliance party (NNA) were actively recruiting for a coup d'état. This solemn announcement was made at the send-off party for then-Lieutenant Colonel Njoku, who was leaving to assume command of the Nigerian Military Training College (NMTC), Kaduna. For the benefit of the doubt, the brigadier general was reported to have graphically illustrated the planned technique for dispatching their victims by making a sadistic gesture against the front of his neck with the edge of his index finger.

The younger well-educated, politically idealistic overwhelmingly southern officers, who had been trained in the finest British military academies, also felt obliged to intervene and salvage a country that was hurriedly going to hell in a handbasket. It would seem that they had ruminated vaguely on the subject for many months, if not years, but it was not until about August 1965 that active planning began. According to Lieutenant Colonel Njoku, the young conspirators became aware of the senior officers' plot in December 1965, and when Brigadier General Maimalari let the cat out of the bag on January 12, 1966, they knew they had to strike without further hesitation.

CHAPTER 6

JANUARY 15, 1966

The coup of January 15, 1966, reportedly had as its objective the overthrow of the NNA-led federal government and its replacement with one that had Chief Obafemi Awolowo at its head. Chief Awolowo was serving time at Calabar Prison for the failed coup attempt of 1962, and Capt. Emmanuel Udeaja, Army Engineers, Kaduna, was scheduled to go and bring him to Lagos as soon as the operations were completed. By a different account, it was Air Force Maj. Theophilus E. Nzegwu, who had served in the Royal Air Force, that was to escort the chief to Lagos. The operation in the North was led by Maj. Patrick Chukwuma Kaduna Nzeogwu, chief instructor at the Nigeria Military Training College (NMTC), Kaduna. In 1963, Major Nzeogwu had become the first indigenous intelligence officer, Army Headquarters, in which capacity he observed the treason trial of Chief Awolowo. As time passed, he apparently kept his fingers on the pulse of the nation's politics.

As chief instructor, Major Nzeogwu could plan and execute training exercises which involved troop movements and the use of live ammunition without arousing suspicion. One such exercise, "Damisa" (for Leopard) was officially billed as training in the use of newly acquired weapons but, in reality, was the rehearsal for a coup. When, in the early hours of January 15, 1966, he led a detachment of troops to the vicinity of the official residence of the premier of Northern Nigeria, they believed it was yet another training excursion until he told them what the mission was. They reportedly all agreed to participate, and he took only three Northern noncommissioned officers with him in the assault on the premier's lodge. The premier, his bodyguard, and one of his wives were killed.

The other leader of the coup in the North was Maj. Timothy Onwuatuegwu, who was an instructor at the NMTC. He led troops to the home of Brig. Gen. Samuel Ademulegun, Commander 1 Brigade, Kaduna. The general and his wife were killed. He then went and arrested the governor Sir Kashim Ibrahim. The governor was reportedly treated with the utmost respect and courtesy by Majors Onwuatuegwu and Nzeogwu, the latter personally apologizing for having had him arrested. However, the Northern soldiers in his guard detail were reportedly demanding that he be shot, presumably because he was just another embodiment of the despised establishment. Major Onwuatuegwu nevertheless insisted that the governor must come to no harm. In due course, Sir Kashim Ibrahim issued a written transfer of power to Major Nzeogwu and was flown home to Maiduguri at his request.

At Ibadan, the coup was carried out by officers and men of Abeokuta Garrison Organization led by Capt. Emmanuel Nwobosi, officer commanding, Second Field Battery. It would seem that the inevitability of military intervention was a foregone conclusion in the minds of politicians in the West of the era, given the failure of civil authorities to maintain law and order in the region in the early 1960s. As a result, they were more attentive to the numerous rumors of such an event that had been circulating since the period of emergency. Some politicians actually began to actively cultivate personal relationships with senior military officers and the premier of the western region, Chief Samuel Akintola reportedly received firearms training at the hands of Lt. Col. Abogo Largema, the commanding officer of Fourth Battalion, Ibadan. Sir Ahmadu Bello in the North was also widely known to be very close to Brig. Gen. Samuel Ademulegun of 1 Brigade, once gifting him a horse.

Chief Akintola and Colonel Largema traveled to Kaduna on January 14, 1966, to meet with Sir Ahmadu Bello and allegedly warn him of the imminence of a coup. Sir Bello was reportedly somewhat dismissive but recommended that the colonel go to Lagos and share his premonitions with the general officer commanding (GOC), Nigerian Armed Forces. A worried Chief Akintola returned to Ibadan, and that night, his worst fears were realized.

Captain Nwobosi and his troops arrived at Ibadan at about 3:00 a.m. and headed first to the residence of the deputy premier, Chief Remi Fani-Kayode. The deputy premier offered no resistance and was arrested without incident. He was transported to Federal Guards Barracks, Lagos, for detention. Fortunately (and unfortunately) for Chief Akintola, his deputy's wife telephoned to tell him what had happened to her husband, and so he was ready when the coup party arrived at his premises shortly afterward. The chief opened fire on the intruders, and a gunfight broke out with inevitable consequences. According to reports, the round that killed the premier was fired by a Tiv soldier.

There was activity in the East and the Mid-West. Orders from Major Ifeajuna in the small hours of January 15, 1966, were received by Lt. Aloysius Akpuaka for soldiers of the First Battalion, Enugu, to arrest government officials and take over vital installations at Enugu as well as Benin City, since there was no military formation barracked in the latter. The new commanding officer Lt. Col. David Akpode Ejoor was still in Lagos, and his second-in-command (2-i-C) was Maj. Gabriel Okonweze. The troops hesitated, unsure about the legitimacy of the orders. They eventually decided that they were valid, and detachments were sent out to seize the broadcasting house and other key installations. Fortunately for the premier Dr. Michael Okpara, he was playing host to the president of Cyprus Archbishop Makarios III, who was, however, scheduled to depart Enugu that day. Lt. Jerome Oguchi and his troops shadowed the premier and, as soon as the archbishop's plane took off, arrested him. Capt. Joseph Ihedigbo led a detachment of troops to Benin City, where they placed the premier Chief Dennis Chukude Osadebay under house arrest and then returned to Enugu. The commanding officer Lt. Col. David Ejoor flew into Enugu at about midday and took control of the situation. All troops guarding installations in the city were ordered back to barracks. He had his adjutant, Lt. Shehu Musa Yar-

Adua, arrest Lt. Akpuaka and, interestingly, gave instructions to Lt. Yohanna Yarima Kure to use troops to defeat any attempt to release Chief Obafemi Awolowo from Calabar Prison. No politicians were killed in the East or the Mid-West—to which many commentators have pointed as evidence that the coup was an Igbo affair. However, Max Siollun stated that Lieutenant Oguchi was one of the plotters who had made the case for a bloodless operation. One suspects that the story might have been different if the politicians in the East and Mid-West or their security details had offered resistance. In the event, they did not.

In Lagos, Brigadier Zakaria Maimalari, commander, 2 Brigade, was celebrating his remarriage to a third wife, all of fifteen years old. His first wife had been tragically killed in a shooting accident. The second wife who bore his children left him, allegedly for reasons of abuse. The party at his home on Thompson Avenue on January 14, 1966, was high-brow and well-attended by the military and civilian elite. It wrapped up after midnight, and his brigade major, Maj. Emmanuel Ifeajuna, called Orders ("O") Group at his residence. The coup plotters then dispersed across the city to their various assignments.

The group tasked with eliminating the GOC of the Nigerian Armed Forces, Gen. Johnson Aguiyi-Ironsi, was led by Maj. Donatus Okafor, commander of the Federal Guards. They headed over to the general's residence on Glover Road, Ikoyi, but drew a blank. The GOC had not gone home after he left Brigadier Maimalari's party. He went instead to another party on board the MV *Aureol* at Apapa Wharf. That was very bad news for the coup plotters.

Maj. Christian Anuforo (general staff officer II) went after his bosses at Army Headquarters—Col. Kur Mohammed, the chief of staff, and Lt. Col. Arthur Chinyelu Unegbe, the quartermaster general. He had them both shot dead. Lieutenant Colonel Unegbe was the only Igbo officer killed in the January 1966 coup. The allegation that he suffered that fate because he refused to surrender the keys to the armory is patently false because, even as quartermaster general, he never would have the said keys on his person or at home. According to General Njoku, he had been approached by Maj. Emmanuel

Ifeajuna to sign on to the plot, but he declined because he thought it would fail. He was also a close friend of the rampant Brigadier General Maimalari and so guilty by association.

Major Ifeajuna led the group that arrested the prime minister shortly after 2:00 a.m. and took him away in a military vehicle. Only three days before, the prime minister had finished hosting a heads of government meeting of the Commonwealth of Nations, which deliberated on the Unilateral Declaration of Independence by then Rhodesia on November 11, 1965. He reportedly was treated very respectfully by his captors, but Chief Festus Okotie-Eboh, the finance minister who lived next door, was not so lucky. Chief Okotie-Eboh had come to symbolize the excesses of the First Republic far more than most other politicians. His sartorial extravagance especially did not endear him to many. The group that arrested him, led by 2nd Lt. Godfrey Ezedigbo, picked him up, literally threw him into their vehicle, and drove away. Major Ifeajuna and Second Lieutenant Ezedigbo met up at Ikoyi Hotel, where Lieutenant Colonel Largema was staying. They shot him dead and then headed out to a prearranged meeting at the officers mess of the Federal Guards, Dodan Barracks.

After the prime minister was abducted, his domestic staff placed a call to the GOC. So did Ms. Elizabeth Pam, the wife of Lt. Col. James Yakubu Pam, adjutant general of Army Headquarters, after he had been picked up by Maj. Humphrey Iwuchukwu Chukwuka, his deputy. She also called Brigadier General Maimalari. The brigadier was actually in the act of taking the call when the mutineers arrived from the GOC's residence. His guards challenged them, and an exchange of fire broke out. The brigadier fled on foot, shooting a noncommissioned officer as he made his escape. He managed to elude the hit squad that had come for him, but unfortunately, when he desperately flagged down an oncoming car for help at the junction of Second Avenue and Temple Road, it turned out to be a vehicle in Major Ifeajuna's convoy that was returning to Dodan Barracks. They shot him dead.

When the GOC returned home and got the telephone messages, he quickly changed into military fatigues and headed over to Dodan Barracks, arriving there shortly after 3:00 a.m. He had long had his misgivings about the officer corps and was known to complain that they were more politicians than soldiers. The day before, a circular note he had signed warned the participants at a brigade conference to reinforce security and exercise more vigilance when they returned to their units because some army officers were planning to "cause trouble." Within twenty-four hours, it seemed to be happening. He knew the army very well, having enlisted as a private at age eighteen in 1942 and risen to company sergeant major in 1946 before proceeding to Staff College, Camberley, for officer training. He believed he could count more on the noncommissioned officers than their commissioned counterparts for loyalty. At Federal Guards Barracks, he ordered the regimental sergeant major (RSM) to place troops on alert and not follow any orders except those that came from him, the GOC. He then drove across town to the Ikeja Cantonment headquarters of the Second Battalion and checked in first with the RSM whom he also ordered to place the battalion on alert. He called the commanding officer of the battalion, Lt. Col. Hilary Njoku, summoning him to the RSM's residence. When he arrived, the GOC challenged him, pistol drawn, to declare his allegiance. A distraught and disappointed but irked commanding officer could only answer, "I would have liked to arm you if you had no arms." He never expected that his GOC would, under any circumstances, consider his loyalty in question. He nevertheless escorted him to his office, and Lt. Col. Yakubu Gowon joined them there. Lieutenant Colonel Gowon had just returned from a course at Joint Services Staff College, Camberley, and was waiting to assume command of Second Battalion on that day. He had come back to the barracks after the brigade commander's party which he had attended with his Igbo fiancée, Ms. Edith Ike, who was a sister of one of my classmates in medical school. Lieutenant Colonel Gowon showed up at the command office in response to the bugle alert that was sounded. The commanding officer, perhaps in the throes of the mixed emotions he was experiencing over his encounter with the GOC, did not remember to summon him personally as a courtesy. Although Lieutenant Colonel Gowon never shared his feelings on the matter, the commanding officer was convinced that he took it hard and would, in due course, consider it as evidence of a calculated attempt to exclude him from important communication and decision-making.

The GOC proceeded to write down the names of officers he wanted arrested, and Maj. Emmanuel Ifeajuna was the very first. He also identified the very important personalities and installations that needed protection by troops. The commanding officer then prepared his orders and called "O" Group in his conference room. Tasks were assigned, and the business of suppressing the insurrection began in earnest.

When the coup plotters reassembled at the Federal Guards officers' mess, they quickly realized that things had gone badly wrong. The GOC was still alive and at large, and Major Okafor had lost his command. He had tried to have a word with his RSM and was "nearly shot." They drove away from Dodan Barracks, taking their captives with them.

Maj. John Ikechukwu Obienu, whose role was critical to the success of the coup in the Lagos area, had failed to execute. He was the commanding officer of the Second Reconnaissance Squadron, Abeokuta, and was supposed to provide the four armored cars needed for the operation—one for the arrest of the GOC, one for taking over Broadcasting House, and two for seizing Second Battalion Headquarters, Ikeja. For unexplained reasons, he developed cold feet and actually changed sides. Majs. Adewale Ademoyega and Christian Anuforo went looking for him, but he was not at his headquarters at Abeokuta either. Major Anuforo, who had commanded the squadron in the past, was able to commandeer some armored vehicles, and they headed back to Lagos. Unfortunately, as they stopped to refuel en route, the junior officers operating the vehicles heard on the radio that there had been an insurrection in the army but that the majority of troops were still loyal to the GOC and the federal government. They abandoned the majors and returned to base.

By midday, it was clear that the coup in Lagos had failed irredeemably. The broadcast that Major Ifeajuna was expected to make earlier in the day had not happened. He and Maj. Donatus Okafor had dashed across country to Enugu by road, but by the time they arrived, Lt. Col. David Ejoor was in town and in firm control. They went into hiding, and Major Ifeajuna would eventually escape to Ghana. In the North, Majors Nzeogwu and Onwuatuegwu had accomplished their objectives and were in essential control of the 1 Brigade Area of Command. Major Nzeogwu took to the air, speaking in the name of the Supreme Council of the Revolution of the Nigerian Armed Forces. He declared martial law over the northern provinces, suspended the Constitution, and dissolved the regional government and elected assemblies. The "Ten Extraordinary Orders of the Day" were issued, and he proceeded to almost lyrically characterize the enemy he and the council were up against:

> The political profiteers, the swindlers, the men in high and low places that seek bribes and demand 10 percent; those that seek to keep the country divided permanently so that they can remain in office as ministers or VIPs at least, the tribalists, the nepotists, those that make the country look big for nothing before international circles, those that have corrupted our society and put the Nigerian political calendar back by their words and deeds. (Radio Kaduna broadcast, January 15, 1966)

Up until then, never had anyone so passionately diagnosed and denounced the ailments of the country so publicly. The political class had indeed come up short, and the chaos in the West was a lurid testament to that failure. The major then set about consolidating his hold on the North and began making plans to move South.

Major Nzeogwu rounded on the military establishments in Kaduna, taking time to explain the unfolding events to the officers and men everywhere he went. The other significant formations in the north were in Kano (Fifth Battalion, commanded by Lt. Col. Odumegwu-Ojukwu) and Zaria (Nigeria Army Training Depot, commanded by Lt. Col. Wellington "Duke" Umoh Bassey. Lieutenant Colonel Odumegwu-Ojukwu seemed to be monitoring events in Lagos carefully and was calibrating his reactions accordingly. Major

TOWARD UNDERSTANDING THE NIGERIA-BIAFRA WAR AND LINGERING QUESTIONS

Nzeogwu first sensed he might be a problem when he did not send a representative to the Signature Parade. Lieutenant Colonel Bassey, the second Nigerian to receive a commission in the Royal West African Frontier Force (second lieutenant, April 30, 1949, two months ahead of the GOC), showed up in Lagos on January 18, 1966. Curiously, the "Old Soldier" seemed to have a talent for smelling approaching trouble from a considerable distance and making himself unavailable at the exigent moment. He headed out of Zaria on January 15, 1966, leaving his 2-i-C, Maj. Festus Akagha, to "take care of the Depot." Come July 29, 1966, he was again not at his headquarters. On a side note, Lieutenant Colonel Bassey's designation was N/1 instead of N/2. The index Nigerian Army officer (and rightfully N/1) was 2nd Lt. Louis Victor Ugboma (East, Igbo—from Ogbaru in present-day Anambra State). He was a school teacher before he enlisted and was commissioned on August 28, 1948. He reportedly resigned his commission in 1953 and returned to teaching.

Meanwhile, troops needed to be paid. Major Nzeogwu dispatched Capt. Goddy Ude with orders for Lieutenant Colonel Odumegwu-Ojukwu to collect the necessary funds from the Central Bank, Kano "by any means at his disposal." The commanding officer had Captain Ude arrested and detained. Maj. Matthew Olusegun Okikiola Aremu Obasanjo, Field Engineering Squadron, Kaduna, who was on good terms with Major Nzeogwu and apparently so too with the commanding officer, offered to mediate and was flown to Kano by Lt. Dan Suleiman and Lt. Jonathan Asen. On arrival at the airport, they, too, were arrested by Lieutenant Ike Nwachukwu on the commanding officer's orders, and their aircraft was impounded. It took the intervention of Lt. Col. Alexander Madiebo, inspector of artillery, for all detained emissaries to regain their freedom and for funds to be made available for troop payments.

Major Nzeogwu decided to escalate. He divided the forces loyal to him into three groups. One group was to head north to Kano via Zaria to sort out the Fifth Battalion and its commander. Another group would strike out southeast to Makurdi and eventually take Enugu and Benin City. The third group was the main force, and its mission objective was Lagos. It was a mechanized armor outfit to be commanded by 2nd Lt. Juventus Chijioke Ojukwu (no relation of the Fifth Battalion commanding officer) and would operate with air support. When the ground force approached Lagos, the plan was for Piaggio and Dornier aircraft to strafe and soften up targets with machine gun fire. Since they did not have the range to return to Kaduna after operations, a makeshift forward base would have to be quickly set up. Capts. Elendu Ukeje and John Yisa-Doko took off in Dorniers to reconnoiter the roadways around Jebba for a suitable strip. Unfortunately, both aircraft developed radio and mechanical problems in flight and had to return to Kaduna.

In Lagos at about 10:00 a.m., on January 15, 1966, two expatriates, the acting inspector of police Mr. Leslie Marsden and commissioner of police Mr. M. V. Jones arrived at Ikeja Cantonment by helicopter. They shared with the GOC what information they had gathered about the events earlier that morning and asked to know whether the coup had his blessing. After he replied in the negative, they told him the minister of state for the Army in the Ministry of Defense Alhaji Ibrahim Tanko Galadima would like to meet with him at the police headquarters in Lion Building, Moloney Street, Obalende. They left about half an hour later. The GOC subsequently set up a joint operations room at police headquarters, and with him there were Lt. Col. Yakubu Gowon and Maj. Patrick Anwunah, general staff officer I. He operated out of police headquarters until January 29, 1966. Among the senior police officers working with him, there were the British expatriates who, needless to say, had access to the most sensitive information and unrestricted access to him. This was worrisome because the foreign news media, including the British Broadcasting Corporation and Voice of America, seemed to get information on the rapidly unfolding events hours, if not days, before the Nigerian Broadcasting Corporation (NBC). These media organizations were also reporting with bias, if not mischief or both. At a time when the names of the military officers killed had not been released, perhaps for security reasons, the foreign news media already had received and published them. On January 16, 1966, the London-based weekly *West Africa* carried the false news item that Lt. Col. Hilary Njoku was the leader of the coup in the South and that Alhaji Zanna Bukar Dipcharima had been named acting prime minister. A further cause for concern was the GOC's overall composure at the outset. In the unsettled atmosphere of a complex situation that was more political than military, he was described as rattled and somewhat discombobulated. Arguably, he would have been very impressionable, and there is no telling what drivel the British officers might have at least tried to push through his mind during his stay at Police Headquarters.

The other operations room was at Second Battalion Headquarters, Ikeja, where Lieutenant Colonels Njoku (who would have handed over battalion command to Lt. Col. Yakubu Gowon that day) and George Tamuno Kurubo, commanding officer, Third Battalion, Kaduna; Francis Adekunle Fajuyi, who was actually on leave, having handed over command of the First Battalion, Enugu, to David Ejoor and would resume at Abeokuta Garrison Organization; and Maj. Murtala Ramat Muhammed, inspector of signals, held forth. Lt. Col. Victor Banjo assembled the officers of Lagos Garrison Organization at the Command Workshop, Yaba.

At about midday, the Council of Ministers (Alhajis Zana Bukar Dipcharima, Shehu Shagari, Maitama Sule, Ibrahim Galadima, and Nuhu Bamali; Chiefs Hezekiah Davies and Abiodun Akinrele; Drs. Kingsley Mbadiwe and Taslim Elias), Mr. Stanley Wey (secretary to the prime minister), and two British expatriates, Mr. Marsden of the police and Sir Francis Cumming-Bruce, the high commissioner, met with the GOC. They gave him a written order signed by the minister of state for the Army Alhaji Galadima for loyal forces to be used to suppress the rebellion. The ministers also reportedly requested British military assistance but were told by the high commissioner that such a request could only come from the prime minister. At the time, Alhaji Balewa was still missing, and his fate was unknown. The NPC members of the cabinet headed over to the home of the acting president Dr. Nwafor Orizu (the president Dr. Nnamdi Azikiwe was away on vacation) to ask that the most senior member of the Council of Ministers, Alhaji Dipcharima, be appointed acting prime minister. The acting president demurred because the delegation did not include members of the other party in the government coalition, the NCNC. He told them he would have to consult with the NCNC ministers before taking further action. It was at that juncture that the GOC arrived to inform the cabinet delegation that the order he was given was insufficient authority to commit military forces. He needed one signed by the prime minister or his surrogate. During the crisis following the 1964 federal elections at which the Nigeria National Alliance prevailed due to the boycott by the United Progressive Grand Alliance over gross electoral malpractices, the precedent was set that in the event of conflicting orders from the president and prime minister, the Armed Forces would obey those of the prime minister. Therefore, the involvement of any military force of any kind, indigenous or foreign, needed prime-ministerial agency.

Senior military officers convened at about 4:30 p.m. on January 15, 1966, to consider their options. In conference were the GOC, Commodore Joseph Edet Akinwale Wey (chief of naval staff, an Easterner [Efik] whose mother was Yoruba); Lieutenant Colonels Njoku, Kurubo, Banjo, Fajuyi, Gowon; and Maj. Patrick Anwunah. The GOC invited each of them to speak their mind. Lieutenant Colonel Njoku shared that he had already expressed to the GOC earlier in the day at Second Battalion Headquarters that a "constitutional" transfer of power to the Army was the country's only salvation. Lieutenant Colonel Banjo mentioned that he was in contact with the group in Kaduna and endorsed the capitulation of the civil administration to the military. This was echoed by Lieutenant Colonel Fajuyi, and they all waited for Lieutenant Colonel Gowon to make his contribution. In Lieutenant Colonel Njoku's recollection, Lieutenant Colonel Gowon stuttered incoherently for a while and then suddenly requested permission to fly to Zaria, where the Army Training Depot was located. The depot had reportedly not pledged allegiance to Maj. Patrick Nzeogwu, and Lieutenant Colonel Gowon imagined he might be able to muster enough troops there to march on Kaduna. He did not seem to appreciate the operational difficulties of such an undertaking, and they were patiently explained to him. Just before the meeting, Lieutenant Colonel Njoku had received the list of casualties, presumably from his adjutant Capt. Martin Adamu, who would later play a key role in the July 29, 1966, coup. Before then, the only officer who they knew had been killed was Lt. Col. Abogo Largema, commanding officer, Fourth Battalion, Ibadan. Lieutenant Colonel Njoku handed the GOC the list, and he passed it around the table. With the full horror of the events thus far before them, further talk of soldier-on-soldier violence seemed moot, if not inane. The meeting rose at about 7:00 p.m.

The next day, January 16, 1966, the GOC summoned the Council of Ministers to meet with him at the cabinet office. With him were the chief of naval staff and the acting inspector general of police Alhaji Kam Selem. The fresh faces on the civilian side were Chief Richard Osuolale Abimbola Akinjide, Alhaji Ali Mungono, and Alhaji Abdul Ganiyu Folorunsho Abdulrazaq, the legal adviser of the NPC and first Northerner to be called to the bar. The meeting began at about 7:00 p.m. with updates from a more self-assured GOC, who, however, became emotional as he related the fate that had befallen his senior officers. According to Alhaji Shehu Shagari, the GOC admitted that he had been unable to quell the rebellion and the Army was "pressing him to assume power." He confessed that he was reluctant to do so but that "the boys were adamant and waiting outside." The council agreed to cede power, and Alhaji Abdulrazak jotted down a handover note which was signed by Alhaji Dipcharima and Dr. Mbadiwe. At 11:50 p.m., the president of the Senate and acting president of the Republic Dr. Nwafor Orizu broadcast to the nation that the Council of Ministers had unanimously handed over the administration of the country voluntarily to the Armed Forces. It was followed by a brief acceptance speech by the GOC. In Chief Akinjide's interesting take on the situation, the coup actually took place on January 16, 1966, when the acting president Dr. Nwafor Orizu handed over power to General Aguiyi-Ironsi.

The senior officers soon learned that the GOC, now head of the National Military Government and Supreme Commander of the Nigerian Armed Forces, was about to make gubernatorial and other appointments. They were surprised he hadn't sought their input, and just in case he needed it, Lieutenant Colonels Njoku, Kurubo, and Fajuyi compiled the following recommendations and submitted them to him—governors: West, Lt. Col Francis Fajuyi; Mid-West,

Lt. Col David Ejoor; North, Lt. Col. (newly promoted) Hassan Katsina; East, Lt. Col. Hilary Njoku. In the event, it was Lt. Col. Chukwuemeka Odumegwu-Ojukwu, commanding officer, Fifth Battalion, Kano, and first university graduate to receive commission in a combat unit in the Nigerian Armed Forces, who was appointed military governor of Eastern Nigeria. Lieutenant Colonel Njoku was given command of 2 Brigade, Lagos.

Meanwhile at Kaduna, Maj. Patrick Nzeogwu realized that the GOC had regained firm control of the forces in the South, and his plan to take Lagos by storm would be calamitous. He agreed to turn himself in but only on condition of five demands being met, among which were immunization from legal action for all those involved in the "military exercise" and guarantees that the overthrown politicians would not be reinstated. The demands were conveyed to the GOC in Lagos by Maj. Olusegun Obasanjo. Major Nzeogwu then held a joint press conference with the newly appointed military governor, Lt. Col. Hassan Katsina, at which he formally handed over power to him. In the evening of January 17, 1966, Lt. Col. Conrad Nwawo, who was military attaché to the Nigerian High Commission in London, was summoned back to Lagos by the supreme commander. He had been Maj. Patrick Nzeogwu's instructor at the Nigerian Military Training School, Zaria, and was trusted by him. The next day, he flew to Kaduna in a chartered aircraft and returned to Lagos with the major. He received treatment at Lagos University Teaching Hospital for the wounds he sustained during the assault on Government House, Kaduna, and, contrary to the assurances he had been given, was arrested by Majs. Henry Igboba (2-i-C, Second Battalion, Ikeja) and Murtala Muhammed (inspector of signals) and slammed into the maximum-security prison at Kirikiri, Lagos. He was later transferred to Aba Prisons. Thus ended the military coup of January 15, 1966. The politicians were dislodged, but the soldiers who came into power were not those who conceptualized, planned, and executed it.

The coup plotters freely admitted that their goal was to release Chief Obafemi Awolowo from prison and vest him with national political power. It was envisioned that it would redound to the benefit

TOWARD UNDERSTANDING THE NIGERIA-BIAFRA WAR AND LINGERING QUESTIONS

of the country as a whole. When that failed to materialize, it quickly faded from the public discourse, and the coup was spun as an Igbo quest for national domination—the preferred delusional paranoid psychosis into which many Nigerians lapse preparatory to perpetrating unspeakable atrocities on the Igbo. Even Brig. Gen. Babafemi Ogundipe, military attaché to the Nigerian Commission in London, called the minister of state for the Army Alhaji Tanko Galadima to tell him he thought it was an Igbo coup. Further discussion of such speculation will be pursued in a subsequent chapter. At first blush, it was all too easy to serve it up as such, especially if the intent was ulterior and malevolent. Just consider the lineup: Majs. Emmanuel Ifeajuna, Patrick Nzeogwu, Timothy Onwuatuegwu, Donatus Okafor, Christian Anuforo, and Humphrey Chukwuka. And the Igbo did not appear to see a need to vigorously challenge and dispel that misapprehension. Or might it just be that in some strange way, it warmed the cockles of their heart that, even though the coup failed, it was an Igbo officer, Gen. Johnson Aguiyi-Ironsi, who became head of state—never mind that what he had to inherit was a sordid mess. The failed January 15, 1966, coup was clearly not an Igbo coup because if it had been, it would have almost certainly succeeded for two obvious facts. First, the officers in command of all the five battalions of the Nigerian Army on January 14, 1996, were Igbo—First Battalion, Enugu: 2-i-C Major Okonweze (Lieutenant Colonel Ejoor was away in Lagos); Second Battalion, Ikeja: Lt. Col. Hilary Njoku; Third Battalion, Kaduna: 2-i-C Maj. Israel Okoro (Lt. Col. George Kurubo was away in Lagos); Fourth Battalion, Ibadan: 2-i-C Maj. Macaulay Nzefili (Lt. Col. Abogo Largema was away in Lagos); Fifth Battalion, Kano: Lt. Col. Chukwuemeka Odumegwu-Ojukwu, as were the quartermaster general (Lt. Col. Arthur Unegbe) and the commanders of Lagos Garrison Organization, Abalti Barracks (Lt. Col. Ogere Umu Imo), and federal guards, Dodan Barracks (Maj. Donatus Okafor). Second, it was Gen. Johnson Aguiyi-Ironsi, the Igbo GOC of the Nigerian Army who, in the event, gave the orders from Second Battalion Headquarters, Ikeja, for loyal forces to put down the rebellion in Lagos. He wouldn't be neutralizing an insurrection he and his kinsmen were fomenting.

The coup of January 15, 1966, did have active Southern non-Igbo participants, among them Maj. Adewale Ademoyega, Capt. Ganiyu Adeleke, Lts. Fola Oyewole and Festus Olafimihan, 2nd Lts. Harris Eghagha and Dag Waribor. According to one account, at least five Northern officers were involved—Capts. John Swanton and Gibson Jalo and 2nd Lts. T. Katsina, S. Dambo, and John Atom Kpera. Major Ademoyega was a key architect of the insurrection, whereas the rest were relatively junior officers and could claim they were only following orders.

It turned out though that General Aguiyi-Ironsi had been contacted beforehand about the coup by one of the plotters, Maj. Emmanuel Ifeajuna, who presumably told him that it would nevertheless be bloodless. The general reportedly traveled to Bauchi to warn the prime minister. It is not clear why he was not granted audience with the prime minister because he left the information with his secretary, Mr. S. O. Wey, who later passed it on to the minister of Defense Alhaji Inua Wada. According to another account, though, it was the GOC who told the minister and was advised he did not need to make the trip to Bauchi if the information he had was all he wanted to convey to the prime minister. Apparently, the minister minimized the threat and promised the general he would let the prime minister know when he returned from vacation. Curiously, Major Ifeajuna was not apprehended for further questioning. On the morning of the coup, however, he was the very first officer the general penciled down for arrest. It was Lieutenant Colonel Njoku's conjecture that the junior officers, in their planning, had wanted to "borrow" the GOC to lend clout and credence to their project. They would have had him announce authoritatively to the country that the military had seized power then disposed of him.

Regardless, the narrative of an Igbo coup took hold and was baked into the public consciousness. The Fulani panicked, power having apparently slipped from their grasp with some of their political and military champions slain. It had become clear to anyone paying attention that the only condition under which they would remain in the country was with power in their hands. Before long, they would seek to avenge the loss of their leaders and regain political power. General Aguiyi-Ironsi was therefore doomed from the outset. He had the options of acting politically or militarily, neither of which guaranteed a useful outcome though. He seemed to opt for the former, pampering the likes of Lt. Col. Yakubu Gowon, who was given a seat on the Supreme Military Council (SMC), and performing other acts of lavish generosity for the benefit of Northerners in the forlorn hope of soothing their bruised sensibilities. Militarily, discipline quickly began to erode as Northern soldiers got into the habit of dictating appointments and deciding who they would take or not take orders from. In the Federal Guards, for example, they insisted that Capt. Joseph Nanven Garba be appointed 2-i-C to Maj. Ben Ochei. At the Fourth Battalion, Ibadan, Igbo officers, including the commanding officer Maj. Macaulay Nzefili, were chased off barracks. Army Headquarters replaced him with Lt. Col. Joseph Akahan. Maj. David Okafor and Capt. Joseph Ihedigbo were rejected by the Fifth Battalion, Kano, as commanding officer and 2-i-C respectively. Majs. Muhammed Shuwa and James Oluleye were appointed in their place. The prompt and willing responsiveness to orders from properly constituted authority, compliance with regulations, and the understanding that other members of the organization will do the same—define discipline. It is at the very core of military essence and the effort to instill it begins on the very first day of bootcamp. A military organization that lacks discipline is done for and is nothing but a menace to itself and the general public as the Nigerian Armed Forces soon became.

Some have argued that the course of history would have been different had the coup makers been promptly court-martialed and the recommended penalties meted out. It turns out that the Supreme Military Council did indeed take a decision to put the mutineers on trial. The responsibility for that fell on the chief of staff, Army Headquarters, the selfsame Lt. Col. Yakubu Gowon who was a member of the council. No one knows why he sat on it, and we will return to this subject in due course. Understandably, the rebellious majors had become folk heroes in many parts of the country, and the Supreme Military Council would have had to contend with substantial public hostility if they came to harm. However, with the benefit of hindsight, that would have been nothing compared to what was to come. Many years later, Gen. Ibrahim Babangida, recidivist coup maker himself, would be unfazed by even his personal relationship with Gen. Mamman Vatsa in the 1985–1986 Orkar coup.

Chapter 7

Uneasy Interlude

General Aguiyi-Ironsi had promised a quick return to civilian rule but not before the ills that doomed the First Republic had been remedied. Two eminent jurists, Dr. Taslim Olawale Elias and Chief Rotimi Williams, were appointed to steer a commission that will craft a new constitution for the country. Another group, led by the finest economists in the land, Dr. Pius Nwabufo Okigbo and Chief Simeon Olaosebikan Adebo, were charged with economic planning. In what would turn out to be a fateful albeit innocent blunder, the general identified "rigid adherence to regionalism" as one of the ailments and set up a commission headed by Mr. Francis Nwokedi to develop a program for unifying the civil administrative services of the country. Few would argue with the correctness of the diagnosis, but it did not, it turned out, need to be intervened upon, at least not at that time.

In a broadcast on May 24, 1966, Decrees 33 and 34 were promulgated. The first proscribed political, tribal, and cultural associations. The second rearranged the regions, transforming them into "groups of provinces," and unified the public service. Before now, the civil service had been siloed in the regions. Its unification irked Northerners very sorely. The regional disposition had nicely insulated them from competition with Southerners in which they were sure they would not fare well. The secretary to the military government and head of the civil service in Kaduna, Alhaji Ali Akilu, made no secret of his displeasure. British expatriates in the North were just as riled up, if not more. Many of them were colonial officers and had taken up cushy jobs in the region on contract, exploiting the very dearth of trained manpower their colonial policy of valorizing Koranic over Western education in the region had created. If a federal public service arrangement came into effect, they would confront the threat of being swept out of office by equally, if not more, capable Southerners. They began to scheme and peddle fantasies of yet another Igbo plot to dominate the North. With the wounds of January 15 still fresh, they did not have to try very hard. Emirs soon met and literally issued an ultimatum to the supreme commander—that Decree no. 34 be abrogated or the North be allowed to secede.

Lieutenant Colonel Gowon was later to allege falsely that the decree was issued before the Supreme Military Council had finished debating it. According to the attorney-general Mr. Gabriel Onyiuke, draft after draft was discussed at multiple meetings of the SMC, with amendments made along the way. The debate did conclude, and the decision to approve the decree was unanimous.

On May 29, 1966, rioting broke out in the North. The British high commissioner (1963–1966) Sir Cumming-Bruce had paid a visit to the area a few days earlier. The rampage had both an ethnic and a religious character. Easterners, Mid-Westerners, and the non-Muslim southern Northerners were killed in very large numbers. The large market in Kano, where many had their businesses, was torched. Easterners and Mid-Westerners fled south in droves. Law enforcement and 1 Brigade were caught off-guard. The brigade commander Lt. Col. Wellington Bassey was regarded as weak and ineffective, having literally subordinated himself to the military governor of the Northern Group of Provinces who was promoted to lieutenant colonel only months before. None too pleased, the supreme commander sent for him and dressed him down. As he returned to his command, Lieutenant Colonel Philip Efiong, principal staff officer, Supreme Headquarters, was sent after him as deputy brigade commander.

The Intelligence Services identified the masterminds of the mayhem. No arrests were made, but some of the British *provoca-*

teurs were expelled. The supreme commander set up a five-person commission of inquiry, with members drawn from all the groups of provinces and headed by a British judge on the Supreme Court, Sir Justice Lionel Brett. Its first meeting was scheduled to be held on August 01, 1966.

Meanwhile, economic activity across the Northern Group of Provinces ground to a standstill with the exodus of Easterners. In solidarity with their fellow Christians, the business people of the southern North (the Middle-Belt), who had also been victimized, refused to move goods around. The North depended on the railways and heavy-freight road transportation to deliver their main cash products, groundnuts, and groundnut oil to the coastal ports. The railway engineers and transport operators were mostly Southerners, predominantly from the East. The military governor of the North, Lieutenant Colonel Katsina, appealed to the supreme commander as well as his colleague in the East. Lieutenant Colonel Odumegwu-Ojukwu acquiesced and pleaded with Easterners who had fled the mayhem to return. In the spirit of forgiveness and reconciliation, he went as far as appointing Alhaji Ado Bayero, the emir of Kano, chancellor of the University of Nigeria, Nsukka, in June 1966. The supreme commander, for his part, wanted more done. His idea was that the emirs who had instigated the unrest should address their appeal themselves directly to the traditional rulers of the South. For that and other reasons, he ordered that arrangements be made for traditional rulers from all over the country to meet with him at Ibadan on July 28, 1966.

The supreme commander who, in the evening of January 16, 1966, professed personal reluctance as he advised the Council of Ministers to temporarily cede power to him confided in Lt. Col. Hilary Njoku that he planned to retire from the Armed Forces on August 01, 1966. The strain of office had begun to show, and the First Lady Victoria had become very worried for him. But first, the general decided he needed to travel around the country to explain and urge acceptance of the much maligned and misunderstood Decree no. 34. His clarifications thus far that the measures were temporary and would be overridden by whatever relevant recommendations the commission working on the new constitution came up with seemed to have inspired little if any reassurance. The tour began in Lagos on July 13, 1966, at Federal Guards (Maj. Ben Okechukwu Ochei, unit commander). He went to Abeokuta the next day and visited Ibadan on July 19, 1966. He then set off for the North on July 23, 1966. Talk about plots to assassinate the supreme commander was rife. Indeed, there had been one to smite him at dinner in the officers' mess in Kaduna, but, according to the commander, 1 Brigade, Lt. Col. Wellington Bassey, who had tried unsuccessfully to persuade the supreme commander to cancel the engagement, it was scrubbed when the chief imam of the Army Alhaji Ilyasu forbade the plotters from spilling the supreme commander's blood in the North. Presumably, they could do it elsewhere. The supreme commander visited Zaria and Jos and then returned to Lagos.

On July 26, 1966, General Aguiyi-Ironsi left Lagos for what would be the last time on the Mid-West leg of his national tour. Two days later, he flew into Ibadan from Benin City for the meeting of traditional rulers. In the recollection of Lieutenant Colonel Njoku, his performance at that meeting was very memorable. He first read from prepared text then launched *ex tempore* into a peroration on unity and duty to country that Lieutenant Colonel Njoku thought was one of the best he had ever heard. His host, the military governor Lt. Col. Francis Fajuyi, gave a reception in the evening at the government house, and at midnight, the supreme commander went to bed.

Up until then, the plot by Northern officers to kill the Supreme Commander and perpetrate their own coup d'état in revenge for that of January 15, 1966, had been twice postponed. They had actually made no secret of their intentions and plans, often fulminating about them out in the open. The lead mutineer, Lt. Col. Murtala Muhammed, declared that he and his fellow Northern officers would avenge the death of those killed in the coup in January to the hearing of the head of the special branch of the Nigerian Police Alhaji Muhammad Dikko Yusuf. Even more disconcerting was the pledge of the military governor of the Northern Group of Provinces that when northern officers struck, they would do so in open daylight, not furtively under the cover of darkness, like the "cowardly" majors did on January 15. Junior officers on a platoon commander's course in Kaduna abused that professional training opportunity to address a letter to the chief of staff, Army Headquarters, Lieutenant Colonel Gowon, warning that if the killings of January were not avenged, they would take matters into their own hands. Among them were 2nd Lt. Sani Abacha (Third Battalion, Kaduna), Lt. Abdullahi Shelleng (Fourth Battalion, Ibadan), Lt. Haladu Hannaniya (Army Corps of Engineers), and Lt. Yakubu Dambo (Third Battalion, Kaduna). How the chief of staff dealt with this ultimatum remains unknown.

What is known is that the supreme commander's attention had been repeatedly drawn to the peril he faced. He was accused by his detractors of having surrounded himself with his Igbo kinsmen whereas the fact was that he often entrusted his personal safety to soldiers of Northern extraction. Lieutenant Colonel Odumegwu-Ojukwu had pointed out to him that such confidence was gravely misplaced. Lt. Col. Alexander Madiebo, inspector of artillery, alarmed at the incessant meetings Northern army officers were holding at the Zaria campus of Ahmadu Bello University with British faculty, flew to Lagos to warn the supreme commander. It is indeed touching that his Army aide-de-camp Lt. Sani Bello, a Northerner, shared with his supreme commander that an attempt would be made on his life in Ibadan on July 29, 1966. The general reportedly replied that it would be unbecoming of him, a soldier, to cancel the trip because of a threat of harm to his person. Under such circumstances, the prudent step would have been to reinforce and/or reconfigure his entourage. Neither was done, and among his retinue on that fateful trip were Maj. Theophilus Yakubu Danjuma (principal staff officer, Army Headquarters), a coleader of the coup plot, and Lt. William Walbe (Second Battalion, Lagos), another enthusiastic mutineer.

According to Capt. Joseph Nanven Garba (second-in-command, Federal Guards), all Northern officers in Lagos and the West were involved in the coup, but the indisputable leaders were Lt. Col. Murtala Muhammed, Majs. Theophilus Danjuma and Martin Adamu (adjutant, Second Battalion, Lagos). On July 28, Lieutenant Colonel Muhammed reportedly came to the home of Lt. Col. Patrick Anwunah, general staff officer (I) and head of military intelligence, uninvited. The GSO accosted Lieutenant Colonel Muhammed with the information that Southern officers were well apprised of the coup he and his fellow Northern officers were planning and were ready and waiting. Afraid that he had been busted, Lieutenant Colonel Muhammed reportedly gave orders for yet another postponement of the mutiny. His minions disagreed and opted to proceed as planned.

Chapter 8

July 29, 1966

The first shots of the July 29, 1966, coup (codenames: AURE, "Paiko's Wedding") were fired at Abeokuta Garrison Organization (AGO). The commanding officer Lt. Col. Gabriel Okonweze had received a tip from sources in Army Headquarters, Lagos, presumably from the GSO (I), that a coup might happen in the night of July 28, 1966. He preemptively summoned all his officers to the mess. He gave orders that all soldiers be armed as a deterrent, but the armorer Corporal Maisamari Maje issued weapons only to Northern soldiers. While he was still addressing his officers, noncommissioned officers (NCOs) burst into the mess, and their leader, Sergeant Sabo Kwale, shot the commanding officer dead. Also killed were Capt. E. B. Orok of the Second Reconnaissance Squadron; Maj. John Obienu, the inspector of reconnaissance; and 2nd Lt. A. O. Olaniyan of the Second Field Battery. Lt. Col. Hilary Njoku, however, described the events differently. In his recollection, the most senior Northern officer in AGO, Capt. Mohammed Remawa, had lured the officers, including his commanding officer to the officers' mess under the pretext of a dodgy signal purported to have been received from Army Headquarters. His hitmen were waiting, and as the officers sat down to drinks, Major Obienu was shot. The commanding officer fled, but they chased him down and shot him too. Captain Orok had been out to town, but as he arrived back in the barracks, he was pulled out of his car and shot dead.

Capt. Mohammed Remawa telephoned Lieutenant Colonel Gowon to let him know what had happened. According to Max Siollun, the chief of staff, Army Headquarters, then began to call military establishments across the country to alert them to the goings-on. The intent of those calls and whom he spoke to are of interest even as the details are not entirely known. Take for instance, though, the one he made to the government house in Ibadan. He reportedly asked to speak to Lt. Col. Hilary Njoku, but it was Major Danjuma who took the call. Major Danjuma told him that he was there to arrest the supreme commander, and the chief of staff's reply was the question, "Can you do it?" Enough said.

Capt. Rowland Ogbonna, officer commanding, "A" Company, AGO, had also been out in town breaking in his new car. He returned to the barracks and went to the mess, literally and figuratively. The body of Major Obienu was still in seated posture at a table. Captain Ogbonna saluted before his eye caught the pool of blood. He quickly sized up the situation correctly and fled back to town where he called First Battalion, Enugu; Second Battalion, Ikeja; and Fourth Battalion, Ibadan, from the police station. The call to the East reached the commanding officer, Lt. Col. David Ogunewe, in a timely fashion. Unfortunately, his message to Second Battalion was received by mutinous officers and passed on to their leaders, Lt. Col. Murtala Muhammed and Maj. Martin Adamu. Now that the ball had begun to roll, they quickly took charge, ordering the troops at AGO to split into two groups, one led by Lt. Pam Mwadkon to head to Ibadan and the other under Lt. D. S. Abubakar to Lagos. Lieutenant Mwadkon was one of the armored vehicle operators whose refusal to join Majs. Ademoyega and Anuforo in the attempt to salvage the January 15 coup in Lagos after Major Obienu's betrayal doomed that effort.

Thanks to Captain Ogbonna, the "Paul Revere" (the eighteenth-century Bostonian silversmith patriot who galloped across the Massachusetts countryside one night in April 1775 warning about the advance of the British) of the crisis, the First Battalion was able to take precautions. The commanding officer secured the armory, and nobody but him was allowed to bear arms. When the order from Lieutenant Colonel Muhammed came for the operation to commence, the call was taken by an Igbo officer fluent in Hausa and so was not propagated. Meanwhile, the designated coordinating officer for the coup in the East, Capt. Baba Usman, general staff officer II (military intelligence), was still away at Aba. The commanding officer was eventually able to convince the Northern officers led by Lt. Shehu Musa Yar'Adua, already in their combat fatigues, that it was not worth their time running amok. The military governor Lieutenant Colonel Odumegwu-Ojukwu had by this time called the government house in Ibadan on learning of the disturbance at Abeokuta. He spoke to Lt. Col. Hilary Njoku and the supreme commander then left to take refuge at the police headquarters in Enugu. There was no bloodshed in the East.

Captain Ogbonna's call to Fourth Battalion was, like the one to Second Battalion, received by a mutineer, the unit adjutant Lt. Garba "Paiko" Dada, who alerted Major Danjuma. They mustered about two dozen Northern troops and headed for the government house. On arrival there, they disarmed all the guards on duty and dismissed those who were not Northerners. The Northern guards joined forces with the mutineers, and reinforced by the contingent from Abeokuta, they surrounded the government house and laid siege.

It would seem that Captain Ogbonna's conversations at Abeokuta Police Station were overheard by the police officers there, and the police headquarters in Ibadan was duly contacted. The commissioner of police Mr. Joseph Adeola telephoned the supreme commander at the government house at about 4:00 a.m. to inform him about the events at Abeokuta. The supreme commander got dressed in his military uniform. His host, Lt. Col. Francis Fajuyi, joined him, and they summoned Lieutenant Colonel Njoku, who was billeted at an adjacent chalet on the grounds. After Lieutenant Colonel Njoku was briefed, he began making calls to his subordinate commanding officers, Lt. Col. Henry Igboba of the Second Battalion, Ikeja, and Lt. Col. Joseph Akahan of the Fourth Battalion, Ibadan. Lieutenant Colonel Igboba told him some armed men had been seen loitering around the communications room at his headquarters, but he was taking necessary security measures. Lieutenant

Colonel Akahan acknowledged awareness of the mutiny at Abeokuta but reported that all was calm and no action needed to be taken. He was lying. The lieutenant colonel was in on the plot. In a few days, he was to succeed Lieutenant Colonel Gowon as chief of staff, Army Headquarters, and one year later, on August 05, 1967, he was killed in the first recorded Nigerian Air Force helicopter crash at Gboko. When Lieutenant Colonel Fajuyi saw the headlamps of two vehicles approaching the government house, he sent his aide-de-camp, Lieutenant Umar, to investigate. A few minutes later, he came back upstairs to report that there was nothing amiss. He, too, was lying. He had run into the mutineers who strangely had no difficulty persuading him to join their ranks. Lieutenant Colonel Njoku decided it would be best if he returned to Lagos as he would be more effective in dealing with the situation from his headquarters. Lieutenant Umar was sent down again to go and arrange for a civilian car for the trip. The brigade commander followed a few minutes later. It was about 6:00 a.m. but still rather dark. As he stepped out the front door, he could make out the shapes of three soldiers and an officer standing between two parked vehicles of the supreme commander's escort party. He advanced toward them, but when he got to a range of 10–15 yards, they opened fire. He was hit in the left thigh. He turned and fled, limping. After he had put some distance between himself and them, he turned again, whipped out his service revolver, a 9mm Beretta, and returned fire. His riposte must have pinned down his assailants and bought him time. He resumed his flight, made it to the eight-foot-high perimeter fence which he scaled, and escaped into the woods. He emerged at the home of an expatriate who, apparently knowingly and with no questions asked, drove him to University College Hospital (UCH) where, by good fortune, he was received and treated by Drs. Ogbede Nwachukwu, Milan Jaja, and Andrew Onukogu, all Easterners. Word eventually reached the Fourth Battalion that the brigade commander was at UCH, and they sent over a hit squad to get him. The doctors were, however, steps ahead of them, spiriting him off and taking him to the home of one of them. Later that evening, Dr. Onukogu drove him over to the major seminary of Ss. Peter and Paul, Bodija, where the rector,

TOWARD UNDERSTANDING THE NIGERIA-BIAFRA WAR AND LINGERING QUESTIONS

Rev. Patrick Ugboka, kept him until July 31, 1966, when he made arrangements for him to leave for the East, disguised in clerical garb.

Meanwhile at the government house, the supreme commander's two aides-de-camp were sent down to investigate and were arrested by Major Danjuma's men. The supreme commander made a call to Kaduna just before 9:00 a.m. to speak to the commander, 1 Brigade, Lt. Col. Wellington Bassey. It turned out that three days prior, he had taken "urgent leave" and traveled to Lagos to sort out matters related to a building construction project. It was to his deputy, Lt. Col. Philip Efiong, that the supreme commander spoke and was also informed that the military governor, Lt. Col. Hassan Katsina, was not on station as well, having flown to Kano to play polo on the same day that the brigade commander left town. He briefed Lieutenant Colonel Efiong and asked him to have the military governor return to Kaduna to help monitor the situation. He also called 2 Brigade Headquarters and spoke to the deputy assistant adjutant / Quartermaster general (DAA/QMG), Maj. Clement Obioha. Lieutenant Colonel Njoku had apparently been able to reach his headquarters by phone from one of the doctors' offices at UCH, and his DAA/QMG had told him that efforts were being made to send a helicopter to the government house in Ibadan to extract the supreme commander and the other hostages, who included his twelve-year-old son, Thomas. According to John de St. Jorre, the police headquarters did eventually send a helicopter, but it arrived at the government house after the fact.

Shortly after 9:00 a.m., Lieutenant Colonel Fajuyi came downstairs and out of the building himself. He was arrested by Major Danjuma, who, grenade in hand and accompanied by another mutineer, Lt. Titus Numan, led him back inside and upstairs to where the supreme commander was sitting. He was placed under arrest and taken away with his host. They were driven off in separate minibuses, escorted by troops in a three-ton lorry and a Land Rover vehicle. Apparently, Major Danjuma was in the Land Rover vehicle, and when the convoy came to a fork in the road, it took the turn to Letmauck Barracks while the rest proceeded toward Iwo. Just outside Ibadan, they stopped and led the supreme commander, his Air Force aide-de-camp Lt. Andrew Nwankwo, and Lieutenant Colonel

Fajuyi into the forest where they tortured and tried to "interrogate" them. The supreme commander reportedly denied involvement in the January 15 coup and would say no more to his tormentors, to their utter frustration. By all accounts, he carried himself with the utmost dignity and refused to be humiliated. We know that much to be true firsthand because his Air Force ADC was an eyewitness. However, as they were diverted by their concentration on the supreme commander, and the governor, his Army coeval, the self-same Lieutenant Bello who had warned the supreme commander about the prospect of trouble on the Ibadan trip, helped him escape. At about 10:30 a.m. on July 29, 1966, Company Sgt. Maj. Useni Fegge gave the order, and a firing squad executed the head of state of Nigeria and supreme commander of the Nigeria Armed Forces Maj. Gen. Johnson Thomas Aguiyi-Ironsi, Member of the Royal Victorian Order (MVO), Member of the British Empire (MBE). Lt. Col. Francis Adekunle Fajuyi, Military Cross (MC), British Empire Medal (BEM), had been shot minutes earlier. The other mutineers present were Lt. Titus Numan, Lt. William Walbe, Lt. Garba Dada, Warrant Officer I. Bako, and Sergeant Tijani.

At Second Battalion Headquarters, Ikeja, matters got out of hand very quickly soon after Lts. Nuhu Nathan and Malami Nassarawa relayed the contents of Captain Ogbonna's call to the coup leaders. The group from AGO, led by Lt. D. S. Abubakar, arrived, and they surrounded the home of the commanding officer Lt. Col. Henry Igboba, but not before he managed to flee to the safety of the Police College Ikeja. They then went berserk and set upon other Igbo soldiers. Capt. John Chukwueke, the unit education officer, was shot in the presence of his nursing wife, their children, and his mother-in-law. Lt. Godson Mbabie, the unit quartermaster; his wife; and brother-in-law were shot—Ms. Mbabie survived. Only about four of the fourteen Southern officers resident in the barracks escaped death that morning. Scores of troops of other ranks were also killed, at both Ikeja and Abeokuta.

Lieutenant Colonel Gowon went over to Ikeja Cantonment in the morning of July 29, 1966, but it remains unclear what time he did so. By one account, he went very early to see things for himself and was purportedly arrested and held by the mutineers. By another account, it wasn't until late morning that he went and had been directed to do so by Brigadier General Ogundipe for the purpose of negotiating with the coup makers, who had established their headquarters at the cantonment. Soon after his arrival, he called his boss to report that the mutineers had taken him into custody. Lieutenant Colonel Gowon made at least two other telephone calls that morning, one at about 8:45 a.m., to Lt. Col. Philip Efiong of 1 Brigade to report the loss of Second Battalion, Ikeja, and the other to the government house, Ibadan, shortly after 9:00 a.m. when he spoke to Maj. Theophilus Danjuma. If he had gone to Ikeja early in the morning, then he, the chief of staff, Army Headquarters of the Nigerian Army, would have been making those calls and conducting the business of his office from the headquarters of a rebellion.

By about 11:00 a.m., it would seem that Brig. Gen. Babafemi Ogundipe, chief of staff, Supreme Headquarters, had sensed that the supreme commander was missing, perhaps dead. He let it be known to officials at Supreme Headquarters, including the attorney-general Mr. Gabriel Onyiuke, that he had assumed control of the military government. He would tell the nation and the world as much later that day, but first, there was the "small matter" of restoring order, at least in Lagos. Matters quickly got interesting when he ordered the officer commanding Pay and Records, Lt. Col. Rudolf Trimnell, to put down the rebellion at Second Battalion, Ikeja, with a motley rifle company comprising diverse tradesmen—cooks, clerks, drivers, the band corps. The lieutenant colonel, some would say understandably, refused to carry out the order. The general then assigned the task to Capt. Ephraim Opara, the adjutant of Lagos Garrison Organization (LGO). As Captain Opara advanced toward Ikeja Airport, he and his troops ran into an ambush laid along Ikorodu Road by the mutinous Northern soldiers and were mauled. Among the casualties were two expatriate bystanders, one British and one German. The other military formation in Lagos was the Federal Guards at Dodan Barracks. Its loyalty had been in question since before the Supreme Commander's trip to the North. Intelligence had been received that there was suspicious activity in the unit on account of which the brigade commander Lt. Col. Hilary Njoku had summoned all the officers to a meeting at his headquarters. He learned that their grievance was that no disciplinary action had been taken regarding the January 15 coup. The brigade commander had told them it was a matter for the Supreme Military Council (SMC) and advised that they await the decision of that body. Unbeknownst to him, the SMC had since decided to court-martial the officers detained in connection with the January 15 coup, and the matter was in the hands of the chief of staff, Army Headquarters, Lieutenant Colonel Gowon. The second-in-command of the unit, Capt. Joseph Garba, was a key plotter of the July 29 coup. When Brigadier General Ogundipe ordered him to lead troops to reinforce the embattled Captain Opara, he refused. According to the historian Max Siollun, it was at this juncture that the chief of Staff Supreme Headquarters sent Lieutenant Colonel Gowon to Ikeja to negotiate with the mutineers. On arrival, Lieutenant Colonel Gowon was reportedly placed under guard but nevertheless was able to start a conversation with the coup leaders. Soon enough, he elicited their conditions for a cease-fire, and they were the repatriation of Northerners and Southerners to their respective regions of origin and the secession of the North from Nigeria. He passed them on to General Ogundipe, who shared them with the military governor of the Eastern Group of Provinces when the latter called for an update. On learning the terms of the mutineers, the military governor reportedly replied, "If that is what they want, I agree. Let them go."

Lieutenant Colonel Gowon never left the Ikeja Cantonment again to rejoin General Ogundipe. Like the missing supreme commander six months before, the general moved and set up shop at the police headquarters in Lion Building, Obalende, Lagos. According to Max Siollun, Lieutenant Colonel Gowon was "pressed by his junior colleagues to join their rebellion." A secession speech Lieutenant Colonel Muhammed and Major Adamu had written was given to Lieutenant Colonel Gowon to read to the nation in his capacity as the most senior Northern officer. He asked a Northern judge, Justice Mohammed Bello, to review it and also sought the counsel of the head of the Special Branch of the Police Alhaji Yusuf. They were

TOWARD UNDERSTANDING THE NIGERIA-BIAFRA WAR AND LINGERING QUESTIONS

among the civilian Northern elite who had also begun to converge on the Ikeja Cantonment. They raised the prospect of practical problems such as funds with which to pay soldier salaries after secession, whereupon the coup makers sent troops to secure the Central Bank. They were also reminded that whomsoever took over from General Aguiyi-Ironsi might attack the North with the help of friendly neighboring countries.

In the North, the carnage was off to a rather late start. Days before, Lt. Buka Suka Dimka of Nigeria Military Training College (NMTC) Kaduna had taken troops on clandestine nocturnal reconnaissance of vital installations in the city. He was arrested, briefly interrogated, and fatefully, released. The brigade major Maj. Samuel Osaigbovo Ogbemudia, who traveled to Benin City to visit briefly with his mother and returned to Kaduna on July 29, decided he would investigate the matter himself and submit a report within twenty-four hours. Lt. Col. Alexander Madiebo, inspector of artillery, had for long had premonitions about the coup. The reception to his suggestion that every soldier be disarmed was mixed as some felt they needed their personal weapons to protect themselves. Specifically, Regimental Sgt. Maj. Ahmadu Bello of Third Battalion discouraged his commanding officer Lt. Col. Israel Okoro from such action. Nevertheless, the deputy brigade commander Lieutenant Colonel Efiong issued orders at about 10:00 a.m. that only officers on security guard duty should bear arms and that all officers should remain together in their messes or orderly rooms. When he called Lieutenant Colonel Okoro for a situation report later in the day, he had gone home and had last seen his officers at about 3:00 p.m. to the alarm of his commander. He was ordered back to his mess and to reconvene his officers there. It was reported that earlier in the afternoon, the commanding officer had given a pep talk to his officers who assured him of their loyalty and pledged to stay out of mischief. Shortly before midnight, his RSM called to tell him his attention was needed in the guardroom. When he got there, he was shot by Lt. Buka Dimka and Lt. Yakubu Dambo. His killing flagged off the coup in the North. Muster was sounded, and after soldiers had formed up on the parade ground, the Igbo were sorted out, taken in trucks to a location about sixteen miles from Kaduna along the Kaduna-Jos road, and shot dead.

Soon after midnight, after multiple failed attempts to reach the Third Battalion, the deputy brigade commander received word from the telephone operator at First Reconnaissance Squadron (unit commander, Maj. Ukpo Isong) that Lieutenant Colonel Okoro had been killed. When he passed on the news to the officers closeted with him at Brigade Headquarters, all but his brigade major rose and deserted, fearing the worst. Command and control of 1 Brigade of the Nigerian Army had collapsed.

Lieutenant Colonel Efiong and Major Ogbemudia remained together at Brigade Headquarters until about 1:30 a.m. before deciding it was too obvious a target and would very likely to be hit next. The major also correctly reasoned that his deputy commander's home would be no safer. So he drove the lieutenant colonel to the residence of a townsman of his in the government reservation area and returned to brigade headquarters. It transpired that a hit squad had come to the deputy commander's house at about 2:05 a.m. When they did not find him, they roughed up his guard detail and took two of them to Maj. Abba Kyari, unit commander, field artillery, Kakuri, Kaduna, for questioning.

Lieutenant Colonel Efiong contacted an American Peace Corpswoman of his acquaintance from his townsman's home and was put in touch with the American Consul. The diplomat arranged for him to transfer to the residence of the bishop of Kaduna (unstated denomination, presumably Catholic) at which he arrived at about 4:45 a.m. About eleven hours later, his sartorial disguise, complete with red fez and dark glasses, was ready. He was driven to the railway station by an expatriate, where he boarded a congested train headed for Lagos. It pulled away from the platform just before 6:00 p.m., July 30, 1966. The two most senior Eastern officers in the Nigerian Army had fled, one from the West to the East and the other from the North to Lagos.

Back in Lagos, a group of permanent secretaries went to Lion Building, Lagos, to meet with Brigadier General Ogundipe for instructions. He told them he could not provide any since he did not

TOWARD UNDERSTANDING THE NIGERIA-BIAFRA WAR AND LINGERING QUESTIONS

know the whereabouts of the supreme commander, had lost control of the armed forces, and had been told by the attorney-general that there was no constitutional provision for the chief of staff, Supreme Headquarters, to assume power in the absence of the supreme commander. He directed them to the coup makers at Ikeja Cantonment to whom they went, escorted by Capt. Joseph Garba. What followed were forty-eight hours of debate described by Max Siollun as "apocalyptic and emotionally explosive." Needless to say, the most vociferous was the coup leader, Lieutenant Colonel Murtala Muhammed. He was also the least constructive. Also involved was the chief justice of the Supreme Court Sir Adetokunbo Ademola. The military governors of the Northern and Mid-Western Groups of Provinces joined by phone. The views of the military governor of the Eastern Group of Provinces were not sought, but he reportedly did call Lieutenant Colonel Gowon. The only Igbo who participated were three permanent secretaries—Messrs B. A. Okagbue, T. C. M. Eneli, and P. C. Asiodu (Mid-West).

At some point, Lieutenant Colonel Muhammed ceded leadership to Lieutenant Colonel Gowon with the remark, "You are the senior, go ahead," according to Capt. Joseph Garba. The British high commissioner Sir Cumming-Bruce and the United States ambassador Mr. Elbert Matthews weighed in to drive home the message that secession should be taken off the table. Senior Northern politicians and the mutineers also cashiered the prospect of a non-Northerner succeeding to the position of supreme commander. One of the coup leaders, Maj. Martin Adamu, nominated Lieutenant Colonel Gowon for head of state. That was a no-brainer, but there were at least seven officers senior to Lieutenant Colonel Gowon in the army hierarchy, including Brigadier General Ogundipe, Col. Robert Adebayo, Col. Wellington Bassey, and at least four Igbo lieutenant colonels. Among them, according to John de St. Jorre, was the military governor of the Eastern Group of Provinces, Lieutenant Colonel Odumegwu-Ojukwu, who continued to insist that hierarchy should be strictly followed in military tradition. The military governors of the Mid-Western Group of Provinces and Lagos (Maj. Mobolaji Johnson), however, acquiesced to the appointment of Lieutenant Colonel

Gowon as head of state and supreme commander. Lieutenant Colonel Odumegwu-Ojukwu never recognized Lieutenant Colonel Gowon in that role or designation. The Supreme Military Council resigned itself to acceptance that he had "been elected by a majority of members" of the council. Nevertheless, Lieutenant Colonel Ojukwu promised to continue to cooperate with the SMC to restore order and end the ongoing massacre of the Igbo and other Easterners.

After he dismissed the permanent secretaries on July 30, Brigadier General Ogundipe remained with his headquarters staff until one of them, an Igbo officer, brought him the information that mutineers were headed his way. He took off, and his officers followed. Thereafter, command and control from Supreme Headquarters ceased to exist. The mutineers did turn up, but their targets had already bolted. The brigadier fetched up on a frigate of the Nigeria Navy and eventually reached London. He was reportedly very pained that Lieutenant Colonel Gowon did not keep faith with him. He had sent him as his emissary to the soldiers in rebellion, and he ended up as their leader. Before the coup, he had been scheduled to attend a Commonwealth Heads of Government conference in London in September 1966. The Gowon government let him do so then demobilized and kept him on there as high commissioner to the Court of St. James.

By the time the dust settled, 40–45 officers and 200–250 noncommissioned officers lay dead or were unaccounted for. By some accounts, the Murtala-Gowon-Adamu-Danjuma coup of July 1966 was one of the bloodiest in recorded history. In his August 01 broadcast, Lieutenant Colonel Gowon thanked God for reinstating a Northerner at the helm but wouldn't disclose the whereabouts or fate of the erstwhile helmsman, General Aguiyi-Ironsi.

Thus Lt. Col. Yakubu Gowon met his destiny but certainly not along a road he took to avoid it. Whether he foresaw that he would fetch up in the position he found himself on August 01, 1966, is not known for certain, but he must have been aware for a long time that he was a blue-eyed boy of the establishment. A few years before, the young, handsome, and dapper Gowon was being held up to Northern secondary school pupils by the Ministry of Defense on recruitment drives as the model of who they too could become if they "worked hard." Paradoxically, it wasn't "hard work" that got Lieutenant Colonel Gowon to where he was. No accounts of the era can be found in which Lieutenant Colonel Gowon was described as a "hard worker" before, during, or since. It just happened that, through no fault or effort on his part, he checked off the "right" boxes. Ethnically, he is Angas in the Middle Belt of the predominantly Muslim North, but his father was a Christian minister of religion. He enlisted after secondary school and so did not have a university education which the colonial masters and his other superiors might have found potentially threatening. He, however, received officer training at the Royal Military Academy, Sandhurst, which gave him elite credentials. Physically, he was not an imposing figure in any discernible way and, in a crowd, would need to be pointed out if not distinctively attired. After the January 15, 1966, coup, he became the most senior officer of Northern extraction. General Aguiyi-Ironsi appointed him chief of staff of the Army and gave him a seat on the Supreme Military Council. Another coup had taken place, and there he now was, riding its wave surrounded by mutineers, many of whose careers in the military he had inspired.

The story of the two coups in 1966 has been told and retold *ad nauseam*. However, no excuse is made for retelling it here at considerable length for two reasons. First, it was one of the final key pieces in the jigsaw tableau at the background of the calamity that was to follow. The second is that one despairs, reading some of the accounts written from the jaundiced, presumptuous, and hubristic perspective of "the side that prevailed." The perpetrators of the July coup, when they felt like it, believed they could tell their stories however they chose. For the most part, they have been serially mendacious and are unfazed when the very foundations upon which they based their actions are shown to be fallacious. Some of the otherwise respectable chroniclers who have written from that viewpoint have also been disingenuous, if not almost intellectually dishonest, massaging and spinning the facts, imputing ambiguity if not benign motives to malevolent undertakings and suggesting excuses for even the very worst of them.

The reasons given by the Fulani-Hausa for their orgy of killings are often posited as almost perfectly valid and fully exculpatory. In essence, the Igbo deserved to be slaughtered in their thousands because of their uppityness. That being ambitious and hardworking qualified you for having your throat slit. That asking to compete was wanting to take over and dominate. When it became widely known that the Supreme Military Council had reached a decision for the court-martial of the January 15 coup plotters long before July 29, one apologist wrote that the matter had already been investigated by the Special Branch of the Nigeria Police. In other words, that Lieutenant Colonel Gowon, chief of staff, Army Headquarters, sitting on his orders on a matter that had so vexed him and his kinsmen, was of no consequence. That the Northern officer corps was honor-bound, if not by duty, to avenge the killing of their senior colleagues in January 1966. Even though military and civilian jurisprudence never comingle, the fact that the investigations had already been completed by the police raises even more worrying questions why the chief of staff chose not to proceed even more expeditiously to court-martial.

Vindictiveness is never a virtue. It diminishes both parties, perhaps more so the revanchist. He loses the moral high ground and might raise the stakes, as in the case of the July coup, a literally mindless, vandalistic bloodletting which quickly spilled out of the barracks and engulfed the civilian populace, with mixed hordes of Northern soldiers and the Fulani-Hausa slaughtering the Igbo, the length and breadth of the country. It is difficult to see any calibration to the January coup they sometimes claimed they were avenging. Both tragic events were very different in character. In January 1966, a dissident group of predominantly Igbo military officers set out to seize power from the civilian political establishment all over the country but succeeded only in the North. Senior military officers in the South, unaffiliated with the group in the North, demanded and secured the transfer of power from the civilian federal authorities in the South, and the group in the North subsequently surrendered to them. In July 1966, virtually all Northern military officers were implicated in the killing spree targeted at the Igbo, either through active participation or connivance. Seizing power was not on the cards at the outset. They just wanted to spill Igbo blood on an industrial scale, "destroy all symbols of central authority in the South," withdraw to the North, and secede. It was not until senior Northern civil authorities and British and American diplomats talked them out of secession that they accepted the consolation prize of power.

Further comparisons between the January and July 1966 coups are really pointless but irritating, if convenient, commentaries on parallels and divergencies regarding the victims have been made. The top brass of the North were eliminated in January (Brigadier Zakaria Maimalari, 2 Brigade; Col. Kur Mohammed, chief of staff, Army Headquarters; Lt. Col. James Yakubu Pam, adjutant general; Lt. Col. Abogo Largema, Fourth Battalion). In July 1966, most of the top Igbo brass escaped but not for the lack of the mutineers trying to rub them out. They did get the major general and supreme commander, Lt. Col. Gabriel Okonweze (Abeokuta Garrison Organization) and Lt. Col. Israel Okoro (Third Battalion, Kaduna). The top Northern civilian casualty of the January coup was Alhaji Abubakar Balewa. At a personal level, he was held in very high esteem by those who knew and worked with him. According to Alhaji Shehu Shagari, when Dr. Kingsley Mbadiwe learned that the prime minister was missing, he wept inconsolably. Mr. Segun Osoba, staff writer for the *Daily Times*, and his friend Mr. Titus Shokanlu saw the bodies of the prime and finance ministers "about 220 yards from Mile 27 along Lagos-Abeokuta road" on January 21, 1966. The prime minister was clad in white trousers and gown. There was no evidence that he had been shot. Unlike General Aguiyi-Ironsi, who was also Head of the Nigerian State, the prime minister was only head of government. But do any of these distinctions really matter? Most decent-minded people would argue that none does.

All too frequently, human beings revulsed by injustices around them, both perceived and real, have sought to remediate them often abruptly through the use of sheer force and violence, and just as frequently, the outcomes have been monstrous, in the near or long term. The case is often made though that no meaningful change is effected through a gradualist and deliberative approach because the beneficiaries of the maligned *status quo* will usually find ways to neutralize transformative endeavors if given time. Yet the case can be made that humankind is designed to "evolve," not just biologically but also in their political, sociocultural, and other affairs as well. People would like most, if not all, of their best-made plans to come to fruition in their lifetimes, and politicians think on the even shorter time scale of their electoral cycles. However, the initiatives may need much, much longer gestational periods. That is the quandary of the human condition. The recommended attitude would appear to be caution, careful calculation, and circumspection. So, when one voice says, "Hey, we got omelets to make here, need to crack some eggs," another voice should ask, "Sure, but any idea what the omelets are going to look/taste like?"

PART 3

AFTER THE COUPS

Mr. Bernard Odogwu, who later as lieutenant-colonel would become head of the Biafran Directorate of Military Intelligence, remarked that a reliably effective tactic for rattling an opponent is to question his or her bona fides at the very outset. It is bound to keep him or her unsettled for quite a time, and that was the gambit the military governor of the East wrought on Lt. Col. Yakubu Gowon. The coup leader forgot that he was not under any obligation to show the military governor any credentials and that his comeback should have been "what I did was SEIZE power, my friend." Instead, he likely presumed he had some other kind of legitimacy and got talked into agreeing to a meeting of representatives of the military governors of the regions in Lagos on August 09, 1966. Among the decisions taken at that meeting were the rescission of any controversial decrees, repatriation of troops to their regions of origin, formation of a committee to initiate the consideration of the nature of future political association among the regions, and preparations for a meeting of the Supreme Military Council.

The ill-fated Decree no. 34 was promptly abrogated. Troops of Eastern origin were officially redeployed to First Battalion, Enugu (commanding officer, Lt. Col. David Ogunewe), where strict military discipline had prevailed and the *esprit de corps* among the officers had remained intact. As has been mentioned, repeated calls by Lt. Col. Murtala Muhammed on July 29, 1966, in attempts to ignite chaos there were intercepted and thwarted. When the repatriation orders came, the officers sat for a photograph and drank a toast before those from the North left. The departing soldiers all took their weapons with them, and the understanding was that the weapons would be sent back to the First Battalion Armory after the servicemen had reached their new deployments. That never happened. In contrast, returning Eastern troops bore no arms and had barely escaped with their lives. Also, Northern troops did not leave Ibadan, Abeokuta, or Lagos.

The accession of Lieutenant Colonel Gowon to headship of the Nigerian state and supreme command of its armed forces on August 01, 1966, did little to placate the rebelling Northern soldiers. This was understandable because the seizure of power to slaughter and then secede was their objective, not the seizure of power to govern. What in effect he was supremely commanding was a fiendishly murderous rabble. Killings by elements of the Fourth Battalion, Ibadan (commanding officer, Lt. Col. Joseph Akahan), actually intensified both on and off barracks. According to Max Siollun, they were most widespread and indiscriminate in Ibadan and Lagos, with victims subjected to "torture and unprintable degradations" before execution. In the case of Maj. Donatus Okafor, former unit commander, Federal Guards, Lagos, who was in detention at Abeokuta Prisons for his involvement in the January 1966 coup, they buried him alive, apparently to spare ammunition. Then they forayed to Benin City on August 19, 1966, and again they broke into the prisons where some of the participants in the January coup were held. Those of Northern origin were released. Five Igbo warrant officers were tortured to death.

Units in the North were behind the curve but were quick to catch up, especially with the arrival of soldiers posted out of the Fourth Battalion. It was like the spread of contagion but not as if they really needed much coaxing. Killing the Igbo had become a

TOWARD UNDERSTANDING THE NIGERIA-BIAFRA WAR AND LINGERING QUESTIONS

badge of honor in the Nigerian armed forces, and those who were not yet fully in on the action were probably only wondering about timing and scope. Personnel from the Fourth Battalion might have merely told them that there was no reason they could not start or go as far as their sick imaginations would carry them.

Apparently for safety reasons, the commanding officer of Fifth Battalion, Kano, Lt. Col. Muhammed Shuwa—who was Kanuri, not Fulani-Hausa—had decided to segregate the Igbo and non-Igbo troops under his command. He ordered the Igbo officers and men to be transferred to a different camp (Wudil) along the road to Katsina. En route, the Northern soldiers escorting the Igbo soldiers to their new quarters shot and killed twelve of them—four officers including Maj. Joseph Ihedigbo, who had just been replaced as second-in-command, six noncommissioned officers, and two private soldiers.

Nevertheless, the committee to begin deliberations on the political future of the country, as agreed at the meeting of representatives of the military governors in August, met in Lagos on September 12, 1966. Addressing the opening session, Lt. Col. Yakubu Gowon offered them four options: a federal system with a strong center, a federal system with a weak center, a confederation, and a novel unique system. He, however, drew the line at a unitary system and opportunities for secession. Notwithstanding, the delegations from the North, West, and East all recommended that the new constitution should include a clause whereby any region could unilaterally secede. The North and the East opted for a confederal arrangement while the West, Mid-West, and Lagos chose the federal system. Regarding the creation of new states, the East opposed such an exercise "under the present situation in the country" but allowed that provision be made for it in the future constitution. The West and Lagos in contrast proposed "the immediate creation of more states, based on ethnic and linguistic affinities." The creation of new states was also supported by the Mid-West delegation.

Their initial proposals filed, the conference went into recess. Even as the meeting was being held in Lagos, Northerners continued to slaughter Easterners in cities all across the region. With much reluctance, the Eastern delegation returned to Lagos on September

20, 1966, for the resumption of deliberations. To their surprise, the Northern delegation totally disavowed their original position. They now wanted a federal system with a strong center. Secession would be proscribed, and new states could be created, if the West and East were in agreement. Three forces, it turned out, had played on Lieutenant Colonel Gowon and the Northern delegation in the interim—the British government, the Northern minorities, and the Eastern minorities. The British government let it be known that it would not countenance a confederal Nigeria and that if there was a secession clause in the constitution, the East would use it to the singular disadvantage of the North. The minorities of the North and East had always wanted states of their own or, at a minimum, an arrangement with most of the power at the center and not in the regions. The Northern minorities were further comforted by the fact that one of their own was now head of state. The Gowon government could not help but salivate at the prospect of using statehood of the Eastern minorities as a good weapon for dividing opinion and undermining the solidarity of the region. As the delegates deliberated, news was received that yet another tsunami of coordinated massacres had hit multiple cities in the North, beginning September 29, 1966—Kano, Kaduna, Zaria, Jos, Makurdi, Nguru, and others. The conference adjourned for three weeks on October 03, 1966.

In late September, Maj. Abba Kyari replaced Lieutenant Colonel Shuwa as commanding officer, Fifth Battalion, Kano. The massacre of a dozen Igbo officers and men the previous month seemed to have whetted the appetite of his troops for blood. They decided they would celebrate the Sixth anniversary of Nigeria's independence with an open mutiny. They shot and killed the second-in-command Capt. H. A. Auna, and the regimental sergeant major Dauda Mumuni, who was a decorated soldier from the UN operations in the Congo. They then broke into the armory, helped themselves generously, and took their game to town where they rendezvoused with civilian mobs.

Northern cities are planned with separate quarters, Sabon Gari, for nonindigenes. As such, the marauding hordes knew where to find their quarry. Since the July coup, very large numbers of Igbo were leaving the North as quickly as they could wind down their businesses. The railway station was crowded with traveling passengers when the killers arrived. The Igbo were separated out and shot dead. At Kano Airport, they outdid themselves. A Lagos-bound aircraft from London had just made a stopover. The passengers were deplaned, and the Igbo were separated out and shot dead. They also shot and killed Igbo staff and passengers in the terminal and elsewhere in the airport. The mayhem presided over by Sergeant Paul Dickson at Ikeja Airport on July 29, in which Maj. Theophilus E. Nzegwu (who earned his wings in the Royal Air Force) and Capt. P. C. Okafor were killed, paled in comparison. In Kano on that day alone, several thousand Igbo civilians lost their lives due to the joint operations of the Nigerian military and Northern mobs. Even the military governor and emir Alhaji Ado Bayero were alarmed at the hideous ferocity of the carnage. They patrolled the streets for many hours, calling for calm. As fate would have it, they had sown the wind, and now theirs was the whirlwind to reap.

The pattern was consistent in all the massacres that took place across the region—targeted ruthless killing of the Igbo perpetrated by civilian mobs in close collaboration with the military. Most heart-wrenching were the interceptions at Makurdi, the only major railroad crossing over the River Benue and last station before exiting the hostile upper North. The killers would patrol the train wagons, pick out the Igbo, and either shoot or toss them out of the train into the river. They had almost made it to relative safety.

Many who did make it to Enugu bore every stigma of horrific torture imaginable—empty eye sockets, crudely amputated limbs, deep gashes inflicted by machetes. However, it was the headless body and the disembodied head that most graphically encapsulated the depth of depravity to which the North was prepared to sink in the expression of their bestial animus toward the East, especially the Igbo. A young Easterner was killed and beheaded. His headless body was placed in a train bound for Enugu as a warning to Easterners. A dazed young woman arrived at Enugu, and all she was carrying was a lidded enamel bowl. Inside it was the head of her child who had been killed and beheaded before her very eyes. During those difficult days, the military governor Lt. Col. Odumegwu-Ojukwu, with a black band around his left arm, would often go to the railway station at Enugu and stand on the arrival platform, welcoming home pained Eastern humanity, brutalized beyond all reason. He went and saw for himself with his own eyes. He did not just rely on reports written by aides. At some level, he might have considered himself responsible for some of what was happening. After the killings in May 1966, he had accepted the assurances of his colleague, the military governor of the North Lt. Col. Hassan Katsina, and personally pleaded with Easterners who had fled to return.

According to the Gabriel Onyiuke Tribunal of Inquiry, the massacres claimed about fifty thousand lives of people of the East, especially Nd'Igbo, and over 1.6 million fled other parts of the country where they resided and returned to the East. Colin Legum, writing for the *Observer* newspaper, described it as "reminiscent of the in-gathering of exiles into Israel after the end of the last war." The regional government became saddled with problems of unprecedented, almost biblical proportions. Fortunately and unfortunately, there were no vast acreages of refugee tents with which to impress the world press. This bears explaining.

The expectation that somewhere in the homeland, safety will be found comes naturally to the Igbo and is underpinned by the latticework configuration of its extended family structure. It is the same for influx as for internal displacement. As illustrated in Chinua Achebe's *Things Fall Apart*, when the hero, Okonkwo, was forced to flee after an unfortunate firearm accident, he readily found hearth and home in his mother's village, the fictional Mbanta. An itinerant people, the Igbo fully appreciate the value of being made welcome and are themselves impulsively generous with their hospitality. Like a sponge, Igbo society quietly but determinedly absorbed its own. To a large extent, the same could be said for other groups in the East. Nevertheless, there remained questions about unpaid salaries, health care, education, and the other services that needed to be provided. The government of the East hurriedly drew up a three-million-pound refugee resettlement budget and appealed to the federal government in Lagos for financial assistance. The Gowon government offered to provide only 10 percent of the amount budgeted by the East. Overburdened and cash-strapped, the government of the East sought to trim its responsibilities. In October 1966, it asked all non-Easterners, except Mid-Westerners, to leave the region.

The ad hoc constitutional conference was scheduled to resume sitting on October 24, 1966, in Lagos. However, the mass slaughter that had taken place compelled the government of the East to demand that Northern soldiers be removed from Lagos and the West as had been agreed by representatives of the military governors at their meeting on August 09, 1966. The Leaders of Thought of the West sided with the East on the issue, with Chief Obafemi Awolowo describing Northern troops in the West as "an army of occupation." Lieutenant Colonel Gowon refused to redeploy Northern soldiers out of the West and Lagos, whereupon the Eastern delegation refrained from traveling to Lagos out of very genuine safety concerns. Northern soldiers had left no one in any doubt regarding their bloodlust, and there was not a shred of evidence that Lieutenant Colonel Gowon had any power or interest to rein them in. Instead, in a broadcast on November 30, 1966, he summarily dismissed the constitutional conference and promised to appoint members to a constitution drafting committee in due course. He let it be known that his belief was that "the less we talk and the more we act honestly in the interest of the whole nation, the better for every one." And just in case anyone doubted his resolve, he ominously added that "if circumstances compel me to preserve the integrity of Nigeria by force, I shall do my duty to my country." Meanwhile, about fifty thousand of his countrymen and women already lay dead, and at least another 1.6 million had been internally displaced.

Lt. Col. Yakubu Gowon nevertheless accepted the security concerns expressed by the military governor of the East regarding the meeting of the Supreme Military Council to which their representatives had agreed at their August 09, 1966, forum. During the month of December, arrangements were finalized for the meeting to be held in Ghana early in the new year, under the auspices of Gen. Joseph Ankrah, who had deposed Dr. Francis Kwame Nkrumah in a US Central Intelligence Agency-inspired coup on February 24, 1966. The venue was Dr. Nkrumah's erstwhile country retreat at Aburi,

Peduase Lodge, nestled in the hills just north of Accra. The conference was held on January 04 and 05, 1967, and the participants were Lt. Col. Yakubu Gowon as head of the federal military government, the regional military governors (Col. Robert Adebayo, West; Lt. Col. Chukwuemeka Odumegwu-Ojukwu, East; Lt. Col. Hassan Katsina, North; Lt. Col. David Ejoor, Mid-West) and the military administrator of Lagos (Maj. Mobolaji Johnson), the head of the Navy (Commodore Joseph Wey), the inspector general of police (Alhaji Kam Selem) and his deputy (Mr. Timothy Omo-Bare), the secretaries to the regional governments (Mr. Peter Odumosu [West], Chief Ntieyong Akpan [East], Alhaji Ali Akilu [North], the Mid-West sent an undersecretary, Mr. Daniel Lawani), and the permanent undersecretary in the federal cabinet office, Prince Solomon Akenzua. The key issues discussed were the disengagement of troops, command of the armed forces, headship of the federal government and governance, displaced persons and their properties, constitutional review, and future meetings.

Perhaps with Lieutenant Colonel Gowon's truculent speech of November 30, 1966, in mind, the military governor of the East moved a resolution that all parties renounce the use of force and rededicate themselves to discussions and negotiations as the only means to a peaceful settlement of the crisis. It was unanimously adopted. The council agreed that all soldiers should return to their regions of origin to allow tempers to cool and avoid a recurrence of the killings that had happened. Also, area commands would be set up in the various regions, under area commanders who answer to their respective military governors. Regarding the command of the armed forces and headship of the federal government, the military governor of the east pointed out that the whereabouts and fate of the head of state and supreme commander of the Armed Forces of Nigeria General Aguiyi-Ironsi were still not known, whereupon Lieutenant Colonel Gowon informed the council that the general was killed on July 29, 1966. Lieutenant Colonel Odumegwu-Ojukwu went on to say he could not recognize Lieutenant Colonel Gowon as General Aguiyi-Ironsi's successor because he, Lieutenant Colonel Gowon, had at least six officers senior to him, and he, Lieutenant Colonel

TOWARD UNDERSTANDING THE NIGERIA-BIAFRA WAR AND LINGERING QUESTIONS

Odumegwu-Ojukwu, played no part in any process that put him in contention for that position. It was decided that the armed forces would be under the joint command of the Supreme Military Council, whose chairman shall be commander in chief and head of government. The Supreme Military Council would also have the final say over promotions and appointments to very senior positions in the security and civil services as well as the diplomatic corps. For at least six months, the government would function as a military government *sensu stricto*, with no involvement of politicians. The permanent secretaries of the Ministries of Finance would meet within two weeks to draw up proposals for a rehabilitation program for refugees, including the payment of their salaries through the financial year ending on March 31. The recovery of the properties of the displaced persons would be dealt with by the regional police commissioners. The ad hoc constitutional conference that Lt. Col. Yakubu Gowon had dissolved on November 30, 1966, would reconvene as soon as possible, and the unanimous recommendations it had already arrived at would be considered for implementation at a subsequent meeting of the Supreme Military Council. It was also agreed that the next meeting of the Supreme Military Council would be held at a mutually acceptable venue in Nigeria. The decisions reached were signed, then the council members drank to them and departed for home.

According to Kirk-Greene (1975), it was the governor of the East who "made the running." He had gone to Aburi with his mind burdened and tormented by the horrors that had befallen his people. He took matters seriously and was clearheaded as to what steps needed to be taken to relieve the pent-up tension in the body politic. Rather strangely, the other council members appeared to bring a different attitude to the meeting. Its historical importance—the first such meeting after a very bloody insurrection within the military and wanton massacre of tens of thousands of civilians—seemed lost to them. Frederick Forsyth remarked that English observers were inclined to accuse Lieutenant Colonel Odumegwu-Ojukwu of having failed to "play the gentleman" by coming prepared to a meeting that others thought was "just a friendly get-together of brother officers." Brother officers indeed.

At any rate, when Lieutenant Colonel Gowon returned to Lagos, some of his permanent secretaries (among them Ibrahim Damcida, Yusuf Gobir, Ahmed Joda, Phillip Asiodu, and Allison Ayida) were incredulous at the agreements reached, considering them excessive concessions to the East. It amounted, in their judgment, to a weakening of the center, in what was basically a confederal arrangement rather than the federal one which would be more favorable to the North now with power back in their hands. A meeting of federal permanent secretaries and members of the Federal Executive Council on January 20, 1967, produced a document detailing criticisms of the "Accra Decisions." These hostile permanent secretaries had opportunities to make their input before the "Accra Decisions" were reached because even though they did not accompany Lt. Col. Yakubu Gowon to Ghana, the agenda was available to them well before the meeting, and they could have monitored the proceedings from Lagos. A gullible Lt. Col. Yakubu Gowon ingurgitated their recommendations and on January 26, 1967, held a press conference in which he effectively laid waste to the agreements reached at Aburi. He let it be known that he was supreme commander and that the regional military area commands would answer to him. Permanent secretaries of the Ministries of Finance would meet, but revenue allocation would not be on the agenda. He decided that the agreement to pay worker salaries until the end of the financial year was unrealistic and needed to be reconsidered. As for the ad hoc constitutional conference, it would now remain adjourned indefinitely. Naturally, the governor of the East denounced the volte-face and insisted that agreements were agreements and must be implemented as reached. "On Aburi We Stand" became the abiding slogan of the East.

The proceedings at Aburi were eventually released on long-playing vinyl phonograph records, and I had the privilege of listening to them as a fourteen-year-old. The principal of my school, who was a friend of the military governor and contemporary at Oxford University, had received a set from the governor as a present. He made me play and listen to them as homework, with instructions to pay attention to and learn from the governor's use of the English language. The assignment was not for me to understand the policy

TOWARD UNDERSTANDING THE NIGERIA-BIAFRA WAR AND LINGERING QUESTIONS

issues discussed, even though I was curious about them. After all those many years, I still do remember vividly picking up on what I thought was incorrect English by the governor—when he said, "None of these gestures are being made." I reported back to my principal, and he assured me that such usage was permissible colloquially. I suspected the point he was actually making was that the English grammar of an Oxonian was beyond reproach. As a further aside, he had custody of Maj. Patrick Nzeogwu's brother, who, for security reasons, went by the pseudonym Peter Ok———. The major had been transferred to Aba Prisons and came one afternoon to visit. He was unmistakable in his green army fatigues and signature white neck scarf. I greeted him, and he acknowledged with a smile and wave of the hand but not a word in reply. That was the only time I met the historical figure at the center of the most determinative event in postindependence Nigeria up to that point in time. And by the way, that teenager did find time to listen to Lennon McCartney's "Paperback Writer" too—but that was a 45 RPM vinyl single!

Public demonstrations broke out in all the urban centers in the East, and outside the region, the perception was that the government instigated and orchestrated them. Indeed, civil servants were not discouraged from, let alone penalized for, leaving their offices and joining the rest of the populace on the streets in protest. In the event, few, if anybody, needed any instigation. Contempt for the antics of Lt. Col. Yakubu Gowon and his puppeteers was common currency against the background of passions that had already been sorely inflamed. Everybody in the region, especially among the Igbo, had lost at least one close relative in the pogrom. Homesteads were bulging at the seams as they strained to accommodate the returnees who fled with nothing but their lives, abandoning property worth over twenty million pounds. Regardless, they felt safe because they were home. The government struggled to provide succor with what meager resources it had. Most of all was the assurance that nobody would come to hurt them again here in the homeland. The day after he returned from Aburi, the military governor had held a press conference and reassured the people of the East that the meeting had been "more than necessary and worthwhile." Mr. Bernard Odogwu, who would later become head of Biafran Military Intelligence, recalled the military governor enthusing that "if Jack [*sic* Lt. Col. Yakubu Gowon] implements Aburi, then we might be able to salvage Nigeria." Then came the January 26, 1967, press conference, and it was all out the window.

One month later, on February 26, 1967, Lieutenant Colonel Odumegwu-Ojukwu broadcast a warning that if the Aburi Accords were not fully implemented by March 31, 1967, he would feel obliged to give full effect to them in the East. In Lagos, the permanent secretaries prepared a draft decree based on their finagled reinterpretation of the Aburi Accords. A meeting of the Supreme Military Council convened in Benin City on March 10, 1967, to consider the draft decree. There was no prior discussion of or agreement on the venue, and so the military governor of the East did not attend for security reasons. The council nevertheless proceeded to approve the draft and promulgate it as Decree no. 8. One might here mention that the Supreme Military Council had agreed that any military governor not present at any of its meetings would be given the opportunity to express his comments on and concurrence with the decisions taken in his absence before they were implemented. The documents reached Enugu on the same day as the meeting. Much of the hot air ventilated by Lt. Col. Yakubu Gowon at his press conference of January 26, 1967, was missing, but a good deal of extraneous material found its way in. Terminologies like "Supreme Commander" and "President" were used. The membership of the Supreme Military Council was enlarged, and a collateral center of executive and legislative power, the Federal Executive Council, emerged.

For Lieutenant Colonel Odumegwu-Ojukwu, however, the sticking point was the specification that a state of emergency could be declared in any part of the country and that any laws deemed "necessary" or "expedient" for the maintenance of law and order could be passed by the head of the Federal Military Government with the concurrence of at least three of the governors. Such laws would supersede any laws hitherto passed by the regional government. Not only was this not discussed let alone agreed to at Aburi, it opened up the possibility of leaving the safety and security of the people of the East once again to the whims and caprices of an agency outside the East. In the context of the bloodlust with which the North had comported itself since May 1966 and the chaos in the West in the lead-up to and aftermath of the state of emergency of 1962–1963, a mischief-maker or other troubled soul could conceivably be manipulated into fomenting public unrest, and the Supreme Military Council would have its reason to declare a state of emergency. Having pledged to ensure that Easterners would never again be wantonly victimized like they had been in 1966, it would have been irresponsible for Lieutenant Colonel Odumegwu-Ojukwu to accept a decree that could expose Easterners to such vulnerability. Even then, one of the "super-permanent secretaries" at the time, Mr. Phillip Asiodu, opined in a television interview about half a century later that Decree no. 8 contained two lethal clauses from the federal standpoint, namely the creation of regional military commands and the requirement for unanimity among the regions in the conferment of promotions and appointments to very senior positions. According to him, if the East had accepted the decree as promulgated, "Nigeria would have disintegrated within 3 months."

On March 13, 1967, the military governor of the East called a press conference to share his reactions to the deliberations at the Benin meeting of the Supreme Military Council. He explained that he could not attend for reasons of personal safety. He rejected the imminent Decree no. 8 and laid out his rationale for doing so. He reiterated his position that the agreements reached at Aburi were the only basis for progress in the resolution of the crisis and that he would proceed to unilaterally implement them in the East come March 31, 1967, as previously pledged, should the Federal Military Government renege on its obligation to do so. He hastened to advise that such a step not be construed as a threat of secession, which action the East would not consider unless attacked or blockaded. Lagos released Decree no. 8 to the public on March 17, 1967.

As March 31, 1967, approached, the world press gathered in Enugu, and the atmosphere was abuzz with speculations as to what next step Lieutenant Colonel Odumegwu-Ojukwu would take. Some thought he was going to announce the secession of the East.

He instead enacted a raft of edicts, the so-called Survival Edicts, designed to shore up the precarious financial position of the region. They were the Registration of Companies, Revenue Collection, and Court of Appeal Edicts. The Revenue Collection Edict required all companies doing business in the East to pay their taxes to the regional government. It, however, did not affect petroleum revenues since the oil companies paid those in Lagos. Lt. Col. Yakubu Gowon was incensed. In a memorandum (SMC/67/42) dated April 19, 1967, he set out his plans for economic and diplomatic blockades of the East and hinted at military operations. Postal services and all of its external communications routed through Lagos, including telephones, telex, and cables, were severed. Flights of the Nigeria Airways into and out of the region were also discontinued. The total lack of fixed-wing aircraft in the region was a handicap the government decided it had to remedy posthaste. A special task force of the nascent directorate of military intelligence headed by Lt. Col. Louis Chude Sokei was commissioned to solve the problem by any means necessary. An intrepid team comprising Capt. Ibikare Allwell-Brown (Nigeria Airways), Mr. Sam Inyagha (pharmacist), Mr. Onuora Nwanya (Nigeria Coal Corporation), and Mr. Mark Anamelechi Odu (undergraduate at the University of Nigeria) made its way to Benin City by road, and on April 23, 1967, boarded a Nigeria Airways Fokker-27 (5N-AAV) flight to Lagos, which they diverted to Enugu without incident. The following day, Lt. Col. Yakubu Gowon dispatched a saber-rattling letter to his military governors, castigating and threatening Lieutenant Colonel Odumegwu-Ojukwu in very fierce terms.

One last attempt to lower the temperature and ease tension was made by a group that called itself the National (Re)Conciliation Committee. It had a very distinguished membership, among which were the chief justice Sir Adetokunbo Ademola, the governor of the Mid-West Sir Samuel Jereton Mariere, Professor Samuel Aluko, Chief Obafemi Awolowo, and Police Commissioner Emmanuel Olufunwa, his close political confidant. The absence of Northern representation from a national committee was, needless to say, conspicuous. They arrived in Enugu on May 06, 1967, and held talks with the military governor and his advisers, among whom was Lt. Col. Victor Banjo.

TOWARD UNDERSTANDING THE NIGERIA-BIAFRA WAR AND LINGERING QUESTIONS

Unfortunately, the salience of his team, like that of the visitors, was the absence of those who should have been there—the likes of Dr. Michael Okpara, Dr. Nnamdi Azikiwe, Dr. Kingsley Mbadiwe, Chief Matthew Mbu.

The two sides listened politely to each other all day, and late that night, according to Mr. Wole Soyinka, Lt. Col. Chukwuemeka Odumegwu-Ojukwu came with a small coterie of his advisers to Chief Awolowo's chalet asking to speak to him in confidence. The chief, for his part, understandably demanded that another pair of ears sit in on his side and brought in his aide, Police Commissioner Olufunwa. The lieutenant colonel reportedly told the chief that he had come to inform him that the East had decided on secession and that there was no going back. Also, that he agreed to meet with the committee only out of personal respect for him. The Chief then extracted from the military governor a promise to be informed at least two weeks ahead of announcing the decision. However, Lt. Col. Philip Efiong, who was on the Eastern team, sought to dispel the suggestion of a cavalier reception implied in accounts such as the above, by drawing attention to the fact that the chief and the governor did retire to the latter's inner office for further private talks after the public meeting. The following day, the delegation returned to Lagos. They submitted recommendations to Lt. Col. Yakubu Gowon, which included the reciprocal revocation of the federal economic sanctions and the Survival Edicts of the East. On May 23, 1967, Lieutenant Colonel Gowon gave instructions for the sanctions to be lifted. However, in his broadcast on May 27, 1967, he stated that vehicles of the post and telegraphs department that had gone to the East on resumption of services were impounded, citing it as evidence of bad faith and intransigence.

PART 4

BIAFRA AND THE NIGERIA-BIAFRA WAR

After the coup of July 29, 1966, Lieutenant Colonel Odumegwu-Ojukwu had constituted a 335-member consultative assembly comprising ten members (six popular and four *ex-officio* delegates) from each of the twenty-nine administrative divisions and forty-five representatives of the professions. Its inaugural meeting was held on August 31, 1966, and it continued to meet regularly as the crisis unfolded. On a proposal by Dr. Okoi Arikpo, a delegate from Ugep, at one of the consultative assembly meetings, the region was reorganized into twenty provinces, dispensing with the British colonial administrative divisions in favor of a structure more in conformity with ethnic and linguistic affinities. The provinces were also given unprecedented powers in their own administration as well as input to decision-making at the center.

According to Mr. Bernard Odogwu, sometime just before May 26, 1967, Lt. Col. Yakubu Gowon sent the military governor of the East a letter to inform him that the Federal Military Government had decided to partition the country into twelve states, three of them out of the East. On May 26, 1967, the military governor convened the consultative assembly, and after lengthy oration describing the trials and tribulations on the journey thus far, he asked which of three courses of action was the best suited to the road ahead, namely accept Gowon and the terms dictated by the North, continue the stalemate and drift, or assert our autonomy to ensure our survival. That said, he then informed the assembly that he had received a communication from Lt. Col. Yakubu Gowon detailing the structural reconfiguration of the country. It had the anticipated effect of electrifying and incensing the assembly. The military governor then left the members to their deliberations at the end of which they voted unanimously for the third of the options he had given them and authorized him to declare the East "a free and sovereign independent state by the name and title of the Republic of Biafra" at an early practicable date.

The next day, May 27, 1967, Lt. Col. Yakubu Gowon made a broadcast in which he proclaimed a state of emergency throughout the country with immediate effect. He identified "the present structural imbalance" as the main obstacle to future stability and that the item in the political and administrative program of the Supreme Military Council that would guarantee that stability was the creation of states. He stated that demands for states had been made in the North, Lagos, and the East and alleged that minority areas in the East had been "subjected to violent intimidation by the Eastern Military Government." He seemed to acknowledge that a mechanism like plebiscites was the appropriate approach to a matter of the kind under reference but dismissed them because "the present circumstances regrettably do not allow for consultations." He then proceeded to promulgate Decree no. 14, which divided Nigeria into twelve states (Fig. 4). The East was split into three states—a landlocked East-Central for the Igbo, a Rivers, and a South-Eastern for the "minorities." The West and Mid-West were not carved up. There were six states in the North. A unifying forum for them, the Council of Northern States, was to emerge later.

It was an insincere and very dishonest speech. The only reference to the historic bloodbath under his watch was a most oblique one—to the "tragic incidents of 1966," which he had "spared no effort to

TOWARD UNDERSTANDING THE NIGERIA-BIAFRA WAR AND LINGERING QUESTIONS

conciliate the East in recognition of their understandable grievances and fears." Clearly, the main, if not sole, purpose of the state creation exercise was to stoke division in the East and undermine its cohesion by pandering to the strong minority activists and powerful federal permanent secretaries who had him by the short hairs.

On May 30, 1967, Lt. Col. Chukwuemeka Odumegwu-Ojukwu proclaimed the East the Republic of Biafra, citing as reason the failure of the Nigerian nation to protect the people of the East and guarantee their safety. The new nation was named for the body of water, the Bight of Biafra, between the Niger Delta and Cap Lopez in Gabon (Fig. 4).

The central question has been whether the East should have seceded, and the answer, I think, is NO. It was neither necessary for the East to declare formally that it had seceded, nor was the East ready to do so. Easterners had been brutalized beyond all reason, but victimhood and resultant moral indignation alone were not a sufficiently valid basis for taking so extreme a step that had geopolitical ramifications and would certainly be challenged in some or every way—economic, diplomatic, and military. The East had effectively separated itself *de facto* from Nigeria and set up its own civic institutions and other structures. Lieutenant Colonel Gowon had no means of coming to the East to enforce his Decree no. 14. Mr. Isaac Boro and his gang had made their move on February 23, 1966, attacking the police post at Yenagoa and declaring a Niger Delta Republic. They were routed in twelve days by a contingent of the Nigeria Police supported by troops of the First Battalion out of Enugu commanded by Maj. John Obienu (Operation ATUA). In the battle of hearts and minds, I believe it was a lot easier for the government of the East to show the "minorities" that their interests were better served by Enugu than Lagos. Events in the postwar era (the rape at Choba, the sack of Odi, the unending vicissitudes of the Ogoni) have borne out this conjecture. There was no reason why the East could not have just carried on nurturing and strengthening its nascent institutions. The East had the moral high ground and would conceivably be able to attract both sympathy and the material help it needed to deter or fend off further attempts at victimization. Potential benefactors would not have had to hesitate and contemplate the implications of their actions as much as they would do in later years. So, why was secession proclaimed at the time it was? Only the governor of the East; and some say, Mr. Christopher Mojekwu; Professor Pius Okigbo; and Lt. Col. Louis Chude Sokei, who were the governor's closest confidants, would have known. They are all deceased now and left no relevant written records to enlighten us on the question.

To some extent, the above construal may be challenged as a figment of hindsight and that, in the real world at the time, passions had overheated and the momentum toward secession was, to all intents and purposes, unstoppable. Lieutenant Colonel Gowon in Lagos was viewed as weak of character and under the thumb of the hotheads of the July 29, 1966, coup who had brought him to power as well as the shrewd politicians and senior civil servants who saw his regime as an opportunity to exercise power on a scale they hitherto could only dream of. It is very improbable that he and his advisers did not know Decree no. 14 was bound to be very provocative. Arguably, he was spoiling for a fight, having at the time begun to mend fences with Chief Awolowo, thus enabling the North and West to close ranks behind him. Lieutenant Colonel Odumegwu-Ojukwu in Enugu had, months before, stated that the East would not secede unless it was pushed. Carving up the East in the tense aftermath of a pogrom in which tens of thousands of Easterners had been wantonly massacred and over one and half million of them displaced bears interpreting as a shove or worse. Many who ordinarily did not share Lieutenant Colonel Odumegwu-Ojukwu's views agreed that Decree no. 14 was blatant mischief-making under the circumstances. They, however, argue that, tempting as it might have been, formal secession was not the right answer—at the time it was proclaimed.

CHAPTER 9

ECONOMIC CRISIS

Many critics of the East derogatorily opine that the East seceded because of the oil resources in the Niger Delta—as if Federal Nigeria would have been so murderously obsessed with its territorial integrity if it were not for those oil resources.

Prior to 1959, Nigeria exported mainly agricultural products—oil palm from the East, cocoa from the West, and groundnuts from the North. The contribution of minerals (a highly desirable low-sulfur coal from the East, tin and columbite from the Middle-Belt North) was relatively very small. All the revenue from export duties on the mineral and agricultural products were retained by the respective producing regions. On January 15, 1956, the first commercially viable oil field was discovered in Oloibiri in the Niger Delta by Shell D'arcy. Production started two years later at 5,100 barrels/day and grew steadily at an annual rate of about 78 percent. By 1966, Nigeria was ranked the thirteenth largest oil producer in the world, having pumped 152.4 million barrels that year. The massive influx of revenue was a veritable shock to the system. In classic Dutch disease fashion, all other sectors of the economy progressively atrophied, and the entire country became dependent on petroleum. The vices of kleptomania and prebendalism quickly took hold and flourished. A tried and true legerdemain which long endured was compelling foreign companies to deposit the revenue due to the government months ahead of the due date in a nongovernment short-term, high-interest-bearing account. At maturity, the interest would be skimmed off and the invested amount returned to government coffers. See? No money missing! The foreign companies, fearful of losing patronage to the competition, played along. From 1959, the federal government adopted a revenue allocation formula whereby only half of the rents and royalties and none of the profits tax were earmarked to the region of derivation. In 1966, two-thirds of the oil production was from fields in the East, valued at about sixty-seven million British pounds sterling.

In June 1967, the government of Biafra asked Shell-BP to pay the due oil royalties in the amount of seven million British pounds sterling. Shell-BP pleaded *force majeure* and offered to pay only 0.25 million pounds. In the event, the British government intervened and reportedly blocked the remittance of even that token amount to Biafra. However, a Yorkshireman who was a senior accountant with Shell-BP at the time, whose acquaintance I made through a close friend, shared that Shell-BP did in fact make substantial payments to Biafra but under different circumstances. According to him, a top executive of the oil company had visited Enugu for talks on the continuation of its exploration and extraction privileges. Assurances were given, but when the time came for him to depart as originally planned, he was discouraged from doing so and instead advised to stay and enjoy Biafran hospitality for a little longer. A deal both sides were happy with was subsequently agreed.

Biafra had reasonably substantial foreign reserves in July 1967, estimated by the United States Central Intelligence Agency at about $40 million. They were reserves of the government of the Eastern Group of Provinces, the African Continental Bank, and the NCNC held in foreign financial institutions. In addition, about $100 million worth of unissued Nigerian currency was held in bank vaults for the replacement of bills worn in circulation. This subsequently had to be sold overseas for foreign currency, unfortunately at a heavy discount for various reasons, including the requirement that official permission be obtained from Lagos for all foreign payments in Nigerian currency and the issuance of new currency notes by Nigeria in January 1968. War matériel was purchased using these reserves, and by April 1968, they were virtually exhausted. During 1968, Biafra was estimated to have received the equivalent of a total of 7–8 million British pounds sterling in foreign exchange. They included about 2 million pounds from France, 4.3 million pounds from relief and mission organizations in exchange for Biafran currency used to pay for their local operations, and 0.75 million pounds raised by Easterners in the diaspora. In 1968, it was estimated that Nigeria spent five to ten times as much as Biafra in foreign exchange in direct defense expenditure.

Manufacturing accounted for only about 6 percent of Nigeria's gross domestic product (GDP) in 1966, compared to 55 percent for agriculture. Of this output, the East accounted for about 30 percent. With the onset of hostilities, all significant manufacturing activity ceased. However, as the storm clouds were gathering and the saber-rattling began after the abnegation of the Aburi Accords by Lagos, the East began to think in terms of developing its local manufacturing capacity. They concentrated on strategies for furtively repurposing for military and other uses materials that could be legally imported. A "Science Group" which brought together the extraordinary talent of the region began to meet. They were engineers, scientists, technologists, and technicians from the University of Nigeria, the Nigerian Army, the Nigerian Coal Corporation, Nigerian Railways, and the Ministries of Works and Communications. Its first military liaison was Capt. J. Ohaya of the Army Corps of Engineers. In due course, the Science Group evolved into the Biafran Agency for Research and Production (RaP), which was under the command of Col. Ebenezer Ejike Aghanya. The accomplishments of RaP under the conditions of the time (the initial budget of the Science Group was ten Nigerian pounds!) are the stuff of legend. In addition to military ordnance, RaP also manufactured household items such as soap, safety matches, candles, and alcoholic beverages as well as stills used for refining petroleum. The qualities were indifferent to begin with but improved dramatically over time. The quantities, however, were never enough due in large part to disruptions caused by plant dismantling and reassembly as territory shrank with shifting fortunes at the frontlines.

The Igbo are innately entrepreneurial and were to be found in all nooks and crannies of Nigeria doing business. They bought and sold for a profit. To their detractors, that meant they were incurably money-grubbing, and the perverse joke was that if you jingled coins or rustled banknotes in the ear of a critically ill Igbo in intensive care and he failed to revive, pulling the plug at that point was justifiable. The population density of the East was very high (420 per square mile, compared to 156 per square mile for Nigeria as a whole, according to the 1963 census), and the available arable land was not only disproportionately small but also not particularly fertile. This was, at least in part, the impetus for the cultivation of expertise in areas of endeavor other than farming. A significant amount of food used to be imported from the Middle Belt to the North before the conflict. After Biafra seceded, some trade continued across the River Niger, but only for about three to four months. In September 1967, the 2 Division of the Nigerian Army under the command of Lt. Col. Murtala Mohammed set fire to and completely destroyed the Onitsha Market, the largest of its kind in West Africa at the time, in their failed attempts to take the town. Later during the war, some trading did occur across the frontlines during lulls in the fighting ("Ahia Attack"), but the volume was little more than a trickle.

Food shortage was a problem even at the outset. The pogrom in the North sparked an exodus of at least 1.6 million Easterners from all parts of Nigeria, increasing the population of the East by 15 to 20 percent. As early as April 19, 1967, Lieutenant Colonel Gowon had sent a memorandum to his Supreme Military Council seeking their agreement to inflict diplomatic and economic sanctions on the East. When the economic blockade of the new nation went into effect, its sting was attenuated in the early days by the overland access to the Cameroons to the east. The Nigerian Navy, however, was an effective deterrent on the Atlantic coast, and no significant shipping effectively ran the blockade. Fortunately, the same could not be said of the Nigerian Air Force. Biafra remained accessible by air all through the war albeit with increasing difficulty as the conflict progressed. With the fall of Enugu on October 04, 1967, the airport was lost. Lt. Col. Benjamin Adekunle's 3 Division (Marine commando) took

TOWARD UNDERSTANDING THE NIGERIA-BIAFRA WAR AND LINGERING QUESTIONS

Calabar during October 17–19, 1967, and linked up with forces coming down from Ogoja to seal off the border of Biafra with the Cameroons. Port Harcourt airport remained available until May 24, 1968, when it fell to federal forces. Thereafter, Biafra became landlocked, with the airport at Uli ("Annabelle"—all 1,148' × 75' of it) as sole link between it and the outside world. The federal government never consented to the use of the Red Cross airstrip at Obilagu. The strips at Uga and Mbawsi were less elaborate and restricted to military use.

As the military situation continued to deteriorate and Biafra lost territory, the precarious food situation grew steadily worse. The federal government had declared that starvation was a legitimate weapon of war and, according to Mr. Allison Akene Ayida, who was among the group instrumental to the vacation of the Aburi Accords, "we have every intention of using it against the rebels." He was head of the Nigerian Delegation to the Niamey Peace Talks in July 1968, by which time the contours of an epic famine were already taking shape.

In the last year of the war, food supplies flown in by humanitarian organizations were the major source of nourishment for Biafran babies and children. They were hardly sufficient, and that segment of the population became ravaged by extreme protein-calorie malnutrition in what became one of the modern world's most horrid stories of famine. The mercy flights (5,314 missions) delivered about 60,000 tons of supplies, making them the second most massive of their kind in recorded history—just behind the Berlin Airlift of 1948–1949 (which was implemented by the military). Yet after the dust settled, American and British diplomats arrived at the official consensus that "only 1 million (children—*sic*) had died, rather than the 2 million once feared." (*New York Times* August 01, 1987). Of course 1 million are fewer than two million—but only?

There was talk by Nigeria of establishing a land corridor across the frontlines for the delivery of relief supplies to the shrinking Biafran enclave. However, given its declared policy of weaponizing starvation, in the full knowledge that the main victims would be children, women, and the old, it was utterly disingenuous and shamelessly self-serving. It was rejected by Biafra and one would argue, rightly so. The mass starvation effort of Nigeria will be discussed more fully in a subsequent chapter.

Sadly in conclusion, Biafra had no effective means of breaking the blockade. The tactical command of the Biafran Air Force (BAF) made valiant attempts to weaken the stranglehold of the Nigerian Navy and would have been successful if it had the right munitions. The raids by the flying ace, Squadron Leader John Ikeokwu Chukwu, Distinguished Service Cross, deserve specific honorable mention in this context. He was certified on jet fighter aircraft, but his colleagues described him as "a natural" in the air, regardless of machine. Flying just a turbine helicopter (Aerospatiale Alouette II) early during the war, he led daring attacks on the flagship of the Nigerian Navy, the NNS *Nigeria*, in which direct hits were scored. Squadron Leader Chukwu flew more helicopter combat missions than any other pilot in the BAF. The air operations during the war will be discussed in the chapter on the military crisis.

Chapter 10

Diplomatic Crisis

Diplomatically, Biafra was largely isolated. It was the height of the Cold War, and every conflict was examined through that prism. The protagonists were the West and the East. There was also the Non-Aligned Movement comprising mostly nations emerging from Western colonialism and so were suspected of harboring Eastern sympathies. The reality of the era was that these newly "independent" countries simply needed to maintain a grip on the apron strings of their erstwhile masters or risk being destabilized, which was very easy to do since they were, in fact, mere "geographical expressions" according to the leader of the Action Group. And so, the British continued to hold sway in Nigeria, and the British did not like the Igbo. During the process of colonizing Nigeria, they had it easier with the North and the West. They could treat with the emirs and obas with assurance that their subjects would all fall in line. In Igboland, it was different. They had to physically subjugate the people everywhere they went, and that was very hard work. Then in 1929, women took them on in Owerri and Calabar provinces, exhibiting a political consciousness and sophistication that equaled, if not surpassed, that of their own women who had only been granted suffrage the year before. They officially called (and still call) it the Aba Riots, in seeking to portray it as some kind of degenerate activity. Also, no gender reference is made. The Aba Women's Uprising of 1929 will be examined in some depth in a subsequent chapter. Britain in the colonial and postcolonial era did not like the Igbo. Unlike the elite of Western Nigeria and, to a much lesser extent, the North, who went to Britain for higher education, most of those of the East traveled to the United States (Eyo Ita, Benjamin Azikiwe, Mbonu Ojike, Kingsley Mbadiwe, Nwafor Orizu, Okechukwu Ikejiani), where they imbibed such pesky ideas as "liberty," "autonomy," "dignity of man," and "independence." They came back and propagated them, helping to accelerate the demise of British rule. The antipathy of official Britain toward the East and the Igbo in particular was therefore hardly surprising.

One thing was for sure, especially during the Cold War era—any aspiring political entity in the Non-Aligned Bloc must hew Left or Right and have its hands held by one or the other of the superpowers or major players (United Nations Security Council members). That was so because that entity was bound to be tried and tested in very significant ways as soon as it declared itself. Without such patronage, it had no fighting chance whatsoever. But if it had a "godfather," then there would be a force on its side to protect its interests and echo its points of view at global fora. The State of Israel was founded with the support of the United States and Britain. It acquired nuclear technology from France. Agreed the Jews are an extremely resourceful people—as are the Igbo. However, the reason the State of Israel has been able to consistently punch above its weight class and get away with policies that would otherwise draw severe condemnation and reprimand is the kind of relationship it has had with the major Western powers. To the best of my knowledge, Biafra was not successful at cultivating that kind of relationship with any member of the UN Security Council. There had been some cordiality between the civilian government of Dr. Michael Iheonukara Okpara and the Soviet Union before the crisis. Contracts for the construction of the University of Nigeria Teaching Hospital, Enugu, had been awarded to mostly Soviet companies. In April 1967, an unnamed top Soviet diplomat visited Enugu and had audience with the military governor. He then met with General Njoku to share his impressions of the governor and his advisers. Regarding their preparedness for the challenge ahead, he described them as ill-suited and ill-prepared. He presented the general with some books and a movie on counterinsurgency. Shortly afterward, the teaching hospital contracts were canceled. The Soviet Union was later to throw in their lot with Federal Nigeria as strange bedfellows with Britain. It has also been suggested that another reason for shunning the Soviet Union was the confidence of the Biafran leadership at the time that there would be no sustained conflict and so no need to mortgage the future of the new nation in any way. If true, then that was shockingly naive, and one does not make that assessment because of the benefit of hindsight. Even if Lieutenant Colonel Gowon and his colleagues decided not to wage war, there was no way Britain would have let the Nigeria they created for such benefit to themselves to just dismember.

France was sympathetic but never committed to a degree that would certainly have made a decisive difference. It seemed they were merely acting in the context of their usual rivalry with the British, which goes back a very long time. In the eighteenth century, they had sent Guy de Lafayette over to America to help Gen. George Washington's Continental Army defeat the British. Even though Biafra had a fine diplomat in Paris at the time, in the person of Mr. Raph Uwechue, he couldn't move the needle much. The decade of the '60s was a very difficult time all across the Western world, with the rise of youth countercultures which questioned the norms of the post-World War II sociopolitical order in fundamental ways. In May 1968, students at the Université de Paris (Nanterre and Sorbonne campuses) rioted. When the police got involved, workers weighed in on the side of the students, and the crisis quickly spread. All of France was literally paralyzed, and out of fear of revolution, Le Président de La République Gen. Joseph-Marie Charles de Gaulle fled in despair, briefly taking refuge at the French military base at Baden-Baden, West Germany. When the dust settled, he was a chastened and very cautious man. Contemporaneously, the US was up to its gills in Indochina—549,500 troops at a cost of 77.4 billion dollars in 1968. It certainly did not have the stomach for more. As defeat stared him in the face and his presidency was crumbling around him, a frustrated Lyndon Baines Johnson, thirty-sixth president of the United States (POTUS XXXVI), was reported to have once told a

State Department official to "get those (racial expletive) babies off my TV set," referring to starving Biafran children. State Department documents the following year, however, suggest that his successor, Richard Milhous Nixon, and Secretary of State Dr. Henry Kissinger were more sympathetic to Biafra's plight but at a humanitarian level. Officially, the preference of the United States was for an intact federal Nigeria but no active steps would be taken one way or the other.

The United Nations, under the secretary-generalship of U Thant, preoccupied itself with perceived humanitarian concerns, opting for the Organization of African Unity (OAU) to handle the more sticky fundamental problems underlying the conflict. Britain, a member of the security council, made sure matters stayed that way. Besides, the UN had been very badly burned in the Congo Crisis of 1960–1965, which claimed not only the prime minister of the Republic Patrice Emery Lumumba (1925–January 17, 1960, assassinated at Elisabethville, Katanga) but also its second secretary-general, Dag H. A. Carl Hammarskjold (1905–September 18, 1961, killed in an air crash near Ndola, Northern Rhodesia). The OAU was pitifully ill-equipped. Its membership comprised states which, with the exception of Ethiopia and Liberia, were contrivances of the British and French in the late nineteenth to early twentieth century. Ethiopia had very limited colonial experience (1936–1944) when the fascist Italian regime of Benito Mussolini had possession of it. They were beaten with the help of the British (1943), and the Anglo-Ethiopian Treaty was signed in 1944. Freed slaves and freeborn African Americans were transported from the United States to present-day Liberia under the auspices of the American Colonization Society, beginning in the early nineteenth century. The settlement grew steadily and eventually declared its independence in 1847. Interestingly, the settlers constituted themselves into an elite and began to treat the indigenous people in pretty much the same way Europeans dealt with Native Americans in the New World.

Almost without exception, the member-states of the OAU created by the British and French were collages of multiple disparate ethnic entities with next to nothing of substance in common. They were often at loggerheads, and that suited the colonial masters nicely

TOWARD UNDERSTANDING THE NIGERIA-BIAFRA WAR AND LINGERING QUESTIONS

since the precious energies they expended going after each other were resources that might otherwise have been devoted to challenging them. Not surprisingly, they stoked the differences to widen the cleavages in classic "*divide-et-impera*" strategy. Indeed, very few, if any, nation-states are ethnically homogeneous. However, for a nation-state to put down roots and thrive, its peoples must have a shared narrative. It may be that of an actual historical experience, like a war of independence, or some extraordinary act in the common interest, like the agreement by England for the Stuart King of Scotland, James VI, to accede to the English throne in 1603 and become king of England and Scotland (and Ireland). Never mind that European royalty were an inbred lot, but considering the ferocity with which they could go after one another, such a gesture was historically outstanding. Their parliaments though would remain separate for another hundred years. Sometimes, the shared narrative is merely mythical and conveniently buried in the remote past. Nevertheless, it remains effective as a social adhesive for as long as everybody believes in whatever that might be. That belief is very important—to the extent that some nation-states, like the United States, are exclusively creedal. Emperor Napoleon Bonaparte was anything but facetious when he said "history is a set of lies that people have agreed upon."

Unfortunately, the vast majority of African countries do not have the benefit of an inspiring unifying chronicle, real or fictional. Knowing this, one of the chartering postulates of the OAU was that the colonial boundaries would be sacrosanct since none of the members was without ethnic incongruities in its makeup and there would be no end to reconfigurations if a start was made. Even Ethiopia had the boondoggle of Eriteria, which the UN, against the wishes of the Eritrean people, had forcefully federated with it in 1952. Therefore the OAU of the 1960s, on whom the world had come to rely to mediate the Nigeria-Biafra conflict, was no more than a conflicted compromised conglomeration. Its verdict was predictable in that under no circumstance could it, as a body, endorse Biafra's sovereignty since that would amount to loss of Nigeria's territorial integrity. Now, knowing that and lacking meaningful patronage in other diplomatic circles raises the question whether it made sense for

Biafra to continue to insist that its sovereignty was not negotiable. At the start of the conflict on July 06, 1967, Biafra was about twenty-nine thousand square miles of territory. On August 08, 1967, an expeditionary force led by Gen. Victor Banjo crossed the River Niger at Onitsha into the Mid-West and penetrated as far west as Ore and Okitipupa. The 2 Division of the Nigeria Army, under the command of Lt. Col. Murtala Muhammed, counterattacked with equally dramatic success about six weeks later and by the end of September had regained all lost territory. Enugu, the capital city of Biafra, fell on October 04, 1967, to the 1 Division of the Nigeria Army led by Col. Mohammed Shuwa. By August 1968, Biafra had shrunken to about nine thousand square miles, having lost the Cross River basin and Atlantic seaboard (Calabar, October 19, 1967; Port Harcourt, May 24, 1968). Such a track record could evoke pity but very unlikely a surge of diplomatic support and recognition.

As 1968 wore on, the military situation more or less stabilized, and there was clearly a window of opportunity to explore diplomatic options seriously. Well before then though, there had actually been multiple overtures, which made no headway, by the East African Community Conciliation Commission, the Vatican, the Organization of African Unity (OAU) Consultative Commission, and the Commonwealth of Nations (CoN). The efforts of the OAU and CoN at the time were predictably doomed to collapse under the weight of their patent bias and conflict of interest. The OAU began with a statement of condemnation of the rebellion—which quickly dispelled any semblance of objectivity and was obviously not a very good place to start. Even as Mr. Arnold Smith, secretary-general of CoN, went through the motions of brokering talks between Lagos and Enugu in October 1967, the British government had in August pledged military support to the federal side. The fact of the matter is that the CoN is the successor community of the British empire, which had been compelled to dismantle after the Second World War. Between the Balfour Declaration of 1926 and the London Declaration of 1949, it was actually the British Commonwealth and never really got rid of its imperial sensibilities, with their racial undertones. Its duplicitousness never surprised, on reflection.

TOWARD UNDERSTANDING THE NIGERIA-BIAFRA WAR AND LINGERING QUESTIONS

Diplomatically, the months of April and May 1968 were momentous for Biafra, even as it was reeling militarily. In quick succession, diplomatic recognition was conferred by Tanzania (April 13), Gabon (May 08), Côte d'Ivoire (May 15), and Zambia (May 20). Clearly in panic, the CoN quickly arranged for formal negotiations to begin in Kampala, Uganda, on May 23. The Biafran delegation was led by Chief Justice Louis Nwachukwu Mbanefo (called to the bar [Middle Temple] in the mid-1930s, the first lawyer of Eastern origin; judge, International Court of Justice at the Hague, 1962–1966) and that of Nigeria by Chief Anthony Enahoro, the commissioner for Information. A two-item agenda—cease-fire, then a political settlement—had been agreed in preliminary talks in London earlier in the month. The Nigerian delegation prevaricated at meetings or found reasons to change the schedules. It turned out that they were listening for the outcome of the ongoing offensive on Port Harcourt. When word was received that the elements of 3 Division (Marine Commando) of the Nigerian Army had entered the city on May 24, 1968, Chief Enahoro apparently decided it made no further sense to discuss a cease-fire first. He put forward a proposal for a political settlement, which required Biafra to renounce secession and accept the twelve-state reconfiguration before a cease-fire. The Biafran side insisted that the talks stick to the hitherto agreed agenda. Thus deadlocked, the parley ended on the thirty-first of May, 1968.

The OAU Consultative Peace Committee, comprising the heads of state of Ethiopia (chair), Niger, Liberia, Cameroon, Ghana, and Congo Kinshasa, decided to pick up the pieces. It issued an invitation to both the Nigerian and Biafran sides to attend preliminary negotiations in Niamey, the Nigerien capital, in July 1968. That was a paradigm shift as it indicated that the OAU had come to recognize that there were two parties to the conflict and not just one party engaged in the suppression of an internal insurrection. General Gowon flew in on July 16, 1968, and returned to Lagos on the same day. General Odumegwu-Ojukwu arrived two days later and spent twenty-four hours in Niamey. The delegations, Biafra's led by Professor Eni Njoku (first indigenous vice-chancellor of the University of Lagos) and Nigeria's by Mr. Allison Akene Ayida, remained to discuss relief aid and an agenda for substantive peace negotiations to be held in Addis Ababa, the Ethiopian capital.

The Addis Ababa peace conference opened on July 29, 1968. General Gowon did not attend, and Nigeria was represented instead by Chief Anthony Enahoro. General Odumegwu-Ojukwu came himself to state Biafra's case. He clearly was in his element when he rose to give his opening address, speaking for over one hour to an enraptured diplomatic audience, who rewarded him with a standing ovation. The peace negotiations themselves predictably went nowhere, with the Nigerian side, buoyed up by battlefield successes (Aba fell on September 04, 1968), seeing no need to show good faith. The conference ended after about five weeks.

The last major effort by the OAU to broker peace between Nigeria and Biafra played out during April 18 and 19, 1969, in Monrovia, Liberia. The Biafran delegation was headed by the chief justice Sir Louis Mbanefo and the Nigerian contingent by Mr. Lateef Olufemi Okunnu, the commissioner for Works and Housing. As reported by Mr. Frederick Forsyth, each delegation first met with the Consultative Committee in separate closed sessions. Then the Biafran delegation was asked to meet with Presidents William Tubman of Liberia and Hamani Diori of Niger, with the secretary-general of the OAU Mr. Boubacar Diallo Telli in attendance. When asked to set out Biafra's position, Sir Mbanefo stated that her primal instinctive concern was for her security and that of her citizens' lives and property. He added that Biafra was willing to discuss "One Nigeria" but needed to know precisely what that meant. President Hamani Diori then proposed the inclusion of international guarantees for the external and internal security of Biafra in the framework for peace talks. Mr. Diallo Telli was instructed to prepare a version of the proposal in the English language. Unfortunately, the secretary-general was an advocate of the Nigerian cause to which he felt the proposal was unfavorable. He went instead to the other four members of the Consultative Committee and calumniated it. The six members of the committee then retired to huddle, and when they emerged, the document they came up with made no reference to guarantees for Biafra's security. The next day, the chairman of the Consultative

TOWARD UNDERSTANDING THE NIGERIA-BIAFRA WAR AND LINGERING QUESTIONS

Committee, Emperor Haile Selassie, handed Sir Mbanefo the final document which stated that all future peace talks would be predicated on the prior acceptance of "One Nigeria" by Biafra. That effort, like others before it, fizzled. Emperor Haile Selassie was deposed by junior officers of his armed forces on September 12, 1974. State media announced his death on August 28, 1975. Mr. Diallo Telli completed his second term as secretary-general of the OAU in June 1972. He returned to his native Guinea and was named Minister of Justice a couple of months later. On July 18, 1976, he was implicated in a coup plot and arrested. He died in prison seven months later.

One month before the Niamey meeting of July 1968, a Biafran delegation led by Dr. Kenneth Onwuka Dike (eminent historian and first indigenous vice-chancellor of the University of Ibadan) visited Tunisia to plead the Biafran cause. Their host, President Habib Bourguiba, sounded sympathetic but would not be sold on the idea of a sovereign Biafra. He instead floated the model of a loose federal arrangement and asked to know what the delegation thought about it. In the recollection of Mr. Raph Uwechue, Mr. Francis Nwokedi spoke up, shooting it down to the unspoken yet intensely palpable disappointment of Mr. Bourguiba. Mr. Nwokedi reminded their host that such an arrangement had been agreed upon at Aburi, but Nigeria had reneged and now it was too late. When they returned to their hotel, Mr. Uwechue offered the assessment that it was wrong to have been so utterly dismissive of Mr. Bourguiba's suggestion to his face, the more appropriate approach being to have assured him that his views would be relayed to General Ojukwu. Mr. Nwokedi would have none of it, branding such thinking as "surrender." Mr. Francis Nwokedi was very distinguished in many ways, but his judgment and track record raised questions. He was the first Nigerian permanent secretary and was a UN envoy to the Congo, where he helped merge the civil service of Katanga with that of the rest of the country. He and General Ironsi were contemporaries in UN service and when the latter became head of state in January 1966, he was appointed commissioner for Special Duties. His detractors blamed him for the ill-fated Decree no. 34 which the British peddled to the Northern establishment as a machination to deplete their feudal native authority system of its enormous administrative power. That didn't go well. In Biafra, he again had the head of state's ear and interventions attributed to him, such as the above, could hardly be described as wise and well-thought-through.

In a speech on September 09, 1968, President Charles de Gaulle made clear that although his sympathies were with Biafra, France was not about to bestow diplomatic recognition upon it just yet. He suggested that it was for African countries to proceed along those lines as they had begun to do. He then insinuated that some form of confederal arrangement could meet the needs of both sides to the conflict. Biafra again failed to take the hint.

On the face of it, Biafra's diplomacy seemed redolent with, one dares say, ineptitude, which is cause for consternation because such a result was totally inconsistent with the intellectual caliber of the practitioners. In the analysis of Mr. Raph Uwechue, the dissonance was the by-product of the conflation of two interests that were in reality at odds with one another—the survival of Biafra and the survival of the leadership of General Ojukwu. I will return to this subject momentarily.

In August 1968, Dr. Francois Duvalier (public health fellow, University of Michigan, 1943) felt compelled to write to UN Secretary-General U Thant to inform him that he felt kinship with Biafrans, whose ancestors, according to him, played a "capital" role in the Haitian Revolution of 1804 in which the forces of Emperor Napoleon Bonaparte were defeated. The victory of Haiti over imperial France was no mean accomplishment considering that when British Field Marshal Bernard Montgomery of Alamein fame was asked who the top three military commanders in history were, he replied, after a pause to reflect, that "the other two are Alexander and Napoleon"! In February 1969, Dr. Duvalier received Mr. Chukwuma Azikiwe and Dr. Okechukwu Ikejiani in audience and, on March 22, 1969, extended formal diplomatic recognition to Biafra. There was no other diplomatic success until the demise of Biafra.

CHAPTER 11

MILITARY CRISIS

The declaration of war (euphemistically "police action") on Biafra by Federal Nigeria on July 06, 1967, was regrettable yet entirely predictable. War happens when "usual" politics break down and understandings cannot be reached among conflicting interests through verbal jousting. It is still politics but by other means. For Nigeria, the *casus belli* was the proclamation of the independent Republic of Biafra. I have already argued that it was a *faux pas* on the part of the East. A military challenge was bound to come, and the question is, Was Biafra ready to meet it?

The injunction of Theodore Roosevelt, POTUS XXVI, to "speak softly and carry a big stick" can hardly be faulted. One would add though that knowing someone who has a big stick and is ready to wield it on your behalf is just as good, if you don't have one yourself. Both sides of the Nigeria-Biafra conflict did not speak softly. Long before the battle was joined, the military governor of Northern Nigeria, Lt. Col. Hassan Usman Katsina, bragged that federal forces would need "only 48 hours to crush the resistance of Eastern Nigeria" once they were given marching orders. The military governor of Eastern Nigeria, for his part, let it be known that "no power in Black Africa" could subdue the East. According to Raph Uwechue, the hyperbole was aimed at reassuring the bloodied Easterners who had scampered home from all parts of Nigeria that they were now safe at home. That the coastal seabed would be littered with the debris of the Nigerian Navy if an invasion was attempted was, of course, naked bombast. Nevertheless, whatever the intonation, the size of the stick was what really mattered. Federal Nigeria had a big stick (actually a couple), Britain and the Soviet Union, which, in the era of the Cold War, were indeed an odd couple. Biafra found favor of sorts with France and Portugal. Through French influence, francophone Africa became reliably well disposed toward Biafra, with the exception of Cameroon, which would, in due course, receive the Bakassi Peninsula in exchange for its services to Federal Nigeria. Portugal's Sao Tome as a staging post was therefore priceless. When in June 1969 an aircraft carrier of the French Navy (I suspect *Le Clemenceau*) anchored off the coast of Biafra for two weeks after a port call at Libreville, Gabon, the Nigeria Air Force suddenly saw no need to harass air traffic in and out of Uli. Unfortunately, neither France nor Portugal was willing to show a level of sustained commitment anywhere near that of Britain or the Soviet Union to Nigeria. It was always *"le pauvre petit Biafra,"* which underscores the point about "big" and "small" in the context of armed conflict—the population-size factor.

It has struck me as axiomatic in all military history that for a small country to prevail in conflict with a bigger one, it must do so VERY QUICKLY. And if for any reason it is unable to score a quick victory, it must treat or run the risk of losing very badly at the end of a prolonged war. Take the Arab-Israel War of June 1966, which smaller Israel won. It did so in six days. In June 1941, Germany invaded the much larger Soviet Union (Operation Barbarossa), and by December 02, the 258th Infantry Division was within fifteen miles of Moscow, so close that the spires of the Kremlin could be seen. A reconnaissance battalion had actually crossed a bridge on the Moscow-Volga canal at Khimki, a mere five miles from the Soviet capital. Unfortunately, the advance of the Wehrmacht stalled as the notorious Russian winter set in, and they were unable to deliver the *coup de grâce*. On December 05, Soviet forces counterattacked with half a million men, and by January 07, 1942, the Wehrmacht had been driven at least sixty-two miles from Moscow, at the loss of an estimated 830,000 men.

On the subject of size, a possible explanation of the dynamic is that at the beginning of conflict, chances are the smaller side would

TOWARD UNDERSTANDING THE NIGERIA-BIAFRA WAR AND LINGERING QUESTIONS

already have identified most of its finest military talent and fielded them. On the more populous side, such talent could exist (from a purely statistical standpoint), but for reason of the large numbers of incompetents and the less endowed with which they are admixed, they would take a long time to bubble up to the top and take command. The key to success for the smaller side, therefore, is to ensure that the more populous side does not get that time. During the American Civil War, the commander of the main fighting force of the Confederate states, the Army of Northern Virginia, as early as June 1862, was Gen. Robert E. Lee, who had been the superintendent of the United States Military Academy. His nemesis, Brig. Gen. Ulysses Grant at the time, was still fighting under Gen. Henry Halleck in the Western Theater and fending off accusations of insubordination and drunkenness. It was not until March 02, 1864, that President Abraham Lincoln promoted him to the rank of lieutenant general and gave him command of all Union forces. Operation Barbarossa was implemented by the very martial giants who wrote the books on modern mechanized warfare—the likes of Col. General Heinz Guderian (Panzergruppe 2) at the tactical level and strategically Marshal Wilhelm von Loeb (Army Group North), Marshal Fedor von Bock (Army Group Center), and Marshal Carl Gerd von Rundstedt (Army Group South). One of the most brilliant officers of the Wehrmacht, Marshal Erich von Manstein, would later command Army Group South. On the Soviet side, personnel quality was indifferent. The Red Army had fought Finland in the Winter War of November 1939 to March 1940, and although it eventually prevailed (again, big vs. small), the consensus of historians is that it performed very poorly and was almost humiliated. No generals stood out for their tactical or strategic skills. In fact, it was the dismal performance of the Red Army in Finland that convinced Herr Adolf Hitler that the Soviet Union was beatable. But as the winter of 1941 wore on, truly "badass" Soviet commanders came to the fore—Georgy Zhukov, Vasily Chuikov, Konstantin Rokossovsky, and Ivan Koniev. General Chuikov, as commander of the Sixty-Fourth Army, distinguished himself in the Battle of Stalingrad (August 1942 to February 1943). His forces destroyed the Sixth Army of the Wehrmacht and took its commander, Field-Marshal Friedrich Wilhelm Paulus, prisoner in what was considered to be the tide-turning confrontation of the war in the East. In due course, he would accept the surrender of the Berlin City Garrison from Gen. Helmut Weidling on May 02, 1945.

So, for small Biafra, a long drawn-out conflict with big Nigeria was not in its best interest. Also, the involvement on its side of a big stick-wielding sponsor was critical for a favorable outcome. As will be seen, a quick knockout punch was thrown in August 1967, but it did not quite connect. On February 24, 1966, Ghana's Dr. Kwame Nkrumah was overthrown in a United States CIA-backed coup d'état, and the Soviet Union lost its toehold in West Africa. Moscow was therefore on the lookout for new opportunities at the time and did approach Biafra within less than a month after the new nation declared its sovereignty. According to the commentator Waidi Adebayo, citing a cable from the US ambassador to East Germany Dr. Martin Hillenbrand, dated August 08, 1967, Biafran Special Envoy M. C. K. Ajuluchukwu met with the Soviet ambassador to Nigeria Mr. Alexandr Romanov in Moscow. Mr. Romanov set the condition for the recognition of Biafra and military support as the nationalization of western oil companies. The proposition was conveyed to General Ojukwu, who was reported to have responded that Biafra did not have the funds to pay compensation, and so no deal was made. A few weeks later, Nigeria's Information and Labor commissioner Chief Anthony Enahoro traveled to Moscow and signed a "cultural" agreement at the Kremlin.

The Biafran military and its commander in chief

With the influx of soldiers from all parts of the country, the military situation in Enugu was very fraught, with an uncertain command structure. Many of the returnees were senior to the commanding officer of the "native" formation, the First Battalion, Lt. Col. David Ogunewe. Lt. Col. Hilary Njoku for instance had been commander of 2 Brigade, which comprised all the units in the south (including the First Battalion) before the Army went berserk. On October 12, 1966, senior military officers from different parts of the country convened at Benin City to take stock. They were Lt. Cols. Eyo O. Ekpo (military secretary, Supreme Headquarters), Sylvanus B. Nwajei, and Michael C. O. Ivenso (East); Olufemi Olutoye (West); Joseph Akahan (now chief of staff, Army Headquarters); Murtala Ramat Muhammed (leader of the July coup); and Maj. Alani Akinrinade (conference secretary). They resolved to recommend to the Supreme Military Council that the Army be reorganized into regional commands, with each command comprised of only indigenes of the region.

On October 16, Lieutenant Colonel Njoku, who was still nursing a thigh wound, called a meeting of the senior Army officers of Eastern origin. Among those present were Lt. Cols. Ogere Imo, Philip Efiong, Alexander Madiebo, Anthony Eze, Michael Ivenso, and David Ogunewe. There were about three thousand troops present in the region, and Lieutenant Colonel Njoku felt that a command leadership framework needed to be established without delay for the maintenance of proper discipline and morale. However, there was, as is often the case in the military, the delicate issue of hierarchy that had to be negotiated. Although he was the most senior by appointment, Lieutenant Colonels Imo and Efiong were commissioned before him. A vote was taken, and he was elected leader. The next day, he met with the entire officer corps, both commissioned and noncommissioned, to acquaint them with the challenges ahead and elicit their concerns. He then met with the military governor on October 21, 1966, accompanied by Lieutenant Colonels Imo and Efiong, to let him know about the conferences they had held and the problems confronting the Nigerian Army in the East. The meeting progressed amicably until the matter of communications with Lagos arose. The military governor demanded with emphasis that all correspondence with Lagos be routed through his office. The military officers protested because under the Aguiyi-Ironsi administration, the position of governor was a mere military posting and service officers were not under his jurisdiction. This did not change until regional commands were established the following year. The senior military officers who met in Benin City earlier that month agreed to recommend the formation of regional commands, but the

Supreme Military Council did not take up their recommendations until their Aburi Meeting in January 1967. Instead, on November 03, 1966, Supreme Headquarters Lagos published the redeployment of senior officers that reflected the existing structure, with Lt. Col. Olufemi Olutoye now posted to 2 Brigade as acting commander, among others.

Lieutenant Colonel Njoku sent a letter to the military governor on November 11, 1966, suggesting that the East proceed anyway with the formation of an Eastern Command of the Nigerian Army at brigade level organization. He apparently did not receive a reply. He then made two unsuccessful attempts to contact Lieutenant Colonel Gowon by phone, one from Owerri and the other from Enugu. The military governor got wind of this and was none too pleased. He summoned Lieutenant Colonel Njoku and reminded him of the order he had given that all contact with Lagos be routed through his office. As documented by Lieutenant Colonel Njoku, he, in turn, reminded the military governor that troops in the East were still part and parcel of the Nigerian Army and that he, Lieutenant Colonel Njoku, was still the commander of 2 Brigade, Nigerian Army. Technically of course, that was not correct. As of November 03, 1966, Supreme Headquarters had replaced him with an acting commander.

Undeterred by his altercation with the military governor, Lieutenant Colonel Njoku conveyed his proposal for an Eastern command to Supreme Headquarters, Lagos, in a letter dated December 13, 1966. He set out the structure (three battalions— First, Seventh and Eighth) and recommended unit commanders (Lt. Cols. David Ogunewe, Alexander Madiebo, and Ogbugo Kalu respectively). On December 29, 1966, the military governor finally replied to his letter of November 11, directing the immediate establishment of an Eastern command with Lieutenant Colonel Njoku as acting commander. Then at Aburi, Ghana, in January 1967, the Supreme Military Council gave its formal approval to the restructuring of the Nigerian military, with the military governors in control of the area commands over matters of internal security. In a letter dated January 18, 1967, Lieutenant Colonel Odumegwu-Ojukwu informed Lt. Col. Yakubu Gowon that the Eastern Command had been established.

Lieutenant Colonel Njoku and the senior leadership of the Eastern Command took issue with the conflation of the military with the political and, specifically, the subjugation of the former to the latter in the requirement that the line of all upward communication pass through the military governor's office. The least they hoped for was for the military and the political to be kept apart, especially in the case of the East where, like in the North, the military governor was not the most senior military officer. The model of military rule in their heads seemed to be that of Egypt and Pakistan, where the most senior military officer became the chief executive officer (Maj. Gen. Muhamed Naguib after the overthrow of Egyptian King Farouk on July 23, 1952, and Field Marshal Muhammad Ayub Khan, who replaced the president of Pakistan Iskandar Mirza in October 27, 1958).

Junior officers were equally ill at ease. Their representatives, led by Maj. Patrick Nzeogwu, met with the military governor on April 27, 1967, to convey their anxieties about the lack of weapons and uncertainty that the region was ready to fight a war with Nigeria, among other dissatisfactions. The governor dryly reassured them that weapons were "in the pipeline"—an expression that they were to hear again and again in the coming months.

Politically, the military governor and his top military officer were also at odds, and their differences surfaced early. In early February 1967, a strategic committee was formed, and it held its inaugural meeting on the eighteenth of that month. According to Lieutenant Colonel Njoku, the military governor left no one in any doubt that secession from Nigeria was his preferred solution to the crisis. After the meeting, Lieutenant Colonel Njoku decided to sound out some of the members of the committee as well as Army officers and civil servants. The opinions expressed appeared to run the gamut, from "favorable to secession" through "not too keen" to "if you military boys can defend it." He then arranged for a number of "high-caliber" men and women to meet and brainstorm. They were all of the mind that secession was a bad idea, and he conveyed their thoughts to the military governor. Predictably, they were not well received, and so he set them down in the form of a memorandum to be tabled for discussion at the next Strategic Committee meeting.

Lieutenant Colonel Njoku's memorandum made interesting, if curious, reading. In it, he identified the Nigerian problem as Northern "feudalism" whose intriguing tendency was to alternate between domination and separation, as circumstances demanded. He cited the late Alhaji Tafawa Balewa's promise that the Northern people would resume their march to the coast as soon as the British got out of the way. The important point was made that not even the North was monolithic. There was a "nonfeudal" North with aspirations to freedom, democracy, and progressive thought—all of which the East championed. The Alkali courts tormented them, and there had also been the Tiv uprisings of 1960 and 1964, which were brutally put down by the Nigerian military. In fact, the January 1966 coup plotters stated that the brutality of Brig. Gen. Zakaria Maimalari's orders during the Tiv counterinsurgency campaigns was a key reason they penciled him down for elimination. Lieutenant Colonel Njoku then made the case that since the East had always borne the brunt of past sacrifices made for Nigeria's progress, it should do so once again. He stated with emphasis that the East had not "abandoned our duty to our fatherland" and could not "for sheer convenience's sake turn our backs to the rest of Nigeria." In his assessment, "Providence has placed the East in a position to complete the onerous task it has started in shriveling feudal domination. The East cannot abdicate. It must take an effective lead in this matter." He quoted the senator addressing Roman tribunes in Shakespeare's *Coriolanus* thus: "(Peace) is the humane way; the other course will prove bloody." He was no shrinking violet though, stating elsewhere that "in order to bring the yapping feudalists to heel, we have to fight, as long as they want it that way." He affirmed that "the East must remain part of Nigeria" and "avoid being called secessionists, a dirty name in international relations."

Heady stuff! According to Lieutenant Colonel Njoku, the document was reluctantly accepted for presentation at the March meeting of the Strategic Committee. To his surprise, support for it was unanimous. The military governor however overruled the committee but allowed that the material was good grist for propaganda and set up a team to consider its use for that purpose: Professor Anthony Modebe (formerly chair, Department of Agriculture, University of Ibadan), Mr. Cyprian Ekwensi (formerly head of features, Nigeria Broadcasting Corporation; novelist and recipient of the 1968 Dag Hammarskjold Literature Prize), and Lt. Col. Patrick Anwunah (commanding officer, Ninth Battalion, Eastern Command).

The tense and uneasy relationship between the military commander and his governor continued to fester. After a command is set up, the next logical step would be to put the various units through their paces, to see how well they mesh operationally. It usually takes the form of war games or a similar military exercise, and the Eastern Command planned one in three phases (Checkmate I–III) involving the Army, Air Force (commander: Lt. Col. George Kurubo), and the police (commissioner: Patrick I. Okeke). Authorization was obtained from the military governor and Checkmate I (Northern sector) flagged off at 7:00 a.m. on May 06, 1967. At about midday, a helicopter flew into Exercise Headquarters, Abakaliki, with orders from the military governor for the exercise to be called off and the Army commander and commissioner of police to join him at a meeting in State House, Enugu. The Army commander, irate and astounded, refused to call off the exercise out of concern that such an order would have an adverse effect on troop morale. He and the commissioner, however, returned to Enugu by car and, at State House, were ushered into a meeting with a delegation from Lagos led by Chief Obafemi Awolowo. Yet another prioritization of the political over the military, thought Lieutenant Colonel Njoku, and for him, that was the last straw. He promptly resigned his command. As a matter of fact, a couple of days prior, he and a group of senior officers had met with the governor on the subject of the spreading discontent among junior officers and the persistent state of military unreadiness. The governor had become defensive, accusing some of the officers of plotting to overthrow his government. The accused officers just retired from service for their own safety and peace of mind. The Army commander was not one of them, but now, he did not think he could carry on. Lt. Col. Alexander Madiebo however remembered the disagreement between the military governor and the Army commander differently. According to him, the Army commander had wanted a seat on the executive council and, egged on by other senior military officers, framed his demand in terms of his seniority, almost evoking memories of the quarrel between the military governor and Lieutenant Colonel Gowon which, needless to say, would be very unwelcome to the former.

Whatever the reason, the resignation of the army commander would obviously be very bad publicity, from the military governor's perspective. Although getting rid of a commander whose personal loyalty he could not count on would serve his purposes, he would naturally prefer for the choice of when and how to be his. Accordingly, he orchestrated pressure on Lieutenant Colonel Njoku to rescind his resignation from multiple quarters—the adviser to the government Sir Francis Akanu Ibiam; the respected educationist and chairman of the Consultative Assembly Dr. Alvan Ikoku, who was a classmate of Sir Ibiam at Hope Waddell Training Institute, Calabar; elders from Lieutenant Colonel Njoku's hometown of Ikeduru, Owerri; and the Catholic bishop of Port Harcourt Diocese, the Rt. Rev. Godfrey Okoye. Ominously, the guards at Lieutenant Colonel Njoku's residence were withdrawn, whereupon close friends decided to spirit him away to Umuahia on May 08, 1967, for his personal safety. He spent the night at the home of one of my mother's cousins, who was a schoolmaster at Government College.

When Lieutenant Colonel Njoku returned to Enugu, an even larger and more distinguished delegation—dignitaries of Old Owerri Province origin—was waiting for him. This was a tactic the military governor had deployed when Lt. Col. Alexander Madiebo needlessly challenged him over senior appointments at the University of Nigeria Teaching Hospital. He had summoned prominent Awka (Lt. Col. Alexander Madiebo's hometown) citizens to Enugu and told them that one of his "greatest problems" was "your son, Colonel Madiebo" and that he "would not want to hurt him by reacting to his affronts." Now as then, it worked. The Army commander relented and asked to meet with the military governor, accompanied by Sir Francis Ibiam

TOWARD UNDERSTANDING THE NIGERIA-BIAFRA WAR AND LINGERING QUESTIONS

and the chief judge Sir Louis Mbanefo. At the meeting, he assured the military governor that he never had any intention of overthrowing his government, responding to stories purportedly disseminated by supporters of the governor. In betrayal of the contempt he had for the governor, he added darkly that if he wanted to oust him, he could do so without difficulty and dared him to say he couldn't. The governor decided it was time the lieutenant colonel left the region to afford him space to reorganize the command. He offered to arrange for him to proceed on "medical leave" to Switzerland. After all, his left thigh had been badly shot up on July 29 the previous year. Lieutenant Colonel Njoku opted to travel to Dublin, departing on May 15, 1967.

At that point in time, the military governor must have been feeling that he had had enough of the ungrateful senior officers. After all, if not for his obdurate advocacy in demanding that their flight to the East be regularized, they would all be absent without official leave (AWOL) and technically required to return and answer for abandoning their commands. Unfortunately, the step he took to neutralize them was most ill-advised and pernicious—he flew to the patronage of junior officers. The military governor met with junior officers at the University of Nigeria, Nsukka, and shared the stories of his torment at the hands of their seniors. According to Mr. Bernard Odogwu, a close confidante of the military governor, the junior officers closed ranks solidly behind him, pledging not only to support him unreservedly but would deal severely with any officers, senior or junior, who dared to challenge him. This might have created a climate auspicious to the military governor personally but toxic to proper discipline across the institution.

On June 08, 1967, Lieutenant Colonel Njoku left Dublin and headed back to Enugu via the Cameroons. He hadn't been officially summoned to return, and so his status was unclear, especially since the Eastern Command of the Nigerian Army had transformed into the Biafran Army nine days prior. Nevertheless, he reported for duty on June 19, 1967, and Lieutenant Colonel Odumegwu-Ojukwu, now head of state and commander in chief, did not seem to mind. They both met two days later and agreed to a reorganization of the Army along the lines of the Checkmate Exercises, namely Northern Zone (Fifty-First Brigade), Southern Zone (Fifty-Second Brigade), and Central Zone (Enugu Garrison Organization, Eleventh Battalion).

Lieutenant Colonel Njoku convened a unit commanders conference on June 28, 1967, at which they took briefings from the chief of staff, Defense Headquarters, and the principal staff officer "G" duties on the military and political situations. A brigade of Nigerian troops had deployed south of the River Benue. An infantry battalion and its supporting units, including artillery, were in the area just north of Nsukka. Another battalion and its supporting units were concentrated in the Adikpo area, facing Obudu-Ogoja. They had begun launching probing attacks, and a clash had occurred on June 10, 1967, during which a Biafran heavy machine gun position was overrun.

At 5:00 a.m., on July 06, 1967, the Nigerian Army, led by Col. Muhammed Shuwa, attacked the Northern frontier of Biafra in force along a broad front that extended from Ogoja (Maj. Sule Apollo) to Nsukka (Maj. Martin Adamu). The head of state summoned his Army commander to State House. On arrival, a lachrymose commander in chief, glass of brandy in hand, briefed him on the situation. The Army commander asked him if there were caches of arms and ammunition that would now be released and if the support of the West and Mid-West could be counted upon. The answers were "No" and "Don't know" respectively but that Lt. Col. Victor Banjo was working on the latter.

The Biafran Armed Forces were totally outmanned and outgunned. The Nigerian Army had a 4:1 advantage in men and a surfeit of artillery pieces and armored cars. According to the chief of logistics at the time, Lieutenant Colonel Efiong, the Fifty-First Brigade of the Biafran Army had only one cannon—a 105-mm howitzer with an allocation of a grand total of two rounds. The armored vehicles ("Red Devils") were track-mounted, rather poorly maneuverable personnel carriers of World War I vintage that had been refurbished by Biafran engineers and technicians. They did not see action until September 1967. The Biafran Air Force and Navy were similarly underresourced, as will be discussed later. However, the Air Force proved to be very perky at the outset, undertaking both close tactical ground support missions at the forward lines and long-distance strategic bombing raids. The legendary MFI-9Bs did not enter service until the last year of the war.

Typically, the federal forces would open their attack with a barrage of artillery fire and then roll in with their Ferret and Saladin armored cars. Nevertheless, they were a frightened, feckless lot, in the assessment of the Biafran Army commander. When they came under sustained but technically harmless small-arms fire, they would abandon their armored cars and skedaddle. They knew though to take the keys with them as they fled. Fortunately for them, the energy grenades that Biafra had purchased were delivered without adaptors and so were practically useless. It would be months before the Research and Production Directorate built and deployed Biafra's devastating mine system (*Ogbunigwe*). The Nigerian soldiers were also ruthless. They did not take prisoners and consistently scorched any territory they captured. The Biafran Army commander commented also that the Nigerian Army was very diurnal and never for once fought at night during the first three months of the conflict.

Large numbers of civilian volunteers poured into Enugu as the hostilities began. They were mainly from Abam, Abriba, and Ohafia—parts of the country with a reputation for martial traditions. Armed with double-barrel shotguns, machetes, and similar oddities, they were allowed by Defense Headquarters to head out to the forward lines on the Nsukka front to the alarm of the regular forces. When Nigerian machine guns and mortars opened up at them, they took heavy casualties and were routed. The sight of fleeing, bloodied, and frightened humanity had a very demoralizing effect on the troops, many of whom were still coming to terms with their own baptism of fire, with the incessant pounding of Nigerian artillery to which they had no reply.

The Nigerian Army launched a massive assault on July 9–10, 1967, which pulverized Biafran defenses. According to the Army commander, had the enemy exploited their initial success, they would have taken Enugu. The commander in chief and his chief of staff, Army Headquarters (and chief of logistics), Lieutenant Colonel

Efiong went forward and met up with the retreating troops at Ukehe. They tried to rally them to no avail. The troops seemed to have lost all will to resist. Upon their return to Enugu, the commander in chief summoned the army commander and, with tears in his eyes, told him "all is lost." The army commander consoled him and took off to the front to see for himself. He met up with the brigade commander Lt. Col. Anthony Eze and had the troops form up. By this time apparently, their nerves had settled somewhat since Nigerians were not in the habit of pressing their advantage. He gave them a pep talk and ordered them back to their trenches.

It was not all doom and gloom in those early days. There were flashes of brilliance at the level of the fighting man when the command screwups were not interfering. In this regard, Maj. Patrick Nzeogwu and his exploits were noteworthy. There was no love lost between him and the commander in chief who had been a thorn in his side during the coup effort in January 1966. In an interview he gave to Mr. Dennis Ejindu, a journalist who wrote for *Africa and the World*, in May 1967, he had made clear his opposition to secession. After Lieutenant Colonel Njoku left for Ireland, he attempted a reprise of Exercise Checkmate, and the commander in chief banned him from all regular military roles. According to the head of Biafran Military Intelligence Lt. Col. Bernard Odogwu, the commander in chief apparently chose to ignore Maj. Patrick Nzeogwu's utterances initially but soon came under pressure that disciplinary action was called for. He therefore sent the major off on indefinite leave with the option of reporting back for duty after coming to terms with the "true position of things." Major Nzeogwu did apologize for the furor his unguarded statements might have caused but refused to deny or withdraw them because, according to him, they were indeed his views on the matter. So, unlike the other participants in the January 15, 1966, coup, he was never assigned a command. That notwithstanding, he somehow managed to remain actively engaged in the struggle. He would assemble groups of militiamen and policemen and lead them on daring guerrilla raids behind enemy lines on the Nsukka front. So impressed with his exploits was the Army commander that he promoted him to the rank of local lieutenant colonel. After all, his coup companion, Maj. Timothy Onwuatuegwu, was now lieutenant colonel and had command of the Seventh Battalion. The commander in chief would have none of it. He charged the Army commander with "wrong application" of his powers and arraigned him before the Defense Committee on July 24, 1967. The chief justice Sir Louis Mbanefo and Sir Francis Ibiam intervened, and the commander in chief shelved his plan to fire the Army commander.

A few days later, Biafran Forces launched a spirited offensive, and by one account, citing information Col. Joseph Akahan, chief of staff, Nigerian Army, shared with a British Military advisor, they sent federal forces reeling despite their handicap in matériel. Then, all of a sudden, they broke away from the engagement and fell back after they purportedly received a strange order to do so. To this day, the provenance of that order has remained a mystery. It, however, gave federal forces time to regroup and reoccupy the territory they had lost, unbeknownst to fresh Biafran units riding up to join the fight. The terrain became very dangerously confused especially for small units on flanking or behind-the-lines operations. Lt. Col. Chukwuma Nzeogwu and two police officers were caught in an ambush on the Nsukka-Opi road near Queen of the Rosary Secondary School. Information was received at Army Headquarters on July 29, 1967, that the lieutenant colonel was missing. Intercepted Nigerian signals indicated that he had actually been killed and that federal forces had recovered his body. For reasons best known to them, they gouged his eyeballs from their sockets before transporting his remains to Kaduna for burial. The two police officers who had gone on the raid with him managed to escape and reported back to Fifty-First Brigade Headquarters at 7:00 a.m. on July 30, 1967.

In those early days, the going was more favorable on the Gakem-Obudu front. The fighting seemed better coordinated, and when federal troops tried to take a strategic bridge between Obudu and Ogoja on July 07, 1967, they were beaten back with heavy losses. According to an official of the Irish Embassy (Eamon O'tuathail), who visited the Catholic Mission Hospital, Obudu, the next day, the body count was a hundred Nigerian soldiers dead for four Biafran killed and nine wounded. Mr. Tunji Akingbade of the *Daily Times* was almost apocalyptic in his assessment. He wrote that the First Battalion of the Nigerian Army was "almost completely wiped out." Soon though, the tables turned too at that front as the ranks of Biafran Forces were depleted, reportedly largely through desertion by non-Igbo elements who scurried across the border into the Cameroons.

Back on the Nsukka front, the campus of the University of Biafra fell into federal hands on August 09, 1967. Their artillery soon began to pound the strategic road junction, Opi, and after three days of relentless shelling, it was taken on September 08, 1967. A couple of days later, the Biafran Army mounted a vigorous counterattack, with a spearhead of "Red Devils"—tricked-up armored personnel carriers of World War I vintage. Progress was made until the federal side brought their 106-mm recoilless antitank rifles to bear. The ungainly "Red Devils" did not stand a chance. Memorably, one round hit the carrier commanded by Capt. Kevin Megwa (Emekukwu, Owerri) and set it ablaze. The entire crew was killed instantly. It was also in that battle that Christopher Ifekandu Okigbo, perhaps the "most lyrical African poet of the twentieth century," perished. The counterattack failed, and the Nigerian Army consolidated its hold on Opi. A very serious threat to Enugu, the Biafran capital about thirty-two miles to the south, loomed.

After the loss of Opi, the C in C relieved Lt. Col. Anthony Eze of his command of the Fifty-First Brigade and replaced him with Lt. Col. Christian Ude, without input from his Army commander. He actually proceeded to reorganize the Army so as to accommodate his friend Lt. Col. Victor Banjo, who was commander of the Biafran Militia. During the scare of July 10, 1967, the C in C confided in his chief of logistics, General Efiong, that he was seriously contemplating throwing in the towel because he had no officers and no armaments. The chief of staff suggested that he press Lt. Col. Victor Banjo into field service. Lieutenant Colonel Banjo was assigned the rank of brigadier general and given command of the newly created 101st Division comprising the two brigades in the northern sector—Fifty-First (Lt. Col. Anthony Eze) and Fifty-Third (Lt. Col. Alexander Madiebo). Also under his command was the Fifty-Fourth "Independent" Brigade, which was charged with the defense of Biafra's western border from Oguta to Idah. Rather strangely, as commander of the 101st Division, General Banjo reported to the Army commander, General Njoku, but as commander of the Fifty-Fourth Brigade, he dealt directly with the C in C. General Banjo even wanted to keep the reins of the Militia, with the C in C's assent, but the chief of logistics put his foot down.

It is obvious from the above that General Odumegwu-Ojukwu had a very dysfunctional relationship with his military. On a general and nonspecific level, all the senior military officers who rose through the ranks resented the graduates in the combat units who, as events bore out, had enlisted with political premeditations. At the top echelon, only Generals Odumegwu-Ojukwu and Banjo were university graduates. The rest—General Njoku and his ilk—had a clear preference for an arrangement whereby the political head of a region was the most senior military officer from that region. He, General Njoku, was the one recommended for the post of governor of the East in January 1966, and just before the July 1966 coup, General Ogundipe had hinted to him that he was slated to replace Lieutenant Colonel Odumegwu-Ojukwu in an impending reshuffle. Lieutenant Colonel Odumegwu-Ojukwu must have known some, if not all, of this.

Many of the senior officers who returned to the East were senior in rank to the military governor. There were also the plotters of the January 1966 coup who he had to release from detention under popular pressure. He had opposed that coup as commanding officer of the Fifth Battalion, Kano, although his critics allege that at least for a time, he ran with the hare and hunted with the hounds. Nevertheless, he must have felt somewhat insecure with its architects at large. He profoundly distrusted the career officers of the Nigerian Army and never really took them into confidence. Although these soldiers did not mind fighting if it came to that, almost unanimously, they were opposed to secession, some more vocally than others. Since the military governor himself was totally invested in the secession project, on his chosen timetable, it was impossible to visualize a reconciliation of such divergent viewpoints. When armed conflict became almost inevitable and battle simulation exercises were planned, he apparently felt threatened by the troop movements involved and stepped in to cancel them, even though his authorization had been sought and obtained at the outset.

Lieutenant Colonel Odumegwu-Ojukwu was the darling of the "masses" who had been viciously brutalized by the Northerners. He was also idolized by the young elite—university undergraduates and graduates—but did not appear to be particularly popular with the career military. As has been mentioned, he sought to play the junior officers against their seniors so as to keep the latter in check. It has been speculated that one reason the Biafran Militia was established was for him to have a more reliable parallel force at his disposal. The militia officers were drawn largely from the civil service and institutions of higher learning, and the first batch graduated from training in September 1967.

In particular, the relationship between Generals Odumegwu-Ojukwu and Njoku was an incongruous love-hate affair. General Njoku had military gravitas and those who knew (not surprisingly, the foreign intelligence agencies) described him in superlative terms. After meeting with General Odumegwu-Ojukwu in April 1967, a visiting top Soviet diplomat made a point of meeting with General Njoku as well. On July 06, 1967, when the first shots were fired, it was to him that the American Consul in Enugu went to get a sense of what was going on. He did, though, direct the diplomat to the head of state. General Odumegwu-Ojukwu seemed to appreciate General Njoku's military potentials and must have been frustrated by his inability to unleash and harness them. Their differences were too fundamental, yet he kept him on as Army commander for as long as he did. He probably was very wary of the reaction of the other senior military officers who held General Njoku in such high esteem.

The military governor sent Lieutenant Colonel Njoku away to Ireland on medical leave, stating he would use the opportunity of his absence to reorganize the Eastern Command but apparently never did. When the lieutenant colonel returned of his own accord and reported for duty, the military governor, now head of state, did not appear perturbed. At the outbreak of hostilities, Lieutenant Colonel Njoku was the one he called, and at a very low point a few days later, it was to the lieutenant colonel that he turned. Yet he appeared to obtrude into command situations in ways that had the effect of undermining the authority of Lieutenant Colonel Njoku and Army Headquarters. He would issue collateral orders and selectively exclude military formations from the formal chain of command. In a letter to the Army commander dated August 24, 1967, he wrote: "I wish to make it quite clear that it is not my intention to interfere with lesser commands, yet it must be realized that in this war, the ultimate responsibility to the nation is mine."

At a personal level, the courage of the C in C was never in doubt. He was fearless and had no hesitation whatsoever in visiting the forward lines. He had taught tactics at the Regular Officers Special Training School, Teshie, Ghana, in the late 1950s. Yet his philosophy of war is difficult to fathom, especially given how very poorly prepared Biafra was materially at the commencement of hostilities. Between January and July 1967, many thought he was actually building up an arsenal but needed to be secretive about it because of the Aburi Accords. It turned out that weapons acquisition was paltry in the mistaken belief that there would be no war, but if there was one, it would be short-lived. The apparent underlying premise was that Nigeria really had no appetite for a fight. Hence, it could either be beaten or quickly wrestled to a stalemate whereupon she would be compelled to negotiate a settlement. Neither happened. In the same letter of August 24, 1967, to his Army commander, he wrote thus:

> I do, of course, appreciate your difficulties but it must be realized that no war is ever fought in perfect conditions where troops have everything they could wish for. The hallmark of a good officer is his flexibility and a faculty for improvisation which will enable him to overcome technical difficulties.

I read with utter alarm in General Efiong's memoir that the preferred battle tactic of the C in C (whom he curiously kept referring to as "the Governor") was the human wave assault, presumably inspired by his "Chinese experience." In practice, masses of civilians would be assembled and hurled howling at the enemy, who, beholding the cacophonous horde coming at them, would panic and take flight. I am inclined to dismiss this construal as farcical. It did happen once at the Nsukka front at the beginning of the war, and that was an isolated event. It would certainly be egregiously criminal to order civilians to charge an armed enemy.

General Njoku, for his part, did give General Odumegwu-Ojukwu reasons to be genuinely concerned. Until the recognition of area commands by the Supreme Military Council in January 1967, General Njoku could justifiably claim that he answered to Army and Defense Headquarters, Lagos. However, the Area Command structure placed the military commander under the authority of the Military governor. Military discipline required that he obey the governor's orders or relinquish his command, which he did in early May 1967. He was effectively exiled to Ireland but, for unstated reasons, returned of his own accord to what had become Biafra about nine days prior and resumed his command after a five-week hiatus. He had made his opposition to secession clear in his memorandum to the Strategic Committee in March 1967. There is no evidence that he ever changed his views on the subject. It is therefore somewhat confusing and hard to believe that he simply saluted smartly and got on with the business of fighting off Nigerian forces who were seeking to end secession. The fact of the matter was that he and his friends ("the Socialists," as he dubbed them) had other plans as will be discussed in the story of the Mid-West campaign. According to General Njoku, among "the Socialists" were Maj. Patrick Nzeogwu, Maj. Timothy Onwuatuegwu, Dr. Winifred Kaine Egonu (one of Nigeria's first pediatricians), Mr. Jacob Nwokolo, Mr. Christopher Okigbo, "and many others."

Since the C in C and his Army commander held irreconcilable viewpoints on the very essence of the enterprise, namely to secede or not to secede, any discussion of mechanisms for reaching accommodations is rather pointless. It is worth adducing though that historically, the equilibrium in the relationship between commanders-in-chief and their military commanders is almost invariably an

TOWARD UNDERSTANDING THE NIGERIA-BIAFRA WAR AND LINGERING QUESTIONS

unstable one. These personages are usually strong and even quirky characters—how does one ever get that far without being one? As such, the chemistry between them tends to be always fraught but sometimes strangely interesting and even entertaining. In every instance though, it is the military commander who concedes if the C in C is not persuaded. Franklin Delano Roosevelt, POTUS XXXII, never really liked Gen. Douglas MacArthur, and people around the president suspected that but for political pressure, he would have let the Japanese Imperial Army capture him in Corregidor. For his part, the general described his C in C as "a man who would never tell the truth if a lie would suffice." Still, the C in C's orders reaching him through the chief of staff Gen. George Catlett Marshall were dutifully carried out. Soviet general Georgy Zhukov had a temper every bit as volcanic as that of his C in C, Joseph Stalin, but clever man, he picked his battles with him carefully, knowing when to call it quits (Stalin does not relight his pipe after it goes out) and when to press his case (pipe is relit as soon as it goes out). Gen. Bernard Montgomery was the ascetic type who ate little and neither drank nor smoked, for which reasons he described himself as "100 percent fit." When Prime Minister Winston Leonard Churchill visited his headquarters at Tripoli shortly after the victory at El Alamein, he was served a rather austere meal. A gourmand, the prime minister was none too pleased and was heard to say, "I drink and I smoke and I am 200 percent fit." In every case, there was no daylight between the C in C and his Army commander regarding the core issue of concern—the defeat of the Axis Powers.

The Nigerian Army continued its push toward Enugu from the north, and by mid-September, the situation became very dire. In the evening of September 18, 1967, the C in C ordered General Njoku arrested. The next day, he formally relieved him of his command of the Biafran Army for failure to carry out his proposals about the conduct of the war and definite instructions on operational objectives. The letter in part read: "You will accordingly proceed with immediate effect, on an indefinite but restricted leave until the end of the war." His firing was greeted by protest from some members of the council, notably Cdr. Enugu Garrison Organization; Col. David

Ogunewe; Sir Francis Ibiam, adviser to the government; and Sir Louis Mbanefo, chief justice. As will be seen, it had more to do with allegations of the general's implication in a coup plot that turned out to be false. He was released to the custody of Sir Ibiam. On September 26, 1967, the mobile police collected and transferred him to the government guest house at Ikot-Ekpene. Lt. Col. Alexander Madiebo, Commander, Fifty-Third Brigade, was promoted brigadier general and appointed general officer commanding, Biafran Army.

Naval operations

At about 8:00 p.m. on April 22, 1967, there was a blackout at the naval shipyard, Apapa, due to power outage of uncertain etiology. It was about two and half hours before power was restored, and in that time, persons of equally uncertain identities effectively incapacitated the Nigerian Navy by damaging sensitive components of gun systems, navigation and communications equipment, and engine parts in nearly all the vessels, including its flagship NNS *Nigeria*, a Dutch-built frigate commissioned only two years prior. Two days later, about thirty ratings of Eastern origin did not report for muster.

The NNS *Ibadan*, a Ford-class seaward defense boat purchased from the Royal Navy in 1957, was on smuggling interdiction duties in eastern waters in May 1967. A few days after the proclamation of Biafra, her skipper, Lt. Paschal Odu, received an order from naval headquarters to return to his Apapa base. When he replied that many of his crew felt unsafe about returning to Lagos, he was instructed to poll them individually. All the officers and ratings of Eastern origin, with the exception of his first officer, 1st Lt. Promise Fingesi, who was an Okirika native, opted to remain in Biafra. The rest were given safe passage back to Nigeria. As for the vessel, it stayed in Biafra as, according to Lieutenant Commander Odu, "a small share of the national assets" and was rechristened BNS *Ibadan*.

Besides the BNS *Ibadan*, the other assets of the Biafran Navy were assorted watercraft like barges, cutters, and tugboats requisitioned from the ports authority and oil companies. They were repurposed by Biafran engineers and technicians who fitted them with 105-mm howitzers, quick-firing six-pounder antitank guns, or automatic antiaircraft cannons (Bofors). The barges became floating artillery platforms, while the cutters and tugboats were designated "Coastal Patrol Craft" (CPC). The Biafran Navy was commanded by Capt. Wilfred Anuku. He had his headquarters at Kidney Island, Port Harcourt.

Nigeria's foreign backers fully appreciated the critical importance of an effective littoral blockade of Biafra to the success of the federal war effort. An operational maritime force was indispensable in that context, and so very quickly, they repaired or replaced all that was broken on April 22, 1967. This was accomplished with such speed and stealth that the Biafran High Command was taken by surprise when the NNS *Nigeria*, commanded by Capt. Nelson Soroh, who had made a transition from the Inland Waterway Department to the Navy, and the NNS *Ogoja*, a United States World War II vintage corvette thrown in as "sweetener" for the acquisition of the NNS *Nigeria*, began to bombard the island of Bonny at the Bonny River estuary on July 25, 1967. The landing craft NNS *Lokoja* cleverly steamed into the estuary and successfully put ashore troops of 3 Division (Marine commando) on the thinly defended northern part of the island. In the morning of July 26, the BNS *Ibadan*, with the selfsame Lt. Cdr. Paschal Odu on the bridge, was on routine patrol when it sighted the three-ship invasion armada. The NNS *Ogoja*, under the command of Lt. Cdr. Akintunde Aduwo, had also seen the BNS *Ibadan* and opened fire with its three-inch gun as soon as it came within range. What ensued was probably the first ship-versus-ship naval battle of the war. The BNS *Ibadan* returned fire with its 40/60mm Bofors antiaircraft cannon. Unfortunately, the piece had seen better days and had become highly prone to jamming. When it did, the skipper would turn tail and steam out of range for his gunners to free the firing mechanism. He would then steer around again and reengage. The risk involved in such a turning maneuver in a waterway that had a relatively narrow channel of navigable depth was obvious. Soon enough, the BNS *Ibadan* ran aground and became a sitting duck. The NNS *Ogoja* scored a direct hit astern, jamming the propeller and setting the engine room on fire. The officers and ratings of the BNS *Ibadan* abandoned ship and swam ashore with the loss of only one sailor. After two days in the marshes, they came to a fishing village where they negotiated with a canoe man to row them through the creeks back to Port Harcourt.

The federal forces proceeded to consolidate their hold on Bonny Island but were relentlessly harried by all the armed services of Biafra. Lt. Cdr. Paschal Odu who, to all intents and purposes, was the chief of naval operations, quickly rejoined his colleagues and returned to the fray. On August 13, 1967, he had the Biafran Air Force (BAF) destroy the foundered BNS *Ibadan* beyond salvage.

A joint Biafran Army and Navy operation to retake Bonny Island, codenamed "Sea Jack," was launched on September 25, 1967. By ill luck, the landing was made at ebb tide, and the troops lost the element of surprise as they struggled through the mud to get to dry land. However, by October 12, 1967, they had advanced beyond the beaches and were engaging the enemy on Bonny mainland. Although Sea Jack was ultimately unsuccessful, in that federal forces were never completely dislodged, the island was never entirely in their hands until January 1968.

Beginning on October 07, 1967, remote-controlled mines designed and built by the Research and Production Directorate, were laid by the Biafran Navy in the main channel of the Bonny River. Mine watch positions were set up on observation floats, buoys, and on shore. The Biafran Navy also experimented with home-built contact mines. So effective were the defenses that Port Harcourt was never threatened by an enemy approach up the Bonny River.

The Biafran Navy patrolled the creek reticulum on either side of the Bonny River in armed speedboats. When infiltrating parties of the enemy were encountered in fishing villages, they would be attacked, sometimes with support from barge-mounted artillery and BAF helicopters. The daring, heroic exploits of the speedboat patrols and Coastal Patrol Craft took place outside the timeframe covered by the present narrative but it would be remiss not to mention them, no matter how briefly. According to Lt. Cdr. Paschal Odu, Leading Seaman Erefamote "caused more havoc on the Nigerian soldiers operating from Bonny than any other individual in Biafra." He never passed up an opportunity to lay into the enemy and reconnaissance patrols in his speedboat "invariably turned into harassment missions." When Gen. Philip Efiong visited Naval Headquarters on January 19, 1968, he promised action on the appeal made by the service for hand-held rocket launchers, and he delivered. The Navy received 37-mm rocket launchers a few weeks later, and one was issued to Leading Seaman Erefamote and his crew. The rockets were intended for enemy speedboats and troop concentrations, but the leading seaman had other ideas. During a reconnaissance patrol down Boler Creek on February 24, 1968, he and his crew encountered an enemy patrol, which they engaged. They shot and killed six enemy soldiers and then pressed on to Bonny, where the NNS *Nigeria* was at anchor. The leading seaman approached the frigate, took aim, fired his rocket, turned, and sped away. Unfortunately, he reportedly missed. But what if he had hit a magazine? Leading Seaman Erefamote was a non-Igbo Biafran. He survived the war. The other daredevil of similar accomplishments, Lt. Israel Onwubiko, failed to return from a reconnaissance patrol along New Calabar River in late January 1968.

Three CPCs distinguished themselves during the conflict—CPC-101, CPC-202, and CPC-203. Their commanders at various times were Lt. Godwin Kanu, Lt. Obi-Rapu, and Lt. Ebitu Ukiwe. Again and again, they saw off the capital ships of the Nigerian Navy, including its flagship, the NNS *Nigeria*, and Soviet-built frigates. One suspects that the lack of respect for the NNS *Nigeria* was inspired, at least in part, by the knowledge that command competency was very likely low-caliber. Two years prior, its captain, then in the rank of commander, had reportedly "failed woefully" in the exercises testing vessel handling ability in Portland, England. He had even panicked during one maneuver, and command had to be wrested from him by the supervising Royal Navy officer. Whether or not he grew in proficiency in the interval was not known.

Lieutenant Commander Odu wrote in his diary that on April 07, 1968, a Soviet frigate, escorted by two speedboats, ventured into the Main Channel. CPC 202 aimed a shot at it, and it fled back to Bonny. Nine days later, CPC 101 and 202 sighted NNS *Nigeria* and engaged her. After a brief exchange of fire, the frigate broke off and withdrew. The next day, April 17, 1968, both CPC's sailed to Bonny, hoping to catch the frigate at anchor. Unfortunately, it was nowhere to be seen, reportedly having "put to sea in a hurry." On April 25, 1968, the CPCs fought for over two hours with the NNS *Nigeria*, a Soviet frigate and Soviet fast patrol boat. The patrol boat was sunk, and hits were scored on the two frigates. Two days later, all three CPCs of the Biafran Navy caught up with the NNS *Nigeria* near Finima Point on the Main Channel. Once again, it managed to escape to sea. On April 29, 1968, it was learned from intercepted radio messages that the flagship of the Nigerian Navy had left the theater of operations for repairs in Lagos.

Air operations

The fortunes of the Biafran Air Force (BAF) were mixed. It quickly asserted itself soon after the commencement of hostilities and dominated the skies with what meager assets it had. After the fall of Enugu, air supremacy soon passed to the enemy. The BAF gained a second lease on life with the acquisition of MFI-9B (Minicoin) aircraft in 1969 and performed with astonishing brilliance but that phase of the conflict is outside the scope of the present work. It has been elaborately chronicled by one of the gallant flyers who did the country proud at the time, Capt. August Okpe.

The case of the first commander of the BAF, Lt. Col. George Tamuno Kurubo, was rather intriguing. Lieutenant Colonel Kurubo had been head of the Nigerian Air Force and was Ijaw by ethnicity (Bonny, specifically). Nevertheless, he was not spared during the July 29, 1966, coup. So endangered was he that he needed to make his escape from Lagos in a wooden crate. Yet it seemed he left his heart and soul back there and couldn't wait to return. Many Eastern senior officers of the Nigerian military had a question or two about the Biafra project, but perhaps none had more antipathy toward it than Lieutenant Colonel Kurubo. In obvious disrespect and perhaps an attempt to ridicule the head of state, he showed up for this investiture as commander of the BAF in casual attire. Nevertheless, he was allowed to keep that position, in which capacity he continued to

TOWARD UNDERSTANDING THE NIGERIA-BIAFRA WAR AND LINGERING QUESTIONS

attend very important meetings at which the most sensitive matters of state were discussed. Arrangements for weapons acquisition were entrusted to him, including the procurement of combat aircraft. Eventually, on one official trip abroad, he defected and fetched up at a press conference in London on September 05, 1967. Needless to say, he was well-received by Lt. Col. Yakubu Gowon. Perhaps, if he had bolted earlier, he might have been named governor of the Rivers State Lieutenant Colonel Gowon had created four months before. That job went instead to a twenty-five-year-old Lt. Cdr. Alfred Diete-Spiff, and Lt. Col. George Kurubo was consoled with an ambassadorship to Moscow. In Biafra, he was replaced by a close confidante of the head of state, Lt. Col. Louis Chude Sokei.

The assets of the BAF at the outbreak of hostilities were two B-26 bombers, a B-25 bomber, six helicopters (Aerospatiale Alouette II and III in equal numbers), a DC-3, a Fokker F-27, and a Riley-400. The F-27 was acquired from the Nigeria Airways, and the Riley-400 was an executive aircraft which Bristow Helicopters had abandoned at Port Harcourt Airport when they left at the outbreak of war. They and the DC-3 were repurposed for use as bombers.

The bombs dropped by the BAF were designed and built by a division of the Research and Production (RaP) Directorate led by the legendary Mr. William O. Achukwu. He had been trained as an agricultural engineer, but in the domain of explosives, his creativity and ingenuity were astounding. The initial models were somewhat unstable, and priming was rather tediously manual. However, soon after a consignment exploded during transportation, claiming casualties who included an Army captain, RaP devised a safe priming mechanism which activated as the bomb gathered speed falling to its target.

Both the bombers and helicopters were very active in the Nsukka and Ogoja sectors of the war, providing air support to ground troops. The Biafran Air Force was utterly spectacular, and the fearlessness with which the NNS *Nigeria* was repeatedly attacked in helicopter gunships suggested that if they had been armed with torpedoes, that frigate would have been sunk within hours of entering Biafran waters. They set the oil tank farms in Bonny Island ablaze, and the fires burned for months. As has been related, they collaborated with the

Biafran naval patrols in keeping troops of 3 Division (Marine commando) in Bonny bottled up and under constant harassment. Only one helicopter was lost in theater—at Eha-Amufu on August 17, 1967. Besides Squadron Leader John Chukwu, whose heroism has already been described, the other helicopter pilots who distinguished themselves in the early months of the campaign were Squadron Leader Monday Ikpeazu and Flight Lieutenants Uwemedimo Iyoho and Gabriel Ebube.

Strategic bombing operations were also carried out by the BAF. When the Nigerian Army began to deploy troops south of the River Benue soon after the proclamation of Biafra, a preemptive strike to destroy the rail and road bridge over the river at Makurdi was planned. The appropriate bomb for the mission was built and successfully tested. Necessary modifications were made to one of the bombers for its delivery and a tentative date of attack (June 26, 1967) was chosen. Unfortunately, one of the Alouette III helicopters piloted by Capt. August Okpe crashed on June 21, 1967, due to mechanical problems while returning from a patrol flight over the Bight of Biafra with the commander of the Biafran Navy and the principal staff officer "G Branch" (Operations), Army Headquarters, Col. Chris Ude, on board. They sustained injuries of varying degrees of severity from which they all eventually recovered fully. Captain Okpe had been very involved in the planning of the Makurdi operation, and with him out of commission, execution was postponed. Makurdi airport and the railroad bridge would eventually be attacked twice a few months later.

When radio intercepts and other intelligence reports in late July 1967 indicated that Nigeria had taken delivery of Czech L-29 jet aircraft parts and that they were being assembled at Lagos airport, the order was given for BAF to attack. The first raid was carried out by a B-26, and bombs of very large sizes were dropped. Unfortunately, one failed to explode, and the overall damage inflicted was minimal. Another mission was quickly launched, this time with two bombers—a B-26 and the Riley-400. The latter was flown by Capt. Elendu Ukeje and would drop large numbers of smaller bombs. The raid was operationally successful, and both aircraft and their crew returned safely to base. Significant damage was done, but apparently not enough to cripple the targeted activities, as confirmed by intelligence reports. It was decided that a three-aircraft raid was called for. As the planes were being made ready for take-off, fighter jets suddenly swooped in at low level, raked them with machine gun fire, and disappeared into the skies. Too late! The Nigerian Air Force (NAF) jets had become operational. The B-26 and DC-3 were very seriously damaged and had to be taken out of service. The Riley-400 got away lightly and was soon repaired.

The NAF relocated its L-29 jets to the North after the BAF attacks on Lagos Airport. The initial intelligence report received—erroneous it eventually turned out—was that they were now based at Kaduna. A long-range B-26 raid on Kaduna airport was executed. Capt. Phillipe Durang, a veteran of the French Air Force, commanded the mission, and Corporal Anthony Alaribe was his gunner. Ack-ack was heavy, but they managed to destroy the tarmac building and fire station. The main target, the hangar, was also hit, but the damage inflicted was not disabling. Kano was the correct destination of the NAF jets, and it was also learned that the Soviet Union, conformant to its obligations under their "cultural agreement" with Nigeria, had sent thirty MiG-15 jet trainer aircraft in crates to Kano Airport, along with hundreds of Soviet technicians. The other B-26 quickly took to the skies, headed for Kano. The reception was very hostile since the antiaircraft defenses had apparently learned from the Kaduna raid and were on the *qui vive*. The attacking aircraft was just as ready, laying down commensurate suppressive fire—over four thousand rounds in the first pass alone. The tarmac building was destroyed, and parked aircraft were heavily damaged by sustained machine gun fire as Captain Durang had a disconcerting habit of lingering over target for imprudent lengths of time. He eventually set off for home base, arriving with barely enough fuel to land.

The bomber raids seemed to have had very little of the desired effect on the development program of the NAF and its Soviet patrons. In no time, the NAF's jet fleet of L-29s, MiGs, and Ilyushins flown by Egyptian pilots recently humiliated in the June war with Israel was in full commission. By late September, they were already dropping bombs indiscriminately on homes, market places, churches, schools, and refugee camps in Biafra. Resistance in the ground war on the Northern front was also crumbling, and troops of 1 Division of the Nigerian Army were within striking distance of Enugu. The airbase relocated to Port Harcourt, where Capt. Rene Leclerc, formerly of the French Air Force and Aerospatiale but with a long association with the East and subsequently Biafra, came up with the idea of giving the Nigerians a little taste of the medicine they were dispensing to Biafrans from the air. The plan was to mount a "massive" raid on Lagos, attacking specific strategic or military targets (Dodan Barracks, Ijora Power Station, Apapa Wharf, the Oil Depot) and thereafter "targets of opportunity." The commander in chief gave his approval, and on October 04, 1967, the F-27 took off from Port Harcourt for Lagos, carrying a strange motley complement of war fighters (seven) and sightseers (five, one of whom was pregnant!). It was designated Flight 101—for the number of bombs on board. Unfortunately, the mission ended disastrously. According to the residents of Lagos, the aircraft flew in at low altitude and was easily knocked out of the sky by antiaircraft fire. By a different account, it was brought down by the accidental explosion of on-board munitions. It was that same evening that federal troops entered Enugu.

The last hurrah of the bombers during this first incarnation of the BAF was the two-ship attack on Calabar in December 1967. They very severely damaged their targets—the airport and the 3 Division (Marine commando) weapons dump—but took serious ground fire as well. They both made it back to Port Harcourt, but the B-25, experiencing problems with its controls as it tried to land, hit a high-tension power line and plowed into a grove of oil palm trees. Miraculously, only the navigator was killed. The B-26 was unable to lower its undercarriage and was bellied in on the grass shoulder by the runway. Both aircraft were inoperable and abandoned as the base was evacuated before its capture by federal forces in May 1968. When intercepted radio traffic indicated that technical experts working with the enemy had decided to repair and return the bombers to airworthiness, the Biafran High Command issued orders that they be destroyed at all costs. The mission to execute the orders, codenamed

Operation Jefta, was entrusted to a team of five, led by an Army commando captain and four airmen, including the colorful technical sergeant John Emordi. Both aircraft were successfully blasted to uselessness with grenades.

The background of the commander of the BAF, Lt. Col. Chude Sokei, was the Army. He was assigned the Air Force role because he was both an excellent logistician and someone the head of state could trust. In early 1968, however, he became restive, having come to the conclusion that the outcome of the war, one way or the other, would be decided by what happened on the ground, and he wanted to be a part of it. With the consent of the commander in chief, he deployed to the Eleventh Division theater of operations. On March 15, 1968, while huddled with Cols. Conrad Nwawo and Anthony Eze at Tactical Headquarters, they came under mortar fire. All three were injured, Colonel Sokei fatally. Wing-Commander Godwin Ezeilo succeeded him as commander, BAF.

CHAPTER 12

THE MID-WEST CAMPAIGN AND ITS POLITICS

From the very outset, the fighting had not gone well on the northern front. It was, however, thought that the overall situation could still be salvaged by striking out west with no less than Lagos as objective. Not only would the pressure on Enugu be relieved by so doing, such an offensive would also hopefully raise serious questions in the minds of the Northern-led junta in Lagos regarding the point of it all. This was probably the thinking all along behind the expectation of a short war. On August 08, 1967, the Biafran Army made its move.

Operation Zero-Four, as it was codenamed, was launched at 0300 on August 08, 1967, having been postponed from August 04. The expeditionary force was the Fifty-Fourth Independent Brigade (also known as the Liberation Army) comprised of three battalions—Twelfth (Lt. Col. Festus Akagha), Thirteenth (Lt. Col. Michael Ivenso), and Eighteenth (Maj. Humphrey Chukwuka)—and was under the command of Brig. Gen. Victor Adebukunola Banjo (Lt. Col. Emmanuel Arinze Ifeajuna was his chief of staff). The planning had apparently been so very hush-hush that not even the chief of logistics, Biafran Army, Gen. Philip Efiong, knew about it until H-minus 3 hour when Lieutenant Colonel Akagha approached him with a requisition for troop carriers.

TOWARD UNDERSTANDING THE NIGERIA-BIAFRA WAR AND LINGERING QUESTIONS

Conceptually, there must have been at least three different plans with different objectives. The official Biafran plan, set out with admirable crispness in operational orders written by the C in C himself, outlined four phases, namely neutralize the Mid-West, liberate the West, recover territories lost to the enemy, and consolidate national integrity. The other plan was that drawn up by the Army commander Gen. Hilary Njoku and Lt. Col. Patrick Nzeogwu to which many officers had reportedly signed on. According to the Army commander, the strategy was to "set Nigeria on fire" by enlisting the West to the struggle, seizing the Niger crossing at Jebba and advancing into the far North. It envisaged Lt. Col. Nzeogwu or Lt. Col. Conrad Nwawo in a command role, not General Banjo. Unfortunately, this other plan stayed on paper because the Army commander was sidelined. The expeditionary force reported directly to the commander in chief, not Army Headquarters. The third plan was that of General Banjo, which, at least at the outset, resonated in some degree with the official Biafran plan and will be described later.

A small assault unit crossed the River Niger early in the night of August 07–08, 1967, landing at John Holt Beach, Asaba. The troops made their way to the post office and severed all major telephone and telegraphic communications. At H-hour, the invasion force came over the Niger Bridge and quickly overran the Asaba garrison at St. Peter's Teacher Training College. The officers, however, were billeted at the Catering Rest House, and their commander, Major Asama, had time to make his escape. He managed to alert the military governor of the Mid-West, Lt. Col. David Ejoor, as he fled toward Benin City. The expeditionary force pressed on to Agbor then fanned out with the Thirteenth Battalion heading north toward Okene on the Umunede-Uromi-Auchi axis, the Eighteenth Battalion south along the Obiaruku-Warri-Sapele axis and the Twelfth Battalion, the bulk of the troops, continuing the westward thrust. The expectation was that the advance, especially of the Thirteenth Battalion, would cause the Nigerian Army to hesitate viz-a-viz their continued operations in the north of Biafra and so relieve the pressure on Enugu. The Twelfth Battalion was supposed to reach Ikeja within forty-eight hours and lay siege to Lagos, the federal capital.

The Twelfth Battalion entered Benin City at about midday, August 09, 1967, and in twelve short hours, all of the Mid-West was effectively under the control of the Fifty-Fourth Brigade. The military governor of the Mid-West had fled the government house and taken refuge in the residence of the Catholic bishop of Benin Diocese, the Reverend Patrick Kelly. The plan had been for the military governor to be apprehended and persuaded to read a prepared speech on radio, "volitionally" handing over the reins of authority to Lt. Col. Conrad Nwawo before being escorted to Enugu to become a special guest of the State of Biafra. General Banjo did not make that happen. He instead proceeded to deliver a long, winding, and self-serving broadcast he had not cleared with his C in C. The general had gone rogue. Condemnation was universal but muted because of his personal relationship with General Odumegwu-Ojukwu. He was recalled to Enugu ostensibly "for consultations"—euphemism for placement under house arrest. Lieutenant Colonel Akagha assumed command of the Fifty-Fourth Brigade.

The Twelfth Battalion soon crossed into Western Nigeria and, by August 24, had taken Ore and Okitipupa. Three days later, heavy fighting was going on around Owo. To the north, the Thirteenth Battalion captured large quantities of enemy equipment and supplies at Okene. Warri in the south was taken without a fight by the Eighteenth Battalion, and Maj. Adewale Ademoyega, who had been in detention there since January 1966, was released.

Meanwhile, Benin remained paralyzed by political bickering. Lt. Col. David Ejoor managed to slip out of Benin and eventually fetched up in Lagos. Lieutenant Colonel Nwawo's "strong personality and independence of mind" were considered inauspicious, and Maj. Albert Okonkwo, a mild-mannered US-trained physician in the Nigerian Army Medical Corps, was appointed military administrator of the Mid-West instead of him. Militarily, the original plan had been for the Mid-West Command to retain substantial operational autonomy, but General Odumegwu-Ojukwu opted to renege. Disappointed, many of the officers of Mid-Western origin cast their lot with the Nigerian side.

TOWARD UNDERSTANDING THE NIGERIA-BIAFRA WAR AND LINGERING QUESTIONS

To the surprise of many, General Banjo resurfaced in Benin City on September 06, 1967, this time as commander of a new formation, the 104th Division of the Biafran Army, which the C in C had just created. It was made up of two brigades—the Fifty-Fourth, whose command was left to Lieutenant Colonel Akagha, and another whose numerical designation I could not find, commanded by Lt. Col. Ben Ochei. Unfortunately, the momentum had dissipated, and the initiative had begun to pass to the federal forces. The Thirteenth Battalion lost Auchi the day the general resumed his command. By September 17, 1967, the 2 Division of the Nigerian Army, under the command of Lt. Col. Murtala Muhammed, intensified their counterattack along the northern front with heavy artillery and armored support. Their advance east from Ore had been slowed by the demolition of Oluwa bridge by sappers of the Liberation Army. The 3 Division (Marine commando) commanded by Lt. Col. Benjamin Adekunle attacked from the south, taking Warri, Sapele, and Ughelli. They also seized the strategic bridges over the Ethiope River along Sapele-Benin road. For nonmilitary reasons that would come to light in due course, the 104th Division pulled out of Benin City on September 18, 1967. The following day, a prerecorded broadcast by the military administrator of the Mid-West proclaiming that territory, the Sovereign Republic of Benin, was played. Twenty-four hours later, the 2 Division of the Nigerian Army entered Benin City. The Fifty-Fourth Brigade set up new defensive lines at Agbor to the east, and General Banjo returned to Enugu for what was to be the last time.

Under relentless pressure and with command uncertainties at the highest levels, the entire expeditionary force understandably remained off-balance and, by September 25, had begun to pull back from Agbor. By the end of the month, it had been driven all the way to Asaba, with its back to the River Niger. On October 06, the last units of the 104th Division crossed into Biafra and blew up the bridge over the River Niger behind them. By October 08, 1967, Lieutenant Colonel Muhammed's forces were in full control of Asaba.

What followed next was perhaps the most horrific single atrocity of the war, a gruesome butchery of civilians by soldiers of the Nigerian Army on a scale equaling or even surpassing that on the worst days of the pogrom in the North of Nigeria the year before. As soon as Nigerian troops entered Asaba, they wasted no time in beginning to molest the inhabitants, looting, raping, and physically tormenting them. The hapless locals reasoned that if they turned out *en masse* and demonstrated their support and welcome of the federal forces by shouting slogans like "one Nigeria," they would be rewarded with a cessation of harassment. They couldn't be more mistaken. Huge processions did take to the streets, but with a ferocity that beggars belief, troops commanded by Maj. Ibrahim Taiwo set upon them in various areas of town. The worst killings happened in Ogbe Osowa, Ogbeke Square, and Cable Point. The numbers that have been put out for the body count after that senseless slaughter have varied but are consistently in the high hundreds. Among those killed were sprinter Sydney Asiodu, who ran the first leg for the Nigeria 4×100 meters relay at the Tokyo Olympics in 1964, and Mr. Leonard Okogwu, whose daughter Maryam would marry Maj. Ibrahim Babangida in 1969. One chronicler described it as a "terrible event" and helpfully added "a violation of Gowon's Military Code of Conduct" but "not the only example of savagery on both sides during the war." In other words, "too bad, stuff happens, and the other side did it too."

In the Mid-West campaign, two officers distinguished themselves for personal valor: Maj. Joseph Achuzia and Maj. Jonathan Isichei. Major Achuzia was never in the Nigerian Army. He had been working as an engineer at Port Harcourt at the time the crisis began to unfold but, according to Frederick Forsyth, had cut his military teeth in Korea with the British Army in the early 1950s. In the ensuing weeks, he (and Maj. Assam Nsudoh) would thoroughly humiliate Lt. Col. Murtala Muhammed in his attempts to take Onitsha. He grew tremendously in stature, becoming almost mythical. At a tactical level, he, Majs. Theodore Atumaka, William Archibong, and Lambert Ihenacho were arguably the most daring soldiers on the Biafran side of the conflict. Unfortunately, his reputation was tainted by rife reports of brutal punishments he inflicted on soldiers suspected to be exhibiting cowardly behavior in the face of the enemy.

TOWARD UNDERSTANDING THE NIGERIA-BIAFRA WAR AND LINGERING QUESTIONS

The politics of the Mid-West Campaign

Primary sources are few regarding the circumstances surrounding the misadventure of the expeditionary force. As such, speculation has been rife, much of it contaminated by preconceptions. With considerable effort, the driblets of available relevant information have been collated into the reasonably coherent unvarnished narrative here presented.

General Banjo, the central character, was a graduate of the Royal Military Academy Sandhurst, England. He also had a degree in mechanical engineering and enlisted in the Nigerian Army in 1953. According to an interview given by his brother, Professor Adesegun Banjo, he was the brain behind an abortive coup d'état in 1964 to which all senior military officers had signed on. However, at about "H-minus-6" hour, Brig. Gen. Samuel Ademulegun, then one of the four highest-ranking officers in the Nigerian Army (alongside Brig. Gens. Johnson Aguiyi-Ironsi, Babafemi Ogundipe, and Zakaria Maimalari), decided for unstated reasons he would no longer participate. The coup was canceled as a result, and it fell upon Lieutenant Colonel Banjo to spread the word. The good professor also stated that Lieutenant Colonel Banjo did not take part in the January 15, 1966, coup but was invited to become head of state after the dust settled, but he declined. Much else volunteered during the interview was just as fanciful thus calling the credibility of it all into question. What was for sure was that Lieutenant Colonel Banjo was one of the senior officers in the South who, as already described, argued for the military to demand that the Council of Ministers in Lagos hand over power.

According to Gen. Hilary Njoku, Lieutenant Colonel Banjo arrived at the police headquarters in Obalande, where General Aguiyi-Ironsi still had his offices, on January 18, 1966. His escort of armed soldiers waited in a Land Rover troop vehicle on the street while he entered the building with a submachine gun and a Beretta pistol. In the anteroom of the general's office, a scuffle ensued between him and Lt. Col. George Kurubo and Maj. Patrick Anwunah. They overpowered and arrested him. Troops under the command of Lieutenant

Colonel Banjo had been behaving with lack of discipline since the coup three days prior, engendering the suspicion in some quarters that the lieutenant colonel was one of the mutineers. The coup plotters were to later confirm that he was not one of them, but Lieutenant Colonel Banjo was known to have been entertaining coup ideations since 1960. It is not known whether it was ever elicited from him why he wanted to see the head of state bearing arms.

Lieutenant Colonel Banjo was held in Ikot-Ekpene prison, Eastern Nigeria, but as the crisis worsened, he and other detainees were released. It is unclear how far back his relationship with General Ojukwu went, but they were, by all accounts, close friends. They were among the small elite group of university graduates in combat units of the armed forces at the time (others were Emmanuel Ifeajuna, Emmanuel Udeaja, Adewale Ademoyega, Olufemi Olutoye, and Oluwole Rotimi). Lieutenant Colonel Banjo actually lived on State Lodge grounds in Enugu. Soon after the proclamation of the Republic of Biafra, he was conferred with the rank of brigadier general and given the task of raising a militia force. As evidenced by his broadcast to the people of Mid-Western Nigeria on August 10, 1967, he was intensely resentful of the Fulani-Hausa feudal clique, urging "rejection of the fiction that peace in Nigeria is only possible under the conditions that the entire people of Nigeria should be dominated" by them. Drastic structural measures were needed, but operationally, it appeared he had ideas that were uniquely his own. He had set them out in a paper which he shared with General Efiong. It described a Biafra that extended from the Cameroonian frontier in the east to include present-day République de Bénin in the west and bordered by the Rivers Niger and Benue in the north. As such, the Biafra of May 30, 1967, was either a mistake or just a beginning. According to General Efiong, General Ojukwu did not know about any of this, but General Banjo told him he intended to show the C in C the paper as well.

All the indications were that General Banjo enjoyed the utmost confidence of the Biafran C in C and was involved in major sensitive policy and other deliberations. When Chief Awolowo came to Enugu on May 05, 1967, at the head of a National Reconciliation

TOWARD UNDERSTANDING THE NIGERIA-BIAFRA WAR AND LINGERING QUESTIONS

Commission, which sought to persuade the East to attend talks in a last-ditch effort to find peace, then Lieutenant Colonel Banjo participated in the meetings that took place. According to Professor Chinualumogu Achebe, some members of the commission were distinguished and well-meaning, but their mission could hardly be seen as sincere since they hadn't even persuaded Lt. Col. Yakubu Gowon to bring to book the perpetrators of the pogrom in the North. Chief Awolowo and his team left Enugu, their mission unaccomplished. On the eve of his departure, the military governor reportedly confided in him and the police commissioner on his commission, Mr. Emmanuel Olufunwa, that the Rubicon had actually been crossed whereupon the chief asked him for a two-week heads-up before the proclamation was made. Lieutenant Colonel Odumegwu-Ojukwu set up a hotline between the government house, Enugu and Ikenne, the chief's home, and they remained in constant contact.

Another line of communication between Enugu (Lt. Col. Victor Banjo) and the West, which was mediated by the eminent playwright Wole Soyinka (BA University of Leeds 1957; PhD [Honoris Causa], University of Leeds 1972, Nobel laureate, Literature 1986) and Ms. Adetowun Ogunseye (Lieutenant Colonel Banjo's sister and then-lecturer in librarianship at the University of Ibadan), came into existence shortly after the proclamation of the republic. Mr. Wole Soyinka was no stranger to controversy. He resigned his lectureship at the University of Ife in 1964 over the political spinelessness and sycophancy of his colleagues there and, the following year, was involved in the armed takeover of the broadcasting house in Ibadan. Gun in hand, he had persuaded the duty officers at the broadcast desk to replace the premier's audiotape with one he himself had made. His tape played long enough for his accusation of the premier and his government of electoral theft to transmit. He escaped to Enugu, but soon, a police squad dispatched from Ibadan was hot on his heels. The premier of the East Dr. Michael Okpara helped him return to the West and give himself up. He was charged with robbery with violence and tried before Justice Kayode Eso, who acquitted him on a technicality.

Soon after the proclamation of Biafra, Mr. Soyinka attended a conference of African and Scandinavian writers in Stockholm, Sweden. He had hoped to meet his Biafran coevals there to brainstorm the gathering gloom and hopefully come up with a unified opposition to war. In his memoir, he wrote that he was opposed to the secession of Biafra, not because it was an act of moral or political felony but because he had his doubts that Biafra would survive the federal counterpunch. No Biafrans attended the conference, and so he decided he would go to Biafra. Upon his return to Lagos, he convened with his friends in the home of his closest confidante, Mr. Femi Johnson, the elder brother of then Lt. Col. Mobolaji Johnson, governor of Lagos State. Out of their deliberations emerged the concept of a "Third Force." In Mr. Soyinka's Kantian-Hegelian formulation of the dialectic, if Federal Nigeria was the thesis and Biafra the antithesis, the Third Force would be a viable synthesis—if it really had "force."

Mr. Soyinka arrived in Enugu in late July or early August and departed three nights before the Mid-West Incursion. During his stay, he had the opportunity of a meeting with the Biafran head of state during which he appealed for a unilateral cease-fire to allow one more effort at resolving the conflict to be made, and that would entail suspending the secession. According to him, the head of state was noncommittal and, having told him that it was the people who had demanded secession, recommended that he meet with civilian leaders. Mr. Soyinka stated that he eventually did but provided no account of who he met with or the discussion they had. However, his most momentous encounter of the trip was with Lt. Col. Victor Banjo. It would appear that it was the lieutenant colonel who did all the talking, as there was no record of what Mr. Soyinka said. He nevertheless seemed very favorably impressed by Lieutenant Colonel Banjo and described him as "an idealist whose politics were quite close to ours in the Third Force." Lieutenant Colonel Banjo reportedly had harsh words for leaders of the West and "even harsher words" for the Biafran head of state, who was his friend and host.

After his single encounter with the Biafran head of state, Mr. Soyinka decided that his ambition was to "take over the nation" as has since been attested to by some unnamed Biafran historians. According to him, Lt. Col. Victor Banjo knew as much, and the twist was that he, Lieutenant Colonel Banjo, too wanted to "take over the nation, including Biafra." The lieutenant colonel's plan was to pretend to support the Biafran head of state's agenda by leading an expeditionary force of mostly Biafrans clandestinely trained in the Mid-West, through the West, and into Lagos. The allegiance of the Western Area Command was crucial to the success of his scheme because, with its support and him in Lagos, the national "takeover" aspirations of the Biafran head of state would be dashed.

Lieutenant Colonel Banjo then commissioned Mr. Soyinka to convey very important messages to the civilian as well as military leadership of the West, especially to Lt. Col. Olusegun Obasanjo, who had recently been appointed commanding officer of the Western Area Command. He hinted that changes were going to be made in Biafra and determinative of them was Lieutenant Colonel Obasanjo's response to his messages. Lieutenant Colonel Obasanjo had been under his command in the Nigerian Army Corps of Engineers. At the meeting Mr. Soyinka had with Lieutenant Colonel Banjo was Maj. Philip Maya Alale, a Moscow-trained leftist agitator and propagandist, who, according to Gen. Philip Efiong, was married to one of the Biafran head of state's cousins.

Lt. Col. Victor Banjo's message, in essence, as documented by Mr. Soyinka, was thus:

> Let them understand in the West that I am leading not a Biafran Army but an army of liberation, made up not only of Biafrans but of other ethnic groups. Make the governor of the West and other Western leaders understand this. Urge them not to be taken in by any propaganda by the federal government about a Biafran plan to subjugate the rest of the nation, especially the West. (Soyinka 2009)

And specifically for the commanding officer of the Western Area Command,

> Tell Obasanjo that the liberation forces at my command do not wish to fight on Western soil. All we seek is unimpeded passage to Lagos through the Western Region. (Soyinka 2009)

Mr. Soyinka set about discharging his courier mission as soon after his return to Nigeria as possible. He, however, decided not to contact Chief Awolowo, on the intuition that "the approaching conflict was not one in which he should be involved." However, when Lieutenant Colonel Banjo entered Benin City within a few days of his meeting with Mr. Soyinka in Enugu, he was able to establish a telephone link with the chief through British diplomatic auspices. He and Mr. Soyinka also remained in regular telephone contact.

Lieutenant Colonel Obasanjo asked to meet in person after he and Mr. Soyinka had spoken by telephone. Driving around the dark streets of Ibadan one night, writer and soldier mulled their predicament. In Mr. Soyinka's recollection, he did no more than convey Lieutenant Colonel Banjo's message as was given to him and made no attempt whatsoever to sway Lieutenant Colonel Obasanjo one way or the other. However, Lieutenant Colonel Obasanjo remembered their discussion differently and wrote many years later that Mr. Soyinka had tried to suborn him, asking that he name his price for signing on to the Third Force program. Of course he did not take the bait and replied instead that he had sworn an oath of loyalty to the authorities in Lagos. For him, apparently, what mattered was not the orders or who gave them but where they came from. In other words, he would join forces with now Brigadier General Banjo only if the general somehow got to Lagos, established himself as the authority there, and issued an order for the Western Area Command to join his crusade. Facilitating his getting to Lagos, passively or actively, would amount to a betrayal of his oath and so was out of the question.

Mr. Soyinka relayed Lieutenant Colonel Obasanjo's response to General Banjo in Benin City by telephone. It would seem that there

TOWARD UNDERSTANDING THE NIGERIA-BIAFRA WAR AND LINGERING QUESTIONS

was a Third Force Plan "B"—a popular uprising that would ignite as soon as the Liberation Army began its march through the West. Meanwhile, the forward elements of the Liberation Army were dug in at the outskirts of Okitipupa, and night after night, Mr. Soyinka pleaded with the general to unleash them. For unclear reasons, he hesitated. Perhaps, he had counted too heavily on the Western Area Command switching sides and did not care much for the popular uprising.

Soon after Mr. Soyinka returned from his visit to Enugu, the trip came to the attention of federal authorities, and when, a few days later, General Banjo led an expeditionary force across the Niger into the Mid-West, he became a person of interest and went into hiding. After his meeting with Lieutenant Colonel Obasanjo, the latter ran upstairs and shared what he had learned. His admirers would subsequently begin to refer to him as "OBJ," which, to all intents and purposes, might well have stood for "Obedient Boy of the Junta." Coincidentally, General Banjo seemingly became unhinged. He threw all caution to the winds and began to make insecure telephone calls, which greatly increased the risk to his interlocutors of detection and arrest. According to Mr. Soyinka, he even called Gen. Yakubu Gowon and Col. Adeyinka Adebayo, the governor of the West, and the language of those conversations was not polite. The manhunt for Mr. Soyinka became almost frenzied, and he decided it was time to stand down the Third Force and escape into neighboring République de Bénin for safety. He did not make it out and was arrested near the campus of the University of Ibadan. Mr. Wole Soyinka remained incarcerated until January 1969 and would document his prison experience in the book, *The Man Died*.

The speculation by Mr. Soyinka that the ulterior ultimate intention of the Biafran head of state was to "take over the nation" beggars belief. In a letter to General Banjo dated August 22, 1967, which formally detailed the conditions under which Biafran forces were being placed at his disposal for the liberation of Yorubaland, the Biafran head of state clearly stated that "our sovereignty and break with what used to be known as Nigeria are complete and irrevocable. Nothing must, therefore, be said or done by you or any member of the Liberation Army to give a contrary impression." It went on to say that "Biafra (is) determined to maintain and safeguard her sovereignty, and ensure that her integrity and safety (are) never again threatened." There was no language in that letter to suggest that he had any designs on Nigeria beyond the excision from it of the Mid-West and Yorubaland.

The ambitions of Gen. Victor Banjo, on the other hand, were anything but obscure even as his path to their realization seemed incongruous. In his radio broadcast soon after entering Benin City, the general decried the "dismemberment of Nigeria" shortly before stating that "I have fought for Biafra in the struggle of her people to sustain their right to live their lives in peace in their own way and at their own pace." He then proceeded to promulgate a decree setting up an interim administration in the Mid-West with all legislative and executive powers vested in himself. In due course, he said, he would appoint a military administrator and "as soon as it is practicable" return to the war front "to complete the liberation of Nigeria." None of this was a part of the plan at the outset. The Biafran head of state's letter of August 22, 1967, seemed to have been written to refocus the general. His dalliance with Mr. Soyinka's Third Force was also off-script. His remit was to punch through to Lagos, not negotiate a lubricated passage.

It would seem the Third Force adopted General Banjo as its flagbearer. Its political agenda, however, was never clearly articulated, in terms of what would happen after it had overthrown the First Force and abrogated the Second Force. By different accounts, it would seek to actualize the objective of the January 15, 1966, coup, namely the reunification of Nigeria under the prime ministership of Chief Awolowo or emplace some other political arrangement excluding the North with Lieutenant Colonel Banjo as leader of some description (president or prime minister). However, whatever the end, the means to it apparently was to be, at the outset at least, Biafran military muscle, such as there was. And after it had been successfully flexed, that muscle paradoxically would be consigned to the dustbin as Biafra went extinct, according to the plan. Mr. Soyinka did allude to the high improbability that such an outcome could be realized.

TOWARD UNDERSTANDING THE NIGERIA-BIAFRA WAR AND LINGERING QUESTIONS

After the general's advances to the commanding officer of the Western Area Command were spurned, another disjunction surfaced. He was unwilling to do any fighting on Western soil. In other words, omelets would be made but with no eggs broken. In the end, he fell victim to the contradictions of his complex machinations, convoluted thought processes, and insincerities.

With forward elements of the expeditionary force having exploited as far west as Okitipupa, the threat to Lagos was real, and its significance was not lost on the British high commissioner (1967–1969) Sir David Hunt. It has been said that diplomats are otherwise decent people whose job it is to lie for their country. In postcolonial Africa, diplomats of the erstwhile imperial powers did more than lie. They were often utterly evil. In an article published in the *Guardian* newspaper of January 21, 2020, Frederick Forsyth, a British journalist who covered the conflict, remembered Sir Hunt as a snob and racist who "expected Africans to leap to attention when he entered the room—which Gowon did." British diplomats have a tradition of writing frankly in their final dispatch about their service upon concluding a posting, and Sir David Hunt, as he left Lagos for Brasilia in 1969, remarked thus: "Africans as a whole are not only not averse to cutting off their nose to spite their face, they regard such an operation as a triumph of cosmetic surgery."

For more reasons than one, there was no love lost between the high commissioner and Chukwuemeka Odumegwu-Ojukwu. Although Sir Hunt became an Oxford don, his upbringing was relatively plebeian in comparison to that of Chukwuemeka Odumegwu-Ojukwu, whose father was a multimillionaire. The same could be said for his boss, Prime Minister James Harold Wilson, as well, and among the ever so class-conscious British, this counted for much. Further, Sir Hunt's second wife, the niece of Mr. A. G. Leventis, who was a well-known businessman in Lagos, had been Chukwuemeka Odumegwu-Ojukwu's girlfriend. There is no evidence that the relationship between the vivacious Lady Hunt and Chukwuemeka Odumegwu-Ojukwu continued after she married Sir Hunt, but then, there is also no evidence that it did not. If it did, one doubts Sir Hunt would have relished enduring a predicament similar to that of the last viceroy of British India. When the ambassador and Chukwuemeka Odumegwu-Ojukwu met, the latter reportedly extended no more than common courtesy to him, and he was resentful of that. In the festering imbroglio, he saw his chance to teach the "upstart" a lesson.

Soon after the proclamation of Biafra, Sir Hunt had brokered a truce between Chief Awolowo and a pliable Lieutenant Colonel Gowon. One of Chief Awolowo's asking prices was the redeployment of non-Yoruba troops out of the West, and Lieutenant Colonel Gowon was happy to deliver. In addition, he named the chief vice-chair of the Federal Executive Council he inaugurated on June 12, 1967. The portfolio of federal commissioner for Finance was also thrown in. Satisfied, the chief informed his kinsmen that the Fulani-Hausa-inspired federal agenda was now worthy of their subscription. According to one account, when the expeditionary force struck west a couple of months later, word was sent to General Banjo that there was no further need for its ministrations and that any further incursion into Yorubaland would be greeted with hostility and vehement resistance. It would seem though that the general had, by this time, already begun to devote his considerable energies to plotting to overthrow the government of the Republic of Biafra.

Chapter 13

The Plot to Overthrow the Government of the Republic

The indifferent overall performance of the Biafran Army on the northern front, isolated acts outstanding bravery notwithstanding, had been a cause for profound concern to many. There was more than enough blame to go around. The citizenry held the soldiery responsible. Perhaps the most vocal was Mr. Philip Alale who was charged with coordinating the efforts of organized labor from the very early stages of the crisis and would later become political commissar in the rank of major. He was a fiery orator, one of whose spellbinding performances, delivered from atop a Land Rover, I was privileged to watch. He once let it be known in a radio broadcast that there were fifth columnists in the armed forces striving to undermine the State, an allegation that did tremendous damage to morale. The senior officers in the armed forces, for their part, maintained that they were far too poorly equipped, compared to the enemy, to prevail in combat in a consistent manner. To this, the leadership replied with an age-old retort heard in all conflicts, before or since—you go to war with the army you have, not the army you wish you had, then adapt to your circumstances. The Mid-West incursion was a reprieve but all too short-lived. Within a matter of days, it had miscarried. The anxieties returned.

The head of Biafra Military Intelligence, Lt. Col. Bernard Odogwu, documented the intrigues at the highest levels in great detail in his memoir. Before the war, he was in the diplomatic service, and his last posting was to the United States. He returned home to the East on December 29, 1966, because he and other officers of Eastern origin were being treated discriminately. Since the July 29 coup, they were being denied access to diplomatic dispatches and other informational materials to the extent that, according to him, non-Nigerians employed as secretaries in Nigerian missions abroad knew more about what was happening in the embassies than Easterners. In the absence of an external affairs ministry in Enugu, he was required to report to State Lodge with other returning foreign service officers. There, he met and struck up comradeship with several other functionaries who also reported to State Lodge. They saw the military governor daily and eventually gained his trust. What little downtime he had, he would come and chat freely with them on any subject. He let them come and go as they pleased, and they would often sleep in his living room. The members of this so-called "In-Group," besides the head of military intelligence, were Mr. Douglas Ngwube (foreign service), Mr. Samuel Ironka Agbamuche (foreign service), Mr. Christopher David-Osuagwu (head, Film Unit), Mr. Uche Chukwumerije (director of information), and Mr. Michael Ikenze (press secretary). Lt. Col. Bernard Odogwu sought to minimize the power the "In-Group" wielded and to what extent it could influence the course of events, stating that "there was nothing special" about it. He might have forgotten the Ball Rule of Power—nothing propinks like propinquity—but Maj. Phillip Alale apparently did not.

On August 12, 1967, Major Alale asked Lieutenant Colonel Odogwu to convene a meeting of the "In-Group" for the purpose of intervening in the crisis that had developed in the Mid-West campaign with the firing of Gen. Victor Banjo. He came to the meeting with Lt. Col. Emmanuel Ifeajuna, General Banjo's chief of staff. Lieutenant Colonel Ifeajuna had been instructed by Army Headquarters to prepare to deploy to the Ikom front in command of a battalion that was being assembled around the nucleus of a company that had been sent up from Calabar. In the unruly climate of the time, he opted to disregard the order, choosing instead to accompany General Banjo on the Mid-West campaign, knowing full well that he would not come to grief on account of the tension between Army Headquarters and the commander in chief. At the meeting, Major Alale painted a dire picture of the military situation in the Mid-West and made a strong case for General Banjo to be sent back there to stem the tide. He told the "In-Group" that he had "every confidence" in their capabilities and hoped that they "should be able to convince the head of state that Brigadier Banjo is the best man for the job."

The "In-Group" agreed to mediate and raised the subject with the head of state. He first informed them that the matter was closed, but after much persuasion, he relented and promised he would reconsider. The "In-Group" then went and met with General Banjo. He, too, was pertinacious in his rejection of the suggestion that he mend fences with the commander in chief. He complained that he had never before been so humiliated, and worst of all, it was meted out by his friend. Again, after prolonged debate, he came around, agreeing to meet with the commander in chief and promising to get the campaign back on track as soon as he returned to his headquarters. The following day, General Banjo came to see the commander in chief. Wounded pride soothed, he was reinstated to his command and, by midday, was off on his way back to Benin City.

Unfortunately, precious time had been squandered, and by the first week of September, the newly established 2 Division, Nigerian Army, was up and running, commanded by Lt. Col. Murtala Muhammed. They challenged the Liberation Army from the north and the west. The commander of 3 Division (Marine commando) Lt. Col. Benjamin Adekunle was ordered to redeploy units from Bonny in southern Biafra to the delta in the Mid-West to create a southern front. Forces of 1 Division resumed their offensive in northern Biafra and by September 08, 1967, were able to take the strategic Opi junction. Apprehension, if not panic, began to be felt in Enugu, thirty-two miles away.

On September 14, 1967, the "In-Group" met and discussed the worsening situation. They were unanimous that, based on the evidence before them, the country was no longer able to prosecute the war effectively. It could no longer counterpunch and was taking a drubbing. They decided the time had come to solicit the negotiation of a cease-fire by a foreign power, like the United States of America, and asked Mr. Samuel Agbamuche to prepare the draft of a memorandum to that effect for submission to the head of state. In less than twenty-four hours, the draft document was ready and was reproduced in full by Lt. Col. Bernard Odogwu in his memoir. It was a masterfully crafted critical analysis of the military, political, and economic situation. In its penultimate and final paragraphs, references to an urgent need for broadening the "political base of our leadership" were made, with a recommendation that "the new leadership must be a collective one in which members do not owe their offices to the whims or pleasure of one man." As they considered the draft the next day, September 15, 1967, they quickly caught on to the vexed paragraphs, recognizing that they amounted to trifling with a tinderbox and that, for all the willingness of the head of state to tolerate their free-wheeling ideas, they might be crossing a line if they made such a presentation directly to him. They decided the matter of leadership style should be broached with citizens of the highest caliber in the land, and their views ascertained regarding taking it up with the head of state. Among them were Brig. Gen. Philip Efiong (then chief of logistics, Biafran Army), Mr. Patrick Okeke (inspector general of the police), Dr. Alvan Ikoku (chairman, Consultative Assembly), Dr. Akanu Ibiam (adviser to the head of state), Sir Louis Mbanefo (chief justice), Mr. Joseph Emembolu (attorney-general), Rt. Rev. Godfrey Okoye (Catholic bishop of Port Harcourt), and Mr. Felix Iheanacho. Maj. Philip Alale attended the meeting of the "In-Group" that morning and agreed to contact the persons named as well as sound out the leaders of organized labor. After the meeting, however, he instead headed out to Benin City to meet with Brig. Gen. Victor Banjo, accompanied by Lt. Col. Emmanuel Ifeajuna.

Maj. Philip Alale returned from Benin City on September 17, 1967, and went directly to Lt. Col. Bernard Odogwu's office to deliver the incredibly good tidings he had brought from the Mid-West. Gen. Victor Banjo had made contact with the British deputy high commissioner in Benin City and through him secured agreement from the British and United States governments to broker a cease-fire between Nigeria and Biafra, followed by peace talks! He, however, admonished that the news not leak outside the "In-Group" since the plan was for the head of state to hear it directly from General Banjo.

The "In-Group" reconvened in the morning of September 18, 1967, to resume consideration of Mr. Samuel Agbamuche's draft memorandum, with Maj. Philip Alale in attendance. Shortly after they began, Lt. Col. Emmanuel Ifeajuna joined them. He had just returned from Benin City and, like Maj. Philip Alale the day before, bore special tidings but which unfortunately were a spanner in the works. The lieutenant colonel told the "In-Group" that the British and US governments had stipulated that a precondition for their mediation was that the head of state, Chukwuemeka Odumegwu-Ojuwku, would not be party to the negotiations. They briefly debated the new situation, and the majority did not see excluding the head of state from negotiations as a viable proposition. However, Mr. Samuel Agbamuche and Lieutenant Colonel Ifeajuna stood out in their expressed conviction that it would not matter who did the negotiations, given Biafra's predicament. The decision was reached to postpone the discussion until General Banjo, who was expected back in Enugu that evening, met with the "In-Group" and provided more information.

As arranged, all members of the "In-Group" rendezvoused at Maj. Philip Alale's Progress Hotel chalet, where they would await word of General Banjo's arrival then head over to his residence. At this point, it had all begun to smell of so much fish to the intelligence chief that he brought his unobtrusive remotely operated recording equipment. As they waited, Major Alale dropped a bombshell—that he had been reliably informed by Lt. Col. Emmanuel Ifeajuna that the commander, Biafran Army, Gen. Hilary Njoku, had plans to overthrow the head of state that night. He implored that an emissary be sent to alert the head of state posthaste. The lieutenant colonel had arrived at his conclusion on the basis of the "rather suspicious" appearance of three armored vehicles at Army Headquarters and the fact that when he had gone to speak to the officers of a company that had actually been waiting to be posted to his command, he was told by them that they were under the personal orders of General Njoku. They would soon learn that the exchange between Lieutenant Colonel Ifeajuna and the officers was different in content, if it ever took place, and that there was nothing suspicious about the location of the armored vehicles. The "In-Group" argued for a while about who was going to convey the news of the imminent "coup" to the head of state, and eventually, Mr. Douglas Ngwube agreed to run the errand. He went over to State Lodge, passed on the information, and rejoined the "In-Group." The head of state ordered the immediate arrest of the commander, Biafran Army. The plotters of the real coup needed General Njoku out of the way so they could get "a clean shot" at the main target. They had successfully framed and effectively eliminated him.

When Mr. Douglas Ngwube returned and the discussion resumed, Lt. Col. Emmanuel Ifeajuna suddenly became more divulgent. He told the "In-Group" that "Ojukwu must be forced out" and replaced by Gen. Victor Banjo, who would then "negotiate the cease-fire and thereafter, continue the struggle." He had contacted some of his military colleagues in the field, and they were in agreement with the head of state's ouster, for the reasons that he had "fooled" the nation into seceding, gone to war unprepared, and was running a "one-man show." Messrs Uche Chukwumerije and David-Osuagwu reminded him that the head of state's popularity with ordinary Biafrans was stratospheric and asked to know how he and his military colleagues would satisfactorily explain toppling him. The lieutenant colonel replied that the military situation, even as bad as it was, could be manipulated further to exaggerate the peril. By so doing, they would strike mortal fear into the minds of the populace and make them more receptive to change. He wondered out loud about what would happen if the people were to learn that Benin City had been lost and that Asaba was suddenly under threat. Or that the enemy, thought to be at Opi, were already at Ukehe. Major Alale then spoke up, reassuring the "In-Group" that organized labor would be out in the streets all over the country demonstrating in support of the change.

TOWARD UNDERSTANDING THE NIGERIA-BIAFRA WAR AND LINGERING QUESTIONS

Lt. Col. Emmanuel Ifeajuna then proceeded to provide details of the operational plan and apportion roles. The exercise would take place the next day, September 19, 1967. He expected the "In-Group" to have gathered in the head of state's living room by 2130 as it usually did. He would have troops deployed just outside the State Lodge perimeter, and at 2200, Mr. Douglas Ngwube would come and meet him at the main entrance of State Lodge with information about the whereabouts of the head of state and what he was up to. If he had come down to the living room and was lounging with the "In-Group," Mr. Ngwube would go back in and tell him that Lieutenant Colonel Ifeajuna was outside and wanted to share with him in private "a very serious and threatening development in the Army." Given the apprehension of the Army commander only twenty-four hours before, he would almost certainly step outside for the meeting, and once he did, troops under Lieutenant Colonel Ifeajuna's command would arrest and take him into custody. If, however, he was in the conference room, the guards at the gate would be disarmed, State Lodge would be taken by storm, and the head of state seized. According to this fanciful scenario, there would be a cease-fire within days of the removal of General Odumegwu-Ojukwu "to enable us regroup and rearm." He also promised that the execution of the plan would be "bloodless"—if followed to the letter!

With good timing, just as Lieutenant Colonel Ifeajuna was wrapping up his spiel, one of General Banjo's orderlies came to Maj. Philip Alale's chalet at about 9:30 p.m. to announce that the general had arrived from Benin City. They all drove over to the general's residence and sat down once again to more talks. He provided them with updates on the situation at the western front, the most stunning of which was that he had just ordered the withdrawal of troops from Benin City and would establish his headquarters at Agbor. According to him, the troops were in no condition to fight anymore and were retreating at the least contact with the enemy. This, however, was false. Benin City was not under threat as of September 18, 1967. The general's pull-out order was a strategic move to engineer chaos and frighten the daylights out of the citizenry, as hinted at by Lieutenant Colonel Ifeajuna earlier in the evening. He in turn asked to be brought up to speed on the developments in Biafra. Lt. Col. Emmanuel Ifeajuna and Mr. Samuel Agbamuche informed him that a decision had been made to remove both the commander, Biafran Army, Gen. Hilary Njoku, and the head of state, Gen. Chukwuemeka Odumegwu-Ojukwu, so he, Gen. Victor Banjo, could assume both military and political power. He thanked them "for reposing such confidence" in him. They agreed to meet the next day for one last review of the plan for the night while Lieutenant Colonel Ifeajuna and Maj. Philip Alale would touch base with their "collaborator" on the Northern front—no other than Lt. Col. Alexander Madiebo, commander of the Fifty-Third Brigade.

The head of Biafran Military Intelligence returned to his apartment that evening and reportedly weighed his options. They were only two, really. He had in his possession credible evidence of sedition. If he did not report it, then he was party to it and would be remembered ignominiously for all time. For all his promises, Lieutenant Colonel Ifeajuna did not have a reputation for delicacy. He would not hesitate to raze State Lodge if he needed to, and on the other hand, it was most unlikely that the head of state would be seized without stiff challenge. If he reported it, then he would have done his duty. Heads would still roll eventually but probably fewer than in the former scenario. By midnight, his mind was made up. He wrote a report and was joined by Messrs David-Osuagwu and Uche Chukwumerije, who were in agreement with passing on the information to the head of state. The trio headed over to State Lodge, arriving there at about 0145.

The head of state was happy to see them. He had just emerged from an Executive Council meeting but was still bright-eyed. They chatted briefly about the general situation, and it transpired that Gen. Victor Banjo had not bothered to communicate with the head of state since returning to the Mid-West. The head of state did not even know that the general was in town. The intelligence chief then told him that a plot to topple his government was about to unfold in a matter of hours and handed him his report and the tape recording of the meeting of the previous evening at Major Alale's chalet and General Banjo's quarters. The head of state quickly recovered from the shock of the dreadful news, and for the next three hours, they brainstormed for the best course of action that would solve the problem with the least possible perturbation. Eventually, it was the head of state himself who came up with what they agreed was "brilliant" and "perfect." In a nutshell, all concerned would be summoned to State Lodge in the morning and confronted with the evidence, their individual statements would be obtained, and in the evening, the Gang of Four—Gen. Victor Banjo, Lt. Col. Emmanuel Ifeajuna, Maj. Philip Alale, and Mr. Samuel Agbamuche—would be put on a flight to Lisbon, Portugal, where they would be let loose to proceed as they chose. The intelligence chief and his colleagues left State Lodge at 0522 and were told to report back at 0830.

Maj. Philip Alale had visited Lieutenant Colonel Madiebo in the morning of September 15, 1967, at Nkalagu, where he had his tactical headquarters. The major bemoaned the imminent loss of the war and got the brigade commander to agree with him that external mediation of the conflict had become a critical necessity before flying the kite that the nations that were willing to intervene would not do so with Lt. Col. Chukwuemeka Odumegwu-Ojukwu as head of state. He then left for Benin City. Early in the morning of September 19, 1967, the major returned to Lieutenant Colonel Madiebo's tactical headquarters, this time with Lt. Col. Emmanuel Ifeajuna. They pitched the plan again to Lieutenant Colonel Madiebo, who then asked them what would happen if the head of state insisted on leading the negotiations himself. They replied that he would be forced out if he refused to step aside, and the plan was for him to be replaced by Lieutenant Colonel Madiebo! The brigade commander confessed that their scheme filled him with foreboding and that matters of that kind were better left to civilian leaders. He promised he would come to Enugu to meet with senior military officers as well as prominent civilians. Obviously, the conversation had not gone as planned. They had hoped Lieutenant Colonel Madiebo would buy into the plot, agree to collapse the frontline to Ukehe, and make available troops for use in Enugu in the coming days in case there was resistance to the coup that needed to be quelled. As they left Nkalagu, they asked

Lieutenant Colonel Madiebo to ensure that he met with General Banjo when he came to Enugu.

When the head of intelligence and his colleagues came to State Lodge in the morning of September 19, 1967, the head of state greeted them with the information that the agreement they had reached earlier on how to deal with the coup plotters would no longer apply. He had conferred with some senior army officers and civilian leaders and they had strongly recommended that the full weight of the law be brought to bear. There would indeed be a trial, and he asked them to turn themselves in at the police headquarters to assist with the investigations and prosecution.

Also in the morning of September 19, 1967, Lt. Col. Emmanuel Ifeajuna visited Gen. Philip Efiong at his Militia Officer Training Camp offices. He made a request for men and equipment ostensibly for the defense of Obubra. General Efiong, who was also chief of logistics, gave him a patrol of thirty militiamen and an officer, armed with rifles. The next day, he would try again to obtain more troops and arms but was told to direct his request to the commander in chief since all available resources had been earmarked for reinforcement of the Nsukka-Enugu sector. In the event, the militiamen were not sent to the Obubra front but were encamped in the outskirts of Enugu to await instructions.

Lt. Col. Alexander Madiebo came to Enugu on September 19, 1967, soon after Lieutenant Colonel Ifeajuna and Major Alale left his headquarters and went straight to Army Headquarters to meet with the commander, Biafran Army, Gen. Hilary Njoku. Unbeknownst to him, the general had been arrested the night before. He was, however, able to share his information with Cols. Conrad Nwawo, Sylvanus Nwajei, and Patrick Anwuna. It would appear Colonel Anwuna was one of the senior officers the head of state had consulted, and Lieutenant Colonel Madiebo's name did come up as a conspirator. As a result, the colonel initially refused to meet one-on-one with him. Perhaps for the same reason, Dr. Akanu Ibiam, Mr. Alvan Ikoku, and Mr. Christopher Mojekwu had headed out that same morning to Lieutenant Colonel Madiebo's headquarters to hear from him what the situation was in his theater of operations.

TOWARD UNDERSTANDING THE NIGERIA-BIAFRA WAR AND LINGERING QUESTIONS

Not finding him, they returned to Enugu, and Lieutenant Colonel Madiebo learned of their trip while still at Army Headquarters. He went over to Dr. Akanu Ibiam's office, and all three civilian leaders were still there. He told them what had transpired at his headquarters earlier that morning. They arranged for him to meet with the head of state, who was equally satisfied with his assurances of loyalty and commitment to the cause.

The night of September 19, 1967, came and passed without incident. In the evening of September 20, an emergency meeting of the Biafran leadership (executive council, Strategic Committee, and according to General Efiong, the inspector general of police Chief Patrick Okeke, the chief justice Sir Louis Mbanefo, Sir Francis Akanu Ibiam, Dr. Michael Iheonukara Okpara, and Professor Eni Njoku) was convened. Prominent chiefs and elders from Owerri were also invited to attend for the reason that one of their sons, Gen. Hilary Njoku, was "making trouble." His removal was announced, and he would remain in detention for the rest of the war. According to General Efiong, the head of state offered him the position of commander, Biafran Army, but he declined and was appointed chief of general staff instead. Lieutenant Colonel Madiebo was promoted to the rank of brigadier general and given General Njoku's job. The commander in chief informed the meeting about the plot to overthrow the government. They sat all night, recessed briefly in the morning, and then went back into session.

Apparently, the Gang of Four were still at large as of September 21, 1967, because Maj. Philip Alale was seen on State Lodge grounds. Soon afterward, he and his coconspirators were rounded up by the police, deposed, and detained. Two counts were brought against all four and a third for Maj. Philip Alale alone. All the counts were under the Law and Order (Maintenance) Decree of 1967. The first count was "subversion," contrary to Section 13(a), and the second was "act intended to cause a breach of public order," contrary to Section 6(e). Major Alale's additional charge, also contrary to Section 6(e), was that "with intent to cause a breach of public order, did incite trade union leaders to hold mass rallies intended to overthrow the government of the Republic of Biafra." They all denied all the charges and were put on trial before a tribunal chaired by the distinguished jurist, the Honorable George Nkemena. The prosecution was led by the commissioner of police (Security) Mr. William Ugboaja. After he rested his case, Gen. Victor Banjo rose and delivered a stemwinder in defense of himself and his coconspirators. Unfortunately, their machinations were caught on tape. All four accused persons were found guilty on all counts. They were sentenced to death by firing squad on the first two counts. Maj. Philip Alale received a sentence of ten years in prison with hard labor for the third count. The head of state opted not to exercise his prerogative of mercy. On September 25, 1967, six days after the nipped coup would have taken place, they were summarily executed by firing squad at Akpaukwa Barracks, Enugu.

So, why did they do it? For Gen. Victor Banjo, it was the latest iteration of an obsessive quest for power, which, according to Gen. Hilary Njoku, could be traced back to 1960. All accounts of his interactions paint the picture of a frighteningly self-opinionated and ambitious individual. Most damaging was his treacherous disposition. When he contacted Lt. Col. Yakubu Gowon soon after the July 29, 1966, coup to enquire about his fate, he had been told he would be sent back to prison if he made it back to Lagos. The military governor of the then East soon released him from detention and actually gave him living quarters on State Lodge premises as his guest. After the proclamation of Biafra, he accepted the appointment of commandant of the militia and subsequently would agree to lead an expeditionary force through the Mid-West and West to Lagos when in fact, he had a different conflicting plan and was privately disavowing Biafra. He got to Benin City and resumed his negotiations with Lieutenant Colonel Gowon through the British Deputy High Commissioner. Precious time passed, and the window of opportunity closed on the campaign of his Liberation Army. It was at this point the two veterans of the January 15, 1966, coup, Lt. Cols. Ifeajuna and Adewole Ademoyega, who had served as his chief of staff at different times, pitched to him the proposal that he could overthrow the government of the Republic of Biafra, put paid to the rebellion, and use it as a bargaining chip. In his defense at his trial, he would say, "in my opinion, the minimum condition for the continued successful prosecution of the war have ceased to exist…" Indeed it might have, but that predicament was the result of a contrivance—his.

Lieutenant Colonel Ifeajuna's baggage from January 15, 1966, was obviously the impetus that drove him in the direction he went after he reached the conclusion that federal forces would prevail. They certainly would not treat him kindly if they laid hands on him, and his calculation was that if he somehow solved their "Ojukwu Problem" for them, he would be absolved of his sins.

In the critical months after Aburi, Maj. Philip Alale did more than most to whip up public awareness and sentiment, working with the Trades Union movement. When the shooting war started, he was fearless as he rallied troops panic-stricken after their baptism of fire. He was a revolutionary hothead whose politics was even to the left of Karl Marx's. He was committed to Biafra—but to a "proletarian" and not a "bourgeois" Biafra. The rebuff with which the Biafran leadership greeted the overtures of the Soviet Union as the storm clouds gathered must have appalled him. He was convinced that there were fifth columnists in the armed forces and very openly said so, to the intense displeasure of the top brass. The senior officers, whatever their attitudes to the politics of the moment, were professional institutionalists and did not take kindly to his affront. So, it was very poor judgment on his part to approach Lt. Col. Alexander Madiebo for support and laughably dangling before him the reward of head of state. In the end, even his Trades Union comrades, like Mr. Lucius Ezenwugo and Mr. Ebony Okpa, became frightened by his very incendiary rhetoric of violent revolution and testified against him.

Mr. Samuel Agbamuche, like Lieutenant Colonel Ifeajuna, had been actively involved in the January 15, 1966, coup and could expect no mercy from the Nigerian Army if he was captured. Nothing but a most dramatic propitiatory gesture would do, he might have thought. Besides, though, he had his differences with the Biafran head of state and his leadership style, as made clear in the final paragraphs of the draft memorandum he had prepared for consideration by the "In-Group." Unfortunately, he and his coconspirators had their own agenda, and handing the head of state a memorandum was really not one of the items on it. When the head of military intelligence met him on September 16, 1967, and learned that the meeting to continue the review of the draft memorandum would not hold as arranged because Lieutenant Colonel Ifeajuna and Maj. Philip Alale had traveled to Benin City, he anxiously remarked that precious time was being wasted. Mr. Samuel Agbamuche told him that it was possible that the memorandum might not be needed any longer after the pair came back from their consultation with General Banjo.

The Gang of Four, it turned out, was too clever by half. All along, the only use they had for the "In-Group" was to get at the head of state. They knew the members were very cerebral people (with Mr. Agbamuche in both camps) and would be receptive to well-reasoned analysis. As a matter of fact, most of the points set out in the Agbamuche draft memorandum were valid. Unfortunately, the document was merely a kite being flown. They were not even interested in pursuing the very sound advice that some of the criticisms were best left to senior civilian leadership to convey to the head of state. Mr. Douglas Ngwube was used to remove the commander, Biafran Army, Gen. Hilary Njoku. He, too, would have been the one to convey to Lt. Col. Emmanuel Ifeajuna the location of the head of state and the activity he was engaged in on the night of the coup, if not for the intervention of Lt. Col. Bernard Odogwu, Mr. Uche Chukwumerije, and Mr. Christopher David-Osuagwu.

Among them, the Gang of Four dissipated the only real opportunity Biafra had to bring the conflict to a quick resolution. If by August 10, 1967, the Twelfth Battalion of the Liberation Army had reached Ikeja, as was the plan, chances were that Britain would have been compelled to broker a cease-fire, to which Biafra would have reluctantly agreed. Instead, the commanding general halted the advance, opting instead to hold court in the Benin City while hatching the plot of his gang.

After the executions, an atmosphere of debilitating distrust descended and settled like a thick pall over the country. Major Alale had claimed months before that the regular armed forces were contaminated by saboteurs. Before the firing squad let fly on September 25, 1967, the witnesses avouched that they heard Lieutenant Colonel

TOWARD UNDERSTANDING THE NIGERIA-BIAFRA WAR AND LINGERING QUESTIONS

Ifeajuna yell that it was "too late" and that "the Nigerians are already in your midst." Indeed, the following day, the first artillery rounds aimed at Enugu by the Nigerian Army began to find their mark. Everybody—military and civilian—became suspect, and more often than not, the burden of proof was on the accused. If there was a readily available bogey to glibly blame, then the need to thoughtfully analyze failures and shortcomings and learn useful lessons from them no longer existed. This erosion of trust and epidemic of paranoia were probably the most crippling of the catalog of legacies bequeathed to Biafra by the Gang of Four.

Chapter 14

Enugu Falls—the End

After the fall of the strategic road junction, Opi, on September 08, 1967, the way to Enugu was clear. Federal forces of 1 Division (Col. Muhammad Shuwa) launched their assault to take the capital on September 12, 1967, and advanced relentlessly. They were opposed by the Fifty-First (Lt. Col. Chris Ude) and Fifty-Third (Lt. Col. Alexander Madiebo) Brigades of the Biafran Army, mostly fighting a rearguard action. Within two weeks, the outskirts of the city were within artillery range. Civilians began to leave, and by September 29, 1967, the city was largely evacuated.

Leading elements of 1 Division reached 9 Mile Corner on October 01, 1967. When the head of military intelligence and his "In-Group" comrade Mr. David-Osuagwu came to State Lodge that morning, the head of state was alone, other than for his household staff. They stayed with him. The defense of the city naturally fell to its garrison commander Col. David Ogunewe, but it did not appear communications were reaching the commander in chief. In the morning the next day, he sent the head of military intelligence to Army Headquarters to ascertain the military situation from the new general officer commanding (GOC) Gen. Alexander Madiebo. According to the emissary, the GOC was alone in his office, gazing at the ceiling. He was still awaiting the return of runners he had sent to the forward lines and so did not have the information the commander in chief was asking for. The head of military intelligence departed to return later in the day. When he did, Army Headquarters was completely deserted. Command and control of the Biafran Army from its capital city, Enugu, had collapsed.

The head of state was crestfallen, lamenting the continuing betrayal of his senior officers. He freely verbalized suicidal thoughts and refused to abandon his capital. The friends who had stayed with him, Lt. Col. Bernard Odogwu and Mr. David-Osuagwu, finally persuaded him to change his mind, and in the evening of October 02, 1967, General Odumegwu-Ojukwu left Enugu but would retreat no further than Awkunanaw in the outskirts to the south along the Enugu-Agwu Road.

As was its wont, the commander in chief's fighting spirit turned on a dime. No sooner had he arrived at Awkunanaw than he started to plan the defense of Enugu. He needed time to put together a combat unit whose operations he would oversee himself, since the regular armed forces, for all practical purposes, had fallen apart. Word had reached him that his GOC had set up his new headquarters about twenty-four miles to the south at Agbogugu. He would have to rely on "irregular" formations. A special task force commanded by Lt. Obed Onuaguluchi of the Biafran Air Force was encamped at Awkunanaw. He gave them orders to deploy to Milliken Hill and try to slow down the advance of the enemy. Next, he assigned Col. Frank Obioha the task of forming His Excellency's Special ("S") Brigade from predominantly militiamen. The colonel would be brigade commander and answer directly to him, not the GOC, Biafran Army.

Federal troops, led by Lt. Col. Theophilus Danjuma, entered Enugu but not until October 04, 1967. Unlike the regular army that did not contest the capture of the city, "irregular" Biafran forces, namely the militia and rangers, put up valiant resistance. The militia, including Chike Obi (PhD in mathematics, MIT 1950) and led by their commandant himself, engaged federal forces in very fierce fighting at the junction of Uwani, Awkunanaw, and Ogbete Roads near the police college, which action temporarily checked their advance along the Enugu-Awgu axis. A militia battalion, around which the "S" Brigade was being organized, remained at Awkunanaw, ready to ambush any federal forces that might attempt to break out of Enugu on that axis. The militia also stationed troops at Akagbe and, as raiding parties, sortied into the capital to harass federal forces. The rangers were commanded by Lt. Col. Timothy Onwuatuegwu. They also launched repeated attacks in heroic attempts to retake the capital. However, their efforts, too small in scope and sporadic in intensity, were ultimately futile. The effectiveness of the nascent "S" Brigade was also stymied by allegations of sabotage leveled against its commander, no less. Colonel Obioha, of course, had impeccable patriotic credentials, but his accusers were zealots. The head of state yielded to their demand that the commander be redeployed—fruit of the seeds sown by the Gang of Four.

Soon, challenges multiplied, and the recovery of Enugu could no longer receive undivided attention. On October 12, 1967, Lt. Col Murtala Muhammed's 2 Division made his first attempt to take Onitsha from Asaba across the River Niger. They received a drubbing at the hands of Maj. Assam Nsudoh and Maj. Joseph Achuzia. Six days later, 3 Division (Marine commando), commanded by Lt. Col. Benjamin Adekunle, landed an amphibious force at Calabar. The objective of the Biafran Army on the northern front shifted from recovery of lost territory to stabilization.

With the fall of Enugu and the collapse of the Mid-West campaign in the first week of October 1967, Biafra never regained the military initiative, except for a brief period during March–April 1969 when the Sixteenth Brigade, 3 Division (Marine commando) of the Nigerian Army, commanded by Lt. Col. Edet Utuk, was destroyed in Owerri. It had entered the city on September 16, 1968, but was contained and eventually encircled. After six months of punishing raids, the "V" Battalion of Lt. Col. Lambert Ihenacho's Sixty-Third Brigade, commanded by Maj. Cyril Anuforo, moved in to finish off what was left of the invading force. They resisted for less than twenty-four hours then, under cover of darkness, broke south and fled in the direction of Umuguma. The brigade commander, who was related to the Biafran chief of general staff by marriage, made it out alive. His brigade-major, Maj. Ted Hamman, did not. He was cut down by sniper fire on April 19, 1969. According to one estimate, Lt. Col. Benjamin Adekunle's 3 Division (Marine commando) lost approximately 2,700 men in Owerri.

PART 5

MASS STARVATION— NIGERIA AND THE INTERNATIONAL COMMUNITY

The Nigeria-Biafra War was the first conflict on the African continent in which one of the adversaries openly avowed a policy of mass starvation and the consequences were there for the rest of the world to see in real-time. The Canadian scholar Michael Ignatieff described it as the dawn of the "age of televised disaster." At dinner time every day, television brought the unfolding horror into the homes of Europeans and North Americans with the evening news. Before that conflict, there had been instances of the death of large numbers of Africans as a result of government policies that deprived them of access to means of sustaining life, but the numbers were generally under the "great famine" threshold of a hundred thousand or more dead (12,000 Africans [and 20,000 Boers] in British concentration camps during the Anglo-Boer War of 1899–1902; 40,000 Herero and 10,000 Nama in German Southwest Africa [present day Namiba] in 1904) and they occurred in the context of colonial rule. The Nigeria-Biafra War was a civil conflict, and by even the most conservative estimates, the number of Biafrans starved to death was over one million, predominantly children.

Hutter (2015) remarked that anything of value can be weaponized. Since food is essential to sustaining life itself, starvation is a very tempting candidate. Not surprisingly, references to its use as a weapon of war are found in some of the earliest reliable historical documents of warfare itself. In 406 BC for instance, Sparta reportedly starved Athens into submission. More recently, the German Army laid siege to Paris on September 19, 1870, during the Franco-Prussian War, and the city capitulated on January 28, 1871. During the First World War, the Central Powers (Germany, Austria-Hungary, Turkey) were blockaded by the Allies, especially Britain, which was the preeminent naval power of the day. By 1915, German imports and exports had fallen to 45 percent and 53 percent of prewar levels respectively. Seeking to break the blockade, the German High Seas Fleet (Vice-Adm. Reinhard Scheer) mounted repeated challenges to the British Grand Fleet (Adm. John Jellicoe), culminating in the inconclusive Battle of Jutland during May 31–June 01, 1916. Later that year, Hamburg was hit by famine. Berlin, Vienna, and the Rhineland were to suffer the same fate the following year. Germany surrendered on November 11, 1918. The siege of Leningrad began on September 08, 1941, when Army Group North of the Wehrmacht (Mar. Wilhelm von Loeb) reached the head of the Neva River at Lake Ladoga. It lasted 872 days, making it perhaps the longest and costliest in human lives in recorded history. According to Walzer (1977), more civilians died in the siege of Leningrad than the firebombing of Hamburg, Dresden, and Tokyo and the atomic bombing of Hiroshima and Nagasaki combined. The mind boggles at the enormity of such carnage.

In the accepted sense of war as hostile interaction between belligerents, there is no evidence that starvation is an effective weapon. Analysis reveals that in the instances where it seemed to be associated with realization of the intended outcome, it actually had little direct effect on the combatants. The National Guard defending Paris during the siege of 1870 did not lack for food and probably had more than enough to drink. During the First World War, the field rations of German soldiers were intact, and they generally remained in fine fighting fettle, launching major offensives (e.g., Kaiserschlacht) until less than six months before the Armistice. Although the food supplies of troops of the Leningrad Front (Gen. Leonid Govorov) defending the city during the siege of 1941–1944 were drastically cut, they had enough to enable them to stay in the fight. During January 12–30, 1943, they were able to participate in a joint offensive (Operation Iskra) with the Volkhov Front (Gen. Kirill Meretskov), which successfully opened up a tenuous but vital sixteen-kilometer-wide corridor between the two Fronts just south of Lake Ladoga. As was pointed out by Dr. Jean Mayer, tenth president of Tufts University and consultant to the Food and Agriculture Organization (FAO), World Health Organization (WHO), and United Nations International Children's Emergency Fund (UNICEF), "armed men seldom starve." Hence, a party that wields starvation against its counterpart in conflict is really aiming at hurting noncombatants and not legitimate belligerents.

Conley and de Waal (2019) have studied famines and atrocities historically across the world and identified the following as the uses to which starvation has been put: (1) killing en masse, (2) reducing the capacity of a group to resist perpetrator policies, (3) gaining territorial control, (4) material extraction or theft, (5) flushing a group out of a remote area into perpetrator control, (6) coercion of compliance, (7) exploitation of human resources as slave labor, (8) war provisioning, (9) social engineering. Some of these uses overlap (e.g. [2] and [6]), and in some others, starvation is not so much the tool as it is the collateral outcome of some other policy (e.g. [8] and [9]). Nevertheless, their characterization is consistent with the flexibility in their definition of starvation as reflected by the features of the phenomenon they describe.

Conley and de Waal (2019) also highlighted three key features of starvation, namely the diversity of deprivations that qualify as acts of starvation, their intersections, and the fact that starvation is a process that takes time to reach full effect. The deprivation of the ability to obtain food is the key element of starvation. It includes the destruction or denial of access to objects such as food and, in conformity with the Geneva Conventions and the Rome Statute, the prevention or obstruction of activities relevant to food acquisition such as working, trading, or foraging. Additional deprivations include reducing the means and capacities of mothers to care for young children as well as destroying health facilities, habitation, and shelter.

In some instances, the deprivation is brought about by economic policies formulated advertently or inadvertently by the perpetrator which operate to the disadvantage of the victim group. Such policies aggravate inequalities, undermine development, create food insecurity and subvert health-care systems.

The third troubling feature of starvation is that it unfolds slowly, over months or even years. It however declares itself in unmistakable warning signs as it takes hold. In every famine in recorded history, the human toll in misery and slow agonizing death, especially of the most vulnerable in society, has always been well-known for extended periods of time to persons with the power to alter the course of events. It is for this reason that perpetrators, in anthropogenic cases of mass starvation, deserve to be summoned to answer for heinous atrocity. It is against the above background that the use of starvation by Federal Nigeria as a weapon in its war against Biafra will be examined.

Serial pogroms in Northern Nigeria in 1966 of which Easterners were victims set off waves of exodus back to the East, which, according to the 1963 census, was the most densely populated part of the country (420 per square mile). The population grew by 15–20 percent with the influx of 1.6–1.8 million refugees. Contrary to agreements reached at Aburi, Lt. Col. Yakubu Gowon in his press conference on January 26, 1967, reneged on the commitment to pay the salaries of federal workers who had fled for their lives because the federal government had failed to provide them with the security they needed to continue to live and work in parts of the country other than their region of origin. On March 31, 1967, Lt. Col. Chukwuemeka Odumegwu-Ojukwu enacted edicts to enable him to appropriate the federal revenues collected in the East for the purpose

TOWARD UNDERSTANDING THE NIGERIA-BIAFRA WAR AND LINGERING QUESTIONS

of rehabilitating the displaced persons under his jurisdiction whom the federal government had turned its back on. It is worth noting that oil revenues were not affected since they were paid directly to Lagos. Less than three weeks later, Lieutenant Colonel Gowon proposed to his Supreme Military Council that the East be sanctioned economically and diplomatically. He also hinted that military action would be needed for the sanctions to succeed. On May 27, 1967, he proceeded to declare a state of emergency, impose a total blockade on the East and divide the territory into three states. Three days later, the East seceded.

The blockade of the Atlantic seaboard to the south by the Nigerian Navy was hermetic. To the east, the Cameroons were hand-in-glove with Federal Nigeria and were in due course handsomely rewarded with the Bakassi Peninsula in the Maroua Declaration of June 01, 1975. Biafra was invaded from the North on July 06, 1967, and the West across the River Niger during the first week of October 1967. By the end of that year, the fertile Cross River basin in the eastern part of the country had been lost, and by mid-April 1968, the equally rich farmlands in the southern provinces fell to federal forces. Territorial gains by the Nigerian Army continued, and Biafra shrank to about 9,000 square miles by August 1968—from 29,848 square miles at proclamation. In the process, the vast majority of the inhabitants of the occupied areas, estimated at about five million, were displaced inward. The absorptive capacity of the extended family system, long since overtaxed by the influx from the North, was quickly overwhelmed. Schools, which were no longer in session, became refugee camps. Domestic food production became increasingly inadequate as agriculture collapsed. The main sources of protein in the diet, beef from the North and stockfish that used to come in by sea from Scandinavia, had vanished. By mid-1968, the incidence of protein-calorie malnutrition had increased alarmingly. The Catholic charity Caritas, the World Council of Churches (WCC), and the International Committee of the Red Cross (ICRC) took notice.

Now landlocked, the only means for victualing unoccupied Biafra would be a land corridor through federal-held territory and/or an air bridge. On July 08, 1968, Dr. Okoi Arikpo, who was Nigeria's foreign minister, proposed a land corridor that would run from Lagos to Enugu and then to Awgu, where the forward lines were. The supplies would be deposited "in the middle of the road for the rebels" to come and pick up. General Odumegwu-Ojukwu held a press conference at Aba on July 17, 1968, at which he offered two alternatives that Biafra would accept, namely for the relief materials to be brought up the River Niger in barges to the Biafran port of Oguta or for the city of Port Harcourt to be placed under neutral international control to receive them and then convey them the short distance to the forward location just north of the city where the Biafran Red Cross would take delivery of them. At the peace conference convened in Niamey, République de Niger, that month by the Committee on Nigeria of the Organization of African Unity, both delegations had the opportunity to discuss the relative merits of their different proposals. It turned out that the Biafran offer of a riverine corridor to Oguta won out on the basis of all the criteria for a relief corridor to which both sides had agreed beforehand. Flummoxed, the Nigerian delegation declared it was no longer going to deal. Its leader, Mr. Allison Akene Ayida, in his best effort at explaining his delegation's new position, told a horrified world that "starvation is a legitimate weapon of war, and we have every intention of using it on the rebels." Starvation is, of course, not a legitimate weapon of war, and we will return to this blatant admission of inclination to atrocious conduct.

Thus it was that an air bridge became the only means of bringing in relief supplies from the outside world to Biafra. As the alarm bells of an impending cataclysm began to sound, the ICRC made repeated appeals to the federal government to guarantee safe passage to clearly marked Red Cross aircraft, and all were turned down. Caritas and the WCC knew not to bother with Lagos and made their own arrangements. From the earliest days of the conflict, the government of Biafra had contracted with an American, Mr. Henry "Hank" Wharton, to fly in arms and ammunition from Lisbon, Portugal. In gun-running circles, he was known as Hanky-Panky, with its undertone of a potential for perfidy. Mr. Wharton had a monopoly on the route and his three Super Constellation aircraft flew twice a week. Caritas and the WCC had stockpiled large quanti-

TOWARD UNDERSTANDING THE NIGERIA-BIAFRA WAR AND LINGERING QUESTIONS

ties of food and medications from generous European donors and, in the early months of 1968, began to purchase space not taken up by war matériel in Mr. Wharton's aircraft for the purpose of delivering what they could of those relief supplies to Biafra. On April 08, 1968, the ICRC felt compelled to join them.

Port Harcourt and its airport were lost on May 24, 1968, but "Annabelle," the airstrip at Uli, quickly became operational. A few weeks later in June 1968, Mr. Leslie Kirkley, the director of the Oxford Committee for Famine Relief (OXFAM), visited Biafra and was devastated by what he saw. He estimated that unless three hundred tons of relief supplies were brought into Biafra on a daily basis, nearly half a million children would develop kwashiorkor, a protein-calorie malnutrition syndrome, within six weeks and eventually die. Upon his return to London, he briefed ministers of the Labor government of Mr. Harold Wilson. Meanwhile, the reporting of journalists who had accompanied him to Biafra, complete with photographs of emaciated, almost skeletal children, had hit the newsstands. Decent humanity was scandalized, and the Wilson government was shamed into asking Lagos for permission to enable Red Cross planes to fly relief supplies to Biafra. On July 05, 1968, within a day or so of receiving the request, Gen. Yakubu Gowon petulantly replied that he would order any Red Cross aircraft bound for Biafra shot down. Eleven months later, to the day, June 05, 1969, the general made good on his threat. A Soviet MiG 17 jet fighter of the Nigerian Air Force flown by an Australian mercenary shot down in broad daylight an unambiguously marked DC-6 relief aircraft of the International Red Cross. The pilot, Capt. George Brown, was an American veteran of the Second World and Korean Wars. His copilot and flight engineer were Swedes, and the loadmaster was Norwegian. All perished.

Shocked, the international community paused its efforts to win Nigeria's cooperation with the relief effort. With the tacit support of the Wilson government, the Soviet Union, and to a lesser extent the State Department of the United States of America, Nigeria could afford to be intransigent and nonchalant. Its enablers suggested that General Odumegwu-Ojukwu and Biafra were "hyping" the crisis and using it to propaganda advantage. The situation did not need to be "hyped"—it was gruesome enough as it was. All visitors to Biafra went wherever they chose, with the exception, perhaps, of sensitive military installations, without restriction, and all, without exception, came to the same conclusion—that a catastrophe of epic proportions was unfolding before their very eyes. Also, the oft-repeated trope that General Odumegwu-Ojukwu should have accepted the land corridor which Federal Nigeria was comfortable with, if he really cared about suffering Biafran children, is specious. It merely fits in the mold of using starvation to coerce compliance. The counterproposals made by Biafra had more logistic merit on analysis.

A couple of months after Capt. George Brown's plane was shot down, the ICRC drew up a plan for daylight relief flights from Cotonou, the capital of then Dahomey, to Uli during the hours of 0900 and 1800, with the cargo inspected in Cotonou by Nigerian officials for benign content. The Nigerian officials also could accompany the flights into Biafra, if they so wished. In return, Federal Nigeria would provide guarantees that the flights would not be molested during the specified time window. They presented the plan to the Biafran government, which, on August 29, 1969, gave its assent. It was then taken to Lagos, where the Nigerian government promptly expressed misgivings and by September 14, 1969, decided to sign on to it with provisos, chief of which were that the time window would close one hour earlier, that the Nigerian authorities would remain at liberty to order any relief flight to land in Nigeria during its overflight of Nigerian airspace, and that the agreement would not in any way interfere with the military operations against Uli. The ICRC brought back its plan, now amended to incorporate Nigeria's brow-raising conditionalities, to Biafra, and predictably it was rejected.

Relief activities did expand after July 1968, as supplies began to arrive by ship at Sao Tome, the Portuguese island colony about 300 miles off the Atlantic coast of Biafra. Relief agencies purchased their own aircraft, but Mr. Hank Wharton insisted that his contract extended to their use. Only he and his pilots had the vital landing codes for Annabelle. It was not until the end of July 1968 that the

TOWARD UNDERSTANDING THE NIGERIA-BIAFRA WAR AND LINGERING QUESTIONS

Biafran side decided to break his monopoly. The codes were passed on to a representative of the ICRC in Addis Ababa, Ethiopia. The ICRC then shared the codes with the other relief agencies. Mr. Hank Wharton was none too pleased.

The ICRC set up shop at Fernando Po, a Spanish island colony only about forty miles off the Biafran coast and flew its first mission into Biafra on the night of July 31, 1968. In October, Equatorial Guinea, of which the island was a part, gained its independence from Spain and promptly came under pressure from Nigeria to discontinue its collaboration with the ICRC. It succumbed in December, and the ICRC pulled out to Sao Tome and Cotonou. Soon after "gaining their independence" from Mr. Hank Wharton, Caritas, the World Council of Churches and Nord Church Aid merged their operations under the name of Joint Church Aid (JCA). Two other organizations flew mercy missions into Biafra, namely the French Red Cross, independently of its contributions to the ICRC, and Africa Concern, a nongovernmental agency founded by Mr. Aengus Finucane and Rev. Father Raymond Kennedy, to deliver the contributions of the people of the Republic of Ireland. Both ran their shuttles out of Libreville, Gabon, with one aircraft each.

In the month of October 1968, the Nigerian Air Force began to attack Uli Airport at night. They used a Dakota transport plane converted into a bomber, and it was flown by a South African mercenary who hovered for two to three hours each night, dropping bombs at intervals. He introduced himself as "Mr. Genocide" in his radio transmissions for the benefit of relief flight crews to dispel any doubts as to his intentions. The relief flights usually kept their distance until he was done, and none was damaged. Nonetheless, these escapades of Mr. Genocide were nerve-wracking. Their claim to legitimacy was that Mr. Henry Wharton's flights were also coming into Uli, and so they went on for about seven months. On May 24, 1969, the Biafran Air Force destroyed Mr. Genocide's aircraft on the ground in a raid on Benin Airport. The Soviet Union responded almost instantly, providing Nigeria with MiG 19 fighter jets and East German pilots to fly them. They went into action in the night of June 02, 1969, riddling a JCA DC-6 aircraft with cannon fire as it made its final landing approach. By good fortune, there were no casualties and the aircraft was salvaged. The danger to relief flights thus remained.

The justification of attacks on Uli on the basis of Mr. Hank Wharton's operations was obviously a dubious distraction. On August 13, 1968, General Odumegwu-Ojukwu decided to sign over the airstrip at Obilagu to the ICRC for daylight flights dedicated exclusively to the delivery of relief supplies. It was upgraded by Swiss architect Mr. Jean Kriller, who also painted a huge red cross inside each of three sixty-foot-wide white disks on the runway to facilitate identification. Lagos refused to acknowledge its neutrality, and the Nigerian Air Force promptly began to bomb it on August 20, 1968. Paradoxically, the markings that were supposed to protect it made it such an easy target. A few weeks later, 1 Division of the Nigerian Army launched an offensive in the direction of Obilagu, and it fell on September 23, 1968.

Not only did Federal Nigeria refuse to cooperate with ICRC, it actively harassed senior officials of the organization who did not subscribe to its way of thinking. The case of Dr. August Lindt will illustrate. Dr. Lindt was the Swiss ambassador to Moscow when in July 1969, he was asked to take over and coordinate the ICRC effort in the Nigeria-Biafra conflict. After Capt. George Brown was shot down on a daylight mission, the Geneva headquarters of the ICRC suspended all its relief operations. Dr. Lindt, however, did not see why night flights by the ICRC could not continue since the JCA had pressed on without pause. He won the argument and approval to resume was given, much to the displeasure of the authorities in Lagos. On the night of June 10, 1968, Capt. Lofto Johanssen flew two successful ICRC missions into Uli from Cotonou. Earlier that day, Dr. Lindt had traveled to Moscow to retrieve his belongings. When he returned to Lagos four days later, he was arrested at the airport on trumped-up charges and, after a few hours of detention, declared *persona non grata* and expelled. On June 19, 1969, Dr. Lindt resigned from the ICRC.

By the end of April 1968, the number of internally displaced persons in Biafra was estimated at 3.5 million. Empty schools had been converted into refugee camps, totaling about 650. They could house only about a million refugees and were easy targets for the MiGs and Ilyushins of the Nigerian Air Force flown by Egyptian pilots, who had, months before, been humiliated in the Arab-Israeli war. The camps were run by the Biafran Red Cross and peerless Europeans, including fifty nuns of the Order of the Holy Rosary of Ireland and eighty priests of the Order of the Holy Ghost of Ireland for Caritas, forty-seven missionaries and volunteers for the World Council of Churches, as well as sixty-five field personnel for the ICRC. They were paragons of piety, humaneness, and boundless compassion. There was never enough, but they did whatever they could with what there was, and many persevered until the very end.

In the six months following the press conference of June 1968 by Mr. Kirkley of OXFAM, only 14,347 tons of relief supplies were delivered (7,500 tons by the JCA and 6,847 tons by the ICRC), which was about eighty tons a night. Mr. Kirkley had estimated that three hundred tons a night was the threshold volume needed to avert a calamity. The death toll in the refugee camps rose steadily, starting at about four hundred per day and peaking at well over a thousand per day. As 1968 drew to a close, it was estimated that 500,000–750,000 children had died in territory controlled by the Biafran government. In 1969, the tonnage flown in increased. The president of Equatorial Guinea Mr. Francisco Nguema had personally intervened to permit the ICRC to resume operations at Fernando Po. Deliveries were to peak at about four hundred tons per night in the months of March and April 1969.

On June 12, 1969, the US consulate in Geneva called the ICRC and JCA offices, urging them to cancel relief flights that night because they would face grave peril if they did not heed the warning. They would not elaborate that night, but the agencies complied anyway. The following day, US officials revealed that their messaging was based on information received from Lagos that there was "some political trouble in Cotonou." It was, however, misinformation that had almost certainly been fed to gullible or conniving US Embassy staff for transmission to Geneva with the aim of disrupting relief operations. There was no "political trouble" in Cotonou. The ICRC thereafter took no further significant part in the Biafran relief operations. The JCA continued undaunted, shifting nearly two hundred tons per night during the second half of 1969.

Between its government and the people, the role of the United States of America was schizoid. As is often the case in international affairs, the people of the United States were spot-on right while their government wallowed in errancy. Dr. James F. Philips, who was a United Nations forward observer embedded with 3 Marine Commando Division of the Nigerian Army during the war, has remarked that the Johnson administration seemed to have no problem with a "One Nigeria Policy" that sought to unite peoples with millennia of disparate languages, traditions, and histories while stopping at nothing in efforts to keep peoples with millennia of common language, culture, and history divided in Southeast Asia. It, however, sold four C-97 Stratofreighters to the ICRC and JCA for token sums of money, paid for their running costs and other expenses incurred in the delivery of US relief by other means. The Nixon Administration did appoint Dr. Clarence Ferguson, a Rutgers University law professor, ambassador-at-large, and coordinator of the government's relief effort in 1969. His service was, however, anodyne and entirely forgettable. The people of the United States, on the other hand, were matchless in their magnanimity. The generosity of the American people accounted for at least 50 percent of all the commodities flown into Biafra.

By one count, a total of 5,314 mercy missions were flown, delivering about 60,000 tons of supplies. Mr. Frederick Forsyth commented that not one packet of food entered Biafra "legally," i.e., with Nigeria's consent. Everything that came in did so by breaking the Nigerian blockade. The quantities received at best hovered just above starvation level, and at least a million children died a kind of slow, harrowing death that seared itself into the collective consciousness. It all began with the federal government of the Republic of Nigeria under Lt. Col. (later General) Yakubu Gowon and ended with the federal government of the Republic of Nigeria under Lt. Col. (later General) Yakubu Gowon.

The federal government of Nigeria, under Lt. Col. (later Gen.) Yakubu Gowon, did nothing to prevent the waves of pogrom that

TOWARD UNDERSTANDING THE NIGERIA-BIAFRA WAR AND LINGERING QUESTIONS

triggered the mass exodus of Easterners from Northern Nigeria, resulting in the severe overpopulation of their home region.

The federal government of Nigeria refused to provide the refugees with the financial and other support they needed to be able to provide food for themselves.

The federal government of Nigeria imposed an economic blockade on the East, using its navy to prevent the importation of food from abroad, especially of stockfish, which was a major protein source for the people.

The federal government of Nigeria prioritized the occupation of the food-producing areas of Biafra using its army.

The federal government of Nigeria went to extraordinary lengths to thwart the efforts of international relief agencies to bring succor to the people, especially children, of Biafra, including the downing of clearly marked, unarmed aircraft carrying relief supplies by its air force.

The actions of the federal government of Nigeria were therefore fully conformant to a policy of mass starvation deliberately formulated at the highest level and openly proclaimed. That policy was first hinted at by Chief Anthony Eronsele Enahoro, the commissioner for information and labor, at a press conference at the United Nations in New York on July 08, 1968, when he hedged that "some may say that it (mass starvation) is a legitimate aspect of war." A couple of weeks later, Mr. Allison Akene Ayida, head of the Nigerian delegation to the peace talks at Niamey, Niger Republic, was more explicit on the subject as has already been stated. Then on June 26, 1969, the vice-chairman of the Federal Executive Council and commissioner for finance Chief Obafemi Awolowo spoke thus: "All is fair in war, and starvation is one of the weapons of war. I don't see why we should feed our enemies fat in order for them to fight harder."

In discussions of consequences for noncombatants in modern warfare, legal experts and others tend to prevaricate over premeditation and inevitable "collateral damage." Mr. Ayida spared them the quibbling. He used the words "We have every intention of using it on the rebels." Mr. Ayida was an Oxford graduate and fully cognizant of what he was saying in the English language. A case can be made that his utterance met the criterion of *dolus specialis*. Since such a policy implies the willingness to watch children shrivel and die a slow harrowing death, it bespeaks a heinously atrocious mindset of the utmost cruelty and criminality. Without a doubt, if Biafra had prevailed on the battlefield, Gen. Yakubu Gowon, Chief Obafemi Awolowo, Chief Anthony Enahoro, and Mr. Allison Ayida would have been brought to reckoning on the issue of Federal Nigeria's mass starvation policy. Had the conflict ended in a negotiated settlement under international auspices, it is also very likely that no effort would have been spared to ensure that some appropriate accounting for the lives of over one million children would be among the terms.

For all time, Gen. Yakubu Gowon, Chief Obafemi Awolowo, Chief Anthony Enahoro, and Mr. Allison Ayida will be associated with the infamy of a policy tantamount to infanticide on an industrial scale. In the decades after the conflict ended, they all had ample opportunity to acknowledge the depth of inhumanity to which they had sunk and attempt to salvage their reputations. All but the general are now deceased. His window of opportunity remains open.

To Mr. Allison Ayida's point, the purposeful starvation of civilians has actually long been recognized as a violation of the laws of war and was listed as such in the report of the Commission on the Responsibility of the Authors of the War and on Enforcement of Penalties after the First World War. In 1977, thanks in part to him and the horror of the Biafran experience, it was added to the Geneva Convention (Additional Protocols).

PART 6

ASSESSMENT

So, what went wrong? How was it the travelers who set forth so jauntily at dawn became benighted so soon after their first steps were taken? The answers, I believe, are to be found primarily in the failures of the political leadership of the East and, to a lesser extent, of the influential elite, who, even though they did not have their hands on the formal levers of power, should have been more circumspect and vocal.

CHAPTER 15

THE LEADERSHIP

From all indications, political acumen was not Lieutenant Colonel Odumegwu-Ojukwu's strong suit. His military instincts predisposed him to the centralization of key decision-making often in just himself, and to the extent that he sought external input, it was to the wrong kind of people that he turned. This was a serious, and as it turned out, fatal handicap when interacting with very experienced politicians like Chief Awolowo.

Politicians are a unique breed. They speak their own language, often saying things they don't mean or meaning things they don't say. Their loyalties are guided primarily, even exclusively, by their interests. They have no permanent friends or permanent enemies and will fraternize with whomever is instrumental to the furtherance of their interests. These interests are usually personal and collective in varying degrees, and politicians differ on the basis of the locus at which they situate on the spectrum from personal to collective. Chief Awolowo might have had his personal interests but was held in very high esteem among his Yoruba ethnic group because he was seen as guided primarily by collective sensibilities. Lieutenant Colonel Odumegwu-Ojukwu was clearly not in his league, politically speaking. The East had people of Chief Awolowo's stature, namely Dr. Michael Okpara and Dr. Nnamdi Azikiwe, but when the chief and his commission visited in May 1967, neither was invited to participate. I am sure they would have been better able to properly gauge the depth of sincerity of the chief and correctly discern his spoken and unspoken sentiments. Lieutenant Colonel Odumegwu-Ojukwu continued to communicate with Chief Awolowo, and it is plausible that the plan to commit Biafran lives to the liberation of Yorubaland might have been shared with him either directly or through General Banjo. If true, that is astounding. One suspects though that many years after the fact, General Odumegwu-Ojukwu might have come to realize his errancy. His rather clever, tongue-in-cheek remark at the time to the chief's passing in 1987 that he was the "best president Nigeria never had" was a fitting coda.

Arguably, all politicians have a price. Some are so cheap they can be bought for peanuts. Others drive a hard bargain and don't come easy. Regardless, all have a price. When the time came, Chief Awolowo named his price, and Sir David Hunt, the British high commissioner, got Lieutenant Colonel Gowon to pony up. The chief thereafter became literally a crusading convert to the federal cause. On one level, he is blameless. He got what he wanted for himself and his constituents. That is what politicians do, and the onus is on any aggrieved erstwhile partner to have an alternative, if not counteractive, plan B to invoke if and when original arrangements fall through. On another level, it is an inescapable conclusion that advocating and actively pursuing a policy of starvation as a weapon of war like he subsequently did, knowing fully well that the prime victims would be children, pregnant women, the old and infirm, came from a very sinister place.

It really didn't make sense to argue that First Republic politicians created the mess of interethnic animosity in the first place, and as a result, there was no further use for their judgment and ministrations. The fact of the matter was that the January and July 1966 coups did little more than exacerbate long-festering ethnic tensions. The organisms who best understood that kind of swamp and were best equipped to navigate it were the politicians of the ancien régime who inhabited it, and if they hadn't left the scene in other parts of the country, why should the Igbo relegate theirs to the background? It is difficult not to arrive at the conclusion that Lieutenant Colonel Odumegwu-Ojukwu, who, as of 1967, lacked the kind of political smarts needed to interact rewardingly with the likes of Chief Awolowo, either did not bother to seek the counsel of the right kind of political talent available to him or chose to listen to persons lacking in cognate wisdom. Either way, he was at a disadvantage when he began to transact with the chief and was outmaneuvered.

The often-heard contention that the West let the East down at a critical juncture in the crisis is worth revisiting. Here, the fingers point at the four "imperatives" Chief Obafemi Awolowo presented to Leaders of Thought of the West at their meeting at Agodi, Ibadan, on May 01, 1967. According to Mr. Odia Ofeimun, his one-time private secretary, they were that (1) a peaceful solution must be found; (2) the East must be encouraged to remain a part of the federation; (3) if the East was allowed by acts of omission or commission to secede from or opt out of Nigeria, the West and Lagos would also stay out of the federation; and (4) the West and Lagos would continue to participate in the ad hoc committee or any similar body only on the basis of absolute equality with other regions. There is a lot to unpack, but I am hard put to find anything of substance the "imperatives" offered the East, and I doubt that it was their intent.

On May 06, 1967, Chief Awolowo's National (Re)Conciliation Committee arrived in Enugu and held a whole day of talks with the military governor. In my view, the military governor should not have spent more than fifteen to thirty minutes with the delegation. What he owed them was a short welcome address after which he should have departed, leaving them an assurance that they could reach him by telephone should his input be needed. The substantive talking should have been left to the likes of Dr. Michael Okpara, Sir Francis Ibiam, Justice Louis Mbanefo, Dr. Pius Okigbo, and Police Commissioner Patrick Okeke. My reasoning behind this has already been outlined.

Chief Awolowo left Enugu on May 07, 1967, with the information that the East was irrevocably committed to secession. He demanded and got an assurance from the military governor that he would be given an advance notice of at least two weeks before the decision was made public. Mr. Wole Soyinka wrote in his memoir that he asked the chief why he wanted two weeks, but he would not let on. And neither would the only other soul who knew the answer, Police Commissioner

Emmanuel Olufunwa. When Mr. Soyinka continued that "hardly had Awolowo's delegation settled back into Federal territory than Ojukwu declared an Independent State of Biafra" and that "a short while after, Chief Awolowo accepted to serve as Commissioner of Finance under Yakubu Gowon," one is left wondering whether a cause-effect relationship is implied. Chief Awolowo had asked for fourteen days. Between the sixth and thirtieth of May 1967 were twenty-four days.

General Ojukwu also did not get the right measure of General Banjo and proceeded to invest far more trust and confidence in him than was warranted. Agreed the expeditionary force that invaded the Mid-West was by no means Panzer-class, but it was arguably in better fighting shape than any force Federal Nigeria could muster in that theater at the time. The available evidence is that Lt. Col. Festus Akagha's Twelfth Battalion could have readily overwhelmed any resistance as they rode that initial momentum and arrived at Lagos on August 10 or 11. The options open to Lieutenant Colonel Gowon and his junta would have been to either flee North by air or take refuge in the British High Commission. This was widely known by the elite in Lagos at the time, and one of my professors (MD, PhD [Oxford]) told us as much during one of his lectures in the mid-1970s. Interestingly, his lectures were usually about 40 percent medical and 60 percent everything else. You learned a lot from them, and this particular titbit is credible even when you allow that Oxonians are almost invariably a mutual adulation brotherhood.

How about a reassessment after the debacle of the Mid-West and the loss of the capital? Was October 1967 not the logical time to reevaluate then reconceptualize? According to Frederick Forsyth, who covered the war from the Biafran side, General Odumegwu-Ojukwu offered to stand down, but the Consultative Assembly declined and instead passed a vote of confidence in his leadership on October 11, 1967. I know nothing else about that deliberation and resolution, but on reflection, that was a missed opportunity for a critical reassessment of the Biafran leadership. Good leadership requires that the leader embody attributes valorized by the led. People of the East cherish enlightenment and high learning, capacity for hard work, drive, and steadfastness. Chukwuemeka Odumegwu-Ojukwu pos-

TOWARD UNDERSTANDING THE NIGERIA-BIAFRA WAR AND LINGERING QUESTIONS

sessed these attributes and more—he oozed charisma, and his oratorical skills were nonpareil. Also for truly great leadership, the historical circumstance needs to be really momentous as indeed the Nigerian crisis of the mid-1960s was. The most savage massacre in recorded African history up to that time, genocidal in scope by many accounts, had just been inflicted upon the people of the East. It would not be surpassed until the slaughter of the Tutsi by the government-trained Interahamwe and Impuzamugambi militias of their Hutu compatriots during April 07–July 15, 1994 (estimates range from 500,000 to 1,074,017). Did General Odumegwu-Ojukwu rise to the occasion?

The general surely had what it took to be a good, even great leader. However, the realization of potential was a different matter. Unanswered questions that bear upon the big strategic idea and the smaller tactical ones, the power to implement them and maneuver in the process of doing so, and the checks and balances on power swirl around his stewardship. The overarching imperative was that the people of the East, having been treated so horribly in Nigeria, deserved that anything and everything be done to ensure their safety and guarantee that they would never be similarly victimized again. A formal secession was one approach to this end, and I have already argued that its consequences did not appear to have been taken into full account and due consideration given to the alternative that was available. That other course of action was to have taken a rain check on Biafra, remained separate as the East (essentially Biafra in all but name), and just dared Lagos to lift a finger. I have serious doubts that federal forces could have defeated the East without foreign assistance, which would have been difficult for Nigeria to obtain if it could not claim that its territorial integrity had been violated.

Conceptually, therefore, the East started off on the wrong foot, and the empirical corroboration came within a few months. One would have imagined that, having been so badly bloodied on the battlefield, October–November 1967 would have been a "back to the drawing board" moment with EVERYTHING put on the table and reexamined with cold eyes. The head of state's close friends—the "In-Group"—got this idea, and one of them, Mr. Samuel Agbamuche, set it down, brilliantly for the most part, in a memorandum, which, with refinement and in the right hands, would have been a superb working document. Instead, he let it be hijacked by his coconspirators who were obsessed with physically eliminating the head of state.

According to General Efiong, General Odumegwu-Ojukwu strangely enough did contemplate surrender in July 1967 after the Nsukka front collapsed, saying he had no officers or armament. That was probably an extreme but fleeting thought in the exasperation of the moment. Instead, Biafra would in due course settle into a slugfest after the federal forces had picked off all the "low-hanging fruit"—the so-called minority areas. It was difficult for those areas to be defended for many reasons. The terrain, mostly riverine, was more challenging, especially in the absence of adequate equipment. Also the Federal Decree no. 14 of May 27, 1967, which granted them statehood and extricated them from perceived Igbo domination, made many of them eager collaborators of federal forces. However, for every Maj. Isaac Boro, there was a Capt. Ibikare Allwell-Brown; for every Lt. Col. Edet Utuk, there was a Lt. Col. William Archibong; for every Dr. Nabo Graham-Douglas, there was a Dr. Sylvanus J. Cookey; for every Dr. Okoi Arikpo, there was a Chief Matthew T. Mbu. Arguably though, it is easier to destroy than to build, and so, even if there was numerical parity between the opposing agencies, the prevalent effect would be that of those working to tear down Biafra.

Entirely surrounded by October 1967, the reality that Biafra could not defeat Nigeria militarily must have finally sunk in. What then became the strategy going forward? As I understood it, it was to continue fighting until the "conscience of the world" shifted in Biafra's favor. Clearly, that was a plan of action formulated without the benefit of analysis in appropriate depth. The repository of effective world conscience, to the extent that there was such a thing in matters of conflict, was the United Nations or, more precisely, its Security Council. But then, the organization had been very badly burned in the Congo a few years before and opted to stay in the shadows. Even if it had wanted to engage, the conscience portrayed would only reflect the sentiments of the Security Council members, which, in the dichotomous Cold War climate of the time, were predictably formulaic. Paralyzed by polarization, it would do no more than offer relief aid to refugees.

TOWARD UNDERSTANDING THE NIGERIA-BIAFRA WAR AND LINGERING QUESTIONS

Worse still for Biafra, the USSR and Britain, on opposite sides of the ideological Cold War divide, saw it fit to pitch their tents in the same (Nigerian) camp. This made Biafra appear just not worth the candle. Still, Biafra did stir the conscience of ordinary citizens all over Europe and North America, even as their governments looked the other way. At that level, Biafra clearly won the war for hearts and minds through its well-oiled propaganda machine led by Dr. Ifeagwu Eke (PhD [Harvard]) and the agency of MarkPress, the Swiss public relations firm. The British prime minister Mr. Harold Wilson wrote that Biafra "secured a degree of moral control over Western broadcasting systems, with a success unparalleled in the history of communications in modern democratic societies." Jimi Hendrix, perhaps the finest blues-rock guitarist of his generation (and probably still unsurpassed), and Joan Chandos Baez, the renowned folksinger and activist, performed at a benefit concert for Biafra in New York on August 08, 1968. So too the versatile Sammy Davis Jr. in London. On November 26, 1969, John Lennon of the famous rhythm-and-blues group Beatles renounced the Member of the British Empire (MBE) honor that had been bestowed on him and the rest of the group in 1965 and had his chauffeur Les Anthony return the insignia to Buckingham Palace in protest over British "involvement in the Nigeria-Biafra thing." Mass rallies were held in many cities, and ordinary folk raised their voices in condemnation of the carnage. Perhaps saddest of all, Bruce Mayrock, a student at Columbia University, self-immolated on May 29, 1969, at United Nations Headquarters, New York. Unfortunately, the arousal of conscience among the citizenry did not persuade anywhere nearly enough governments to make and act upon policy changes salvific from the Biafran standpoint.

As has been pointed out, the secretary-general to the United Nations U Thant and President Charles de Gaulle of France, Biafra's most highly placed sympathizer, repeatedly made it clear that ultimately, the solution of the Nigeria-Biafra crisis would be a political one and African countries were the ones to take the lead. The majority of African countries, for their part, left no one in doubt that their preference was for a solution that did not undermine the territorial integrity of Nigeria at a time colonial boundaries were worshipped—

in a fetishization of form. Why then did Biafra continue to insist that its sovereignty was not negotiable? Students of this period have variously blamed the person of General Odumegwu-Ojukwu, the general's inner circle, and the Consultative Assembly.

The main personal criticisms leveled against General Odumegwu-Ojukwu were vaulting ambition, overweening pride, obduracy, an autocratic disposition, and even insecurity. The general also had a reputation as an unrepentant ladies' man, and apocryphal reports allege that his amorous impulses fueled his long-running feud with one or some of his senior commanders.

General Odumegwu-Ojukwu was barely thirty-three years old when he was appointed military governor of the East. If that is not a time of life to be ambitious, I do not know when and so am not sure that ambition was the issue. It just happened that, as fate would have it, the stakes were much too high for youthful experimentation in the extraordinary position and circumstances he found himself. His sternest critics allege that the reason he proceeded with the premature proclamation of the Republic of Biafra and refused to negotiate its sovereignty was his personal ambition to be head of state. It would be very sad if that was the case. If negotiating away Biafra's sovereignty was more than he could stand, beyond October 1967, it had become obvious that Biafra could not assert itself through the force of arms or diplomatic clout. That was when it would have made perfect sense for him to step aside, like he eventually did in the night of January 09–10, 1970. Under far less desperate circumstances, a new team would have put sovereignty on the table and chances were, the mediators would have stood a better chance of successfully prevailing on Nigeria to discard Decree no. 14 and settle for a compromise confederal arrangement in exchange. Under such an arrangement, federal forces would have to return to preconflict borders, and outside the stifling embrace of the rest of Nigeria, the East could begin to march to its own drumbeat, which would, of course, include doing whatever it needed to do to ensure that it could successfully resist any attempt to suck it back into close embrace. And let's face it, over time, the East could decide to leave on its own terms, even if there was no secession clause in the compact. General Odumegwu-Ojukwu could

TOWARD UNDERSTANDING THE NIGERIA-BIAFRA WAR AND LINGERING QUESTIONS

return then and vie for leadership, if he chose to. Gen. Charles de Gaulle was head of the Quartrième (Fourth) République from the liberation of France in 1944 until 1946. He then left the political scene but returned in May 1958 as head to the Cinqième (Fifth) République. Even if General Odumegwu-Ojukwu did not return to power, his place in the annals of the history of the East was assured. After all, Moses did not reach the Promised Land with the Israelites.

As military governor, Lt. Col. Odumegwu-Ojukwu was administratively the chief executive of the East. He was also a soldier, and a good number of the senior officers who poured back home from other parts of the country were senior to him in rank in the Nigerian Army. This made for a rather prickly and uneasy relationship. Also among the returnee officers were perpetrators of the January 15, 1966, coup. Specifically, he had had a run-in with Maj. Chukwuma Nzeogwu, who led that coup in the North. He therefore might have felt a need to pick his company cautiously. On military matters earlier on, he relied heavily on the counsel of Lt. Col. Louis Chude Sokei, who operated as a roving inspector of formations and would later become commander, Biafran Air Force, after Gen. George Kurubo abandoned his command and fled to Lagos. Lt. Col. Sokei was killed on March 15, 1968, in the fighting to check the advance of 2 Division from Awka to Onitsha. The head of state subsequently transferred that trust to Lt. Col. Joseph Achuzia, arguably one of the finest tacticians of the war. He would often superimpose him on theater commanders when their sectors came under severe pressure and collapse threatened. I suspect the C in C's affection for Lt. Col. Achuzia was because he was such a "scrapper." All you needed to do was show him a fight and he would go at it with anything available, usually leading from the front. This was in sharp contrast with the regular troops and their commanders who, according to General Efiong, hankered after imported hardware and grumbled because it was in very short supply. The militia and forces under Lt. Col. Achuzia would readily go and do battle with the hand grenades, landmines, and rockets manufactured by the Research and Production Directorate, whose resourcefulness and ingenuity will live forever in the hearts and minds of the people of Biafra. After the war, in a move reminiscent of the Allied effort to keep alive the stupendous advances made by German scientists, especially in rocketry by Dr. Werner von Braun and his Peenemunde colleagues, Maj. Samuel Ogbemudia, then military governor of Mid-West State, dispatched a search party to seek out and lure Biafran scientists to his state with the promise of support and freedom to continue their research. A general staff officer found out and passed the information on to General Gowon. According to General Ogbemudia in the telling (personal disclosure 2016), the allegation was made that he was "trying to reconstitute Biafra." General Gowon called him and ordered a halt to his efforts. Gen. Samuel Ogbemudia was a fully assimilated Bini, but his forebears trace their origins to Igboland. It is worth contrasting his disposition to that of Col. Iliya Bisalla, commander of 1 Division, Nigeria Army, whom Mr. William Achukwu, Biafra's ordnance artificer *par excellence*, had tried to interest in his blueprints. The colonel reportedly ordered them incinerated. On March 11, 1976, he would be executed by firing squad for involvement in the February 13, 1976, coup.

General Odumegwu-Ojukwu had an ocean of superb civilian talent to tap and many distinguished names reverberate throughout the Biafra story—First Nigerian Republic politicians, trailblazers in academia, and highly sophisticated technocrats. Yet as is usually the case, it was the small coterie of advisers who had unhindered access to the head of state and could still talk to him after everyone else has been heard out that carried the most clout in decision-making. Two names stand out—Mr. Christopher C. Mojekwu and Mr. Francis Nwokedi. I have already offered a glimpse of the impact Mr. F. Nwokedi had on at least one of Biafra's lobbying efforts. Mr. C. Mojekwu was the commissioner for internal affairs. Mr. Ntieyong U. Akpan, chief secretary to the government and head of service, described him as "a man of the greatest influence on the Governor." He was likely related to the head of state and at least one account identified him as an uncle. Just about all accounts conclude that he was a malign influence. He was called to the bar at Gray's Inn, London. During the war, he was apparently entrusted with the most sensitive overseas assignments, especially those with significant financial components. He answered directly to the head of state and nobody else. After the war, he reaccredited at Northwestern University Law

TOWARD UNDERSTANDING THE NIGERIA-BIAFRA WAR AND LINGERING QUESTIONS

School, Chicago, and taught politics at Lake Forest College until his death in a motor vehicle accident four days before his sixty-second birthday in 1982.

The Consultative Assembly was the representative body set up to advise the military governor as the crisis unfolded. It comprised nominees of the provincial administrators and delegates nominated on the basis of their personal cognizance by the military governor. This latter category were mostly persons who had distinguished themselves in various fields of endeavor, trade, and student union leaders. There was this apocryphal anecdote about the inaugural sitting of the assembly on August 31, 1966. Dr. Nnamdi Azikiwe, first governor-general and subsequently president of Nigeria, had stood up to speak and let it be known that he felt slighted by his membership as a delegate nominated by his provincial administrator rather than by invitation of the military governor. The president of the student union of the University of Biafra reportedly interrupted him to ask if, other than wallowing in self-pity, he had a substantive contribution to make to the matter under discussion. It probably was downhill from that point on. Indeed, the military governor had deliberately slighted the former president at every opportunity, and it was common knowledge that there was no love lost between them. En route to Niamey, Niger, in July 1968, the Biafran delegation stopped over at Libreville, Gabon, for a meeting with President Albert-Bernard Bongo. When the time came for private talks with the host, General Odumegwu-Ojukwu chose Mr. Christopher Mojekwu, Mr. Francis Nwokedi, and Professor Eni Njoku to accompany him. Dr. Nnamdi Azikiwe and Justice Louis Mbanefo were left to wait in the dining room. A pained "Zik of Africa" remonstrated that the Biafran leadership had no appreciation or respect for his reputation, person, or age.

The story of Dr. Nnamdi Azikiwe's relationship with the Zikist Movement might offer a glimpse into General Odumegwu-Ojukwu's wariness about him. Dr. Azikiwe was very much a "pen is mightier than sword" exponent. Indeed, his trenchant newspaper articles in the 1940s lambasting British colonial rule burnished his nationalist credentials and won him a devoted following among the restive youth who had been chafing at the bit since the Ikoli-Akinsanya crisis of

JOSEPH NNODIM

1941 enfeebled then destroyed the Nigerian Youth Movement. On February 16, 1945, the Zikist Movement was inaugurated by four young men, Messrs. Kola Balogun (founding president), Michael (MCK) Ajuluchukwu, Abiodun Aloba, and Nduka Eze. They adopted Dr. Nnamdi Azikiwe as the embodiment of their nationalistic aspirations. In a matter of a few years, branches of the movement had been established in all major cities across the country, and organizations with similar orientation, like the Kano-based Anti-Color Bar Movement led by Mallam Raji Abdallah and Mr. Osita Agunwa, merged with it. Although affiliated with the NCNC, whose national president Dr. Azikiwe became in 1946, the Zikist Movement occupied a unique niche with a distinct ethos. True to the exuberance of the youthfulness of its membership, it favored direct action and had little patience for the ditherings of the regular political class. In 1948, they decided to expedite the showdown with the much despised imperialist, which they believed was inevitable, using their idol, Dr. Azikiwe, as bait. They reasoned that if they called for civil disobedience, British colonial authorities would arrest Dr. Azikiwe and hopefully throw him in jail, provoking a mass uprising which would render the country ungovernable. Their first move was a public lecture at Tom Jones Memorial Hall, Lagos, on October 27, 1948, delivered by the deputy president, Mr. Osita Agunwa, calling for a revolution. He, two other Zikists, and the chairman of the occasion, who was not a member of the movement, were arrested. The NCNC rallied to the support of movement, and the party executive called a mass meeting on November 07, 1948. In a memorable and passionate speech at the meeting, the president of the Zikist Movement, Mallam Raji Abdallah, described the Union Jack as a hateful symbol of domination, exploitation, persecution, and brutality. Needless to say, the colonial authorities were not amused. They arrested him and nine other leaders of the movement on charges of sedition. Knowingly, they skirted Dr. Nnamdi Azikiwe, not wanting to furnish the militant enterprise with a martyr. Martyrdom was, however, never in Dr. Azikiwe's calculations. He sought to dissociate himself as much as possible from the movement and its methods. The mass meeting of November 07, 1948, was supposed to have been chaired by him, but he failed to attend, pleading fatigue after a party business trip to Ijebu-Ode. Days later, he would describe the Zikists disdainfully as "fissiparous lieutenants and cantankerous followers." Understandably, many Zikists felt betrayed, and this episode was arguably one of the lowest points in the storied career of Dr. Azikiwe. The colonial police thereafter felt emboldened and on February 08, 1950, raided the offices of the movement all over the country, confiscating documents. Ten days later, Mr. Chukwuma Ugokwe made an attempt on the life of Sir Hugh Foot, the chief secretary to the government. He was arrested, tried, and sentenced to a dozen years in jail with hard labor. Two months later, the Zikist Movement was proscribed.

So, quite conceivably, General Odumegwu-Ojukwu might have contemplated the question of how much trust to repose in Dr. Nnamdi Azikiwe, given his track record with the Zikist Movement. It must be said though that in the trust department, the judgment of the general himself did not inspire much confidence, calling to mind his relationships with Chief Obafemi Awolowo, Gen. Victor Banjo, and Gen. George Kurubo. There was no indication that he appreciated that the only basis for durable trust in interactions with politicians happens to be agreement that benefits their self-interest of the time (personal or collective). Generals Banjo and Kurubo's inclinations in the Biafra story were more political than military.

In those heady days, especially after the Aburi meetings, the youth felt the widespread indignation more intensely than other demographic groups. They were literally incandescent, and naturally, the positions they espoused tended to be extreme. They idolized the military governor, and he no doubt drew energy from their adulation. Given the barbarism that Nigeria had inflicted on the East, the atmosphere was giddy, and the cooler heads in the Consultative Assembly must have had a very hard time making themselves heard. As such, the mandate conferred on His Excellency Lt. Col. Chukwuemeka Odumegwu-Ojukwu, military governor of Eastern Nigeria on May 27, 1967, to declare at the earliest practicable date Eastern Nigeria a free, sovereign, and independent state by the name and title of the REPUBLIC OF BIAFRA was probably mood-appropriate. However, May 30, 1967, was by no means the earliest practicable date by any stretch of the imagination. Notably though, on the same day as the

Consultative Assembly resolution, General Gowon broadcast the speech in which he reconfigured the country into twelve states. The sensitive man that he said he was, he invoked the Willink Commission report of 1958 and claimed that minorities had been subjected to violent intimidation by the Eastern Military Government. Was the proclamation of Biafra triggered by General Gowon's broadcast? If it was, it needn't have been. Indeed, tampering with the structural integrity of the East was one of the lines in the sand drawn by the military governor. However, formal secession in response raised the stakes substantially with no perceptible practical benefits to the East. As has been argued earlier, the East could have been better served confronting Federal Nigeria as such—the East, rather than as Biafra.

At subsequent critical stages of the conflict, why didn't the Consultative Assembly intervene with course-corrective injunctions? It would seem that the nature of governance changed drastically as the situation deteriorated and grew more complex. According to Mr. Raph Uweche, a small but cult-like followership developed around the head of state and insulated him from wise input. They were almost idolatrous in their devotion to him and were totally invested in his edification even at the expense of the best interests of the nation. Unable to get through to him, many gave up and gave out. Some who managed to penetrate the cocoon and had the courage to make their thoughts known were often greeted with a most counterproductive, even hostile, reaction. A case in point was the lead-up to the OAU summit meeting of September 1968 when Dr. Nnamdi Azikiwe, Dr. Michael Okpara, Professor Kenneth Dike, and Ambassador Raph Uwechue approached the C in C to make the case for a negotiated resolution of the conflict on the basis of an OAU-guaranteed confederal arrangement. The head of state took profound umbrage at the suggestion and asked some of them (I suspect Dr. Azikiwe and the ambassador) to either recant or resign. Dr. Azikiwe went into exile, and Ambassador Uwechue resigned.

Chapter 16

The Followership

How about the led? Were the ordinary people of the East blameless in all of this? Given the extended family structure of the Igbo and other ethnic groups in the East, the horrors of the pogroms of 1966 were felt in every home and hearth. Just about everybody had a skin in the game, and few needed more than a little prodding to show their indignation. Mass rallies took place all across the East in support of the administration and its policies, especially after Lagos reneged on the Aburi Accords. The slogan "On Aburi We Stand" was emblazoned on every surface. The messaging by the government was masterful, and nobody who lived in that era will forget NewsTalk on the radio which Mr. Okokon Ndem delivered in a uniquely sublime lilting prosody never heard before or since.

When eventually Biafra was proclaimed, she was received enthusiastically by the vast majority of the ordinary folk. For reasons I have already alluded to, opinion was divided in the so-called minority areas at which Federal Nigeria was dangling statehood. Nevertheless, some of the most full-throated endorsements originated therefrom. "Hail Biafra, the Land of Freedom," perhaps the best-selling popular recording of the time, was the handiwork of "Cardinal" Rex Jim Lawson, a Kalabari native. All in all, the majority ethnic group of the East, the Igbo, were naturally out in front and took the hardest knocks before, during, and after the conflict.

The Igbo defy easy analysis, and that is a confession one makes with abundant reason. The Aba Women's War of 1929 will be briefly described to illustrate. The British arrived in Igboland and were promptly confused by its political flatness, namely the absence of the kind of easily manipulable hierarchical organization they had encountered among the Yoruba and Fulani-Hausa. All they had needed to do was subdue or win over the Oba or the Emir and their subjects would fall in line. In Igboland, they were confronted with a political organization and authority pattern which appeared abstruse, even arcane (Dike 1956).

Among the Igbo, the largest political unit is the village group—an agglomeration of villages (*Ama* or *Nchi*) whose inhabitants share remote kinship (e.g., descent from a common ancestor) but intermarry. The village group, Owere (anglicized as Owerri) for instance, is made up of five villages (*Nchi Ise*)—Umurororonjo, Amawom, Umuodu, Umuonyeche, and Umuoyima—and the inhabitants are all descended from Ekwem Arugo. The government of the village group is vested in a representative assembly (e.g., Oha Owere). Each village is represented in the assembly by its custodians of *Ofo Umunna*, the symbol of authority derived from the ancestors. At the lower levels of organization—village, sublineage (*Umunna*), and compound (*Ezi*)—governance takes the form of direct democracy, with all adults participating. Such participation is the normative right of "all who are old enough to talk sense" (Afigbo 1973). Resourceful members of the community may work hard, accumulate wealth, and acquire titles, but authority relations function according to the belief that all members of the social unit are basically equal. Such is the devolution of power and the collective manner in which it is wielded that a predatory system of rule could not develop. Nobody pays or receives taxes or tributes from any other person. All decisions are arrived at deliberatively, and it is contrary to Igbo tradition for a single individual to seek to impose their personal decision on the community, as captured in the saying *Otu onye anaghi awu nnam oha*.

So, what to do? The prospect of transacting with assemblies of adults at multiple levels was unworkable from the perspective of the colonial masters. Fatefully, they decided they would pick and impose

TOWARD UNDERSTANDING THE NIGERIA-BIAFRA WAR AND LINGERING QUESTIONS

warrant chieftains. Some, like my great-granduncle Osuji Njemanze, were accomplished members of the community who had already distinguished themselves in other spheres of endeavor. Others were nondescript. Unfortunately, the Igbo are predominantly unrepentant republicans and have no use for chiefs. However, the colonial masters looked forward to exercising power through their warrant chiefs and using them to extract resources. The stage was thus set for confrontation. The first task assigned to the warrant chiefs was the enumeration of menfolk in their chiefdoms, and that was accomplished in 1926. The following year, the taxation of men was introduced. Naturally, they demurred but very reluctantly complied, with the help of their wives and mothers who were the ones in control of the relatively lucrative trade in palm produce. Men held sway over the trade in the "king crop," yam, which paradoxically fetched comparatively little in revenue. In 1928, women in Ogoja and Onitsha provinces did register their discontent with an exercise they considered to be purloining but by a different name.

It was the Roaring Twenties in faraway United States and Europe, and the irrational exuberance of investors drove share prices into the skies, in the belief that economic growth was boundless. Of course, it was all delusional, and come 1929, the boom burst. The ripples emanating from the stock exchange crash on Wall Street, New York, ravaged economies worldwide. Prices in the oil palm trade were not spared. The colonial master now needed more money, and so they sought to broaden the tax base. The warrant chiefs were sent out again, this time to enumerate the women and their livestock. Women were apprehensive, and in Oloko, Bende Division, they called a meeting on Orie market day at which they resolved to "wait until we heard definitely from one person that women were to be taxed, in which case we would make trouble as we did not mind to be killed for doing so." In mid-November 1929, Warrant Chief Okugo designated a schoolteacher, Mr. Mark Emeruwa, his enumerator. Mr. Emeruwa called at the home of Madam Nwanyieruwa on November 23, 1929, to collect census information. She refused to oblige because she was a woman and did not appreciate why she should provide the requested information. Further, she was a widow and proceeded to ask Mr. Emeruwa whether his own widowed mother had been counted. Mr. Emereuwa was incensed by the affront, and an altercation, in part physical, ensued. Madam Nwanyieruwa ran to the town square where a prescheduled women's meeting was already in progress and related her experience with Mr. Emeruwa. Her testimony was the awaited evidence that the British really meant to actualize their threat to tax women. Messages went out to surrounding villages and were relayed beyond. Women poured into Oloko and besieged Chief Okugo's compound. They sang provocative songs to the effect that, but for "*nwa beke*" (petty white boy, referencing the colonial officer), they would have dealt with him with unspeakable savagery. This was the traditional female martial tactic of "sitting on a man." Members of Chief Okugo's extended family came to his defense and fought off the women. They retreated then returned in greater numerical strength. A deputation was sent to the district officer, who on arrival at Oloko saw a gathering of over a thousand angry women. He tried to backtrack and reassure them that the census was actually not for taxation purposes, but they obviously did not believe him. They demanded that Chief Okugo be arrested and tried for assault. He agreed and took the Chief back with him to Bende on November 29, 1923. The women followed in hot pursuit, their numbers still growing. They set up camp in Bende and, according to the district officer, numbered "over 10,000, were shouting and yelling round the office in a frenzy. They demanded his cap of office which I threw to them." On December 03, 1929, the deposed Chief Okugo was tried and sentenced to two years in prison.

Victorious and jubilant, the women headed for home. They had not only challenged the taxation of women but succeeded in having a warrant chief deposed. News of their triumph spread, and donations poured in to Oloko. The funds were used to travel and spread the news even farther, to all divisions of Owerri Province and into Ibibio country in the neighboring Calabar Province to the south—the Oil Palm Belt.

A similar but deadly scenario played out at Owerrinta in Aba Division, a few days after the incident at Oloko. The enumerator there again tussled with a woman, knocking her to the ground.

TOWARD UNDERSTANDING THE NIGERIA-BIAFRA WAR AND LINGERING QUESTIONS

Unfortunately, she was pregnant and subsequently miscarried. The womenfolk were scandalized, and on December 09, 1929, they "sat on" the warrant chief Mr. Njoku Alaribe. Armed colonial police officers arrived and opened fire on the women, killing two. Their leader was arrested and taken to the prison at Aba. A mass rally was held two days later at Eke Akpara. Attendance was in the thousands, and they decided to take their protest to Aba. As they entered the city, marching down Factory Road, a car driven by the local British physician hit two women in what was reported to be an accident. They would later die from their injuries. Already frayed tempers snapped, and the women sacked the city, badly damaging European businesses, the bank, the courthouse, and the prison, among other targets. True to form, the armed colonial police responded heavy-handedly, inflicting numerous casualties on the women. There was no record kept of how many were killed or wounded.

The resident of Calabar Province had also embarked on an enumeration exercise similar to that in neighboring Owerri Province, and it was equally resented there. The enumerators in Calabar were white cadets in the administrative service, and on their approach, the villagers just fled into the bush with their livestock. However, after word reached women in Opobo district from Owerri that the direct taxation program had been actively challenged at Oloko, they became emboldened. On his next round, the cadet was confronted. The women roughed him up physically and seized his tax register. At nearby Ukam, they, with the support of men, knowingly severed the telegraph wires then destroyed the Native Court and freed the inmates of the local jailhouse. On December 15, 1929, at Utu-Etim-Ekpo, they needed no male assistance as they laid waste to the Native Court, Nigerian products factory and European store. The homes of clerks were also damaged. The women then demanded to meet with the district officer Captain James. Their request was denied, and troops were summoned. The women explained that the district officer was born of woman, and so there was no reason they could not see him. According to the Margery Perham Report, they charged the troops, who then opened fire with a Lewis gun and rifles. It was

231

more likely that they ignored an order to disperse. At any rate, eighteen women were killed and nineteen wounded.

Now that blood had been spilled, matters could only get worse. The next day, throngs of women turned out in Opobo, chanting ominously about the smell of death. The district officer relented and agreed to meet on December 17, 1929, with a delegation of seven women leaders. At the appointed time, there were not seven but several hundred women at the district office. The numbers grew as the morning wore on until there were about 1,500 women. The meeting had to be held outside across a bamboo fence, with the district officer, his military orderly, and a platoon of troops on one side and the women, armed with wooden cudgels, on the other. Then they talked. The women told the district officer to take careful notes of the discussion and that after the meeting, they would ask for his notes to see what he had written. One would imagine some of them were literate. They also demanded that two-shilling stamps would be affixed to copies of the notes, presumably for purposes of authentication and that, for good measure, they should be placed in envelopes. Meanwhile, the women not directly involved in the verbal exchange with the district officer were taunting the troops behind him, reportedly making threatening and obscene gestures at them. They called them "sons of pigs" and dared them to shoot. At some point in time, according to the report, the district officer was attacked. The reason for this escalation was unstated. The district officer's aide, however, deflected the blow and shot the attacker in the head with his revolver at point-blank range. The other women charged the fence, and the troops opened fire. After the smoke cleared, thirty-two women lay dead and thirty-one were wounded.

In all, fifty-five women were killed and just as many of them wounded by British colonial troops. Important symbols of the colonial administration suffered from the wrath of the women. Forty-six prisons were attacked and their inmates released. Ten Native Courts were wrecked. The last British patrol departed Abak Division on January 09, 1930, and the next day, the rebellion was declared as put down.

The British were nevertheless mortified by the experience, having not seen it coming. Tens of thousands of women mobilized across

TOWARD UNDERSTANDING THE NIGERIA-BIAFRA WAR AND LINGERING QUESTIONS

an area of over six thousand square miles and took largely coordinated action of significant magnitude. The colonial administration set up a commission of inquiry on February 07, 1930, to investigate the disturbances. The commission began sitting at Aba on March 10, 1930. They took evidence from 485 witnesses and submitted their report on July 21, 1930. Thereafter, the government anthropologist Dr. C. K. Meek, who was having what by all accounts was a "good time" in docile Northern Nigeria, was dispatched to southeastern Nigeria to study "the social organization of the Ibo" in the context of the theory and practice of "indirect rule." He worked for about two years before quitting for reason of ill health, and his findings were published in the book *Law and Authority in a Nigerian Tribe: A Study in Indirect Rule*, Oxford University Press, 1937. As would be expected, its scholarship is tainted by colonial perspective, and although it is interesting reading, it doesn't enlighten much.

The East, the reader might begin to think, does have a penchant for mortal combat in the defense, albeit futile, of worthy causes. Just like Igbo and Ibibio women, the United States did not stand for "taxation without representation" in the eighteenth century. However, the United States had France. These women had only themselves and were up against a colonial master with no compunction about the use of deadly force. Bringing chopsticks to a gunfight has preordained outcomes and reminds one of the encounter in *Raiders of the Lost Ark*, between the Harrison Ford character and a local person who challenged him to a duel. The Arab twirled his sword skillfully to signal that he was ready to rumble. The American absentmindedly whipped out his revolver and dropped him with a shot from about twenty feet.

The enigma of the Igbo endures. There is, by the way, no such thing as "Ibo" for real. It is an anglicization by those unable to wrap their tongue around "gb," and detractors tend to use it as acronym for "I Before Others"—that the Igbo are selfish, even narcissistic. Also, Igbo is not pluralized with the addition of an "s." It is "the Igbo" or "Nd'Igbo." It rankles that even Igbo scholars are not bothered by such errant usage. On the matter of being before others, the Igbo will gladly plead guilty that they are not shy to take the lead in collective endeavors and contribute more than their fair share to their success. Sadly, the allegation, however, is usually framed in terms of their wanting to "take over" or "dominate."

The Igbo valorize success and, for generations and generations, recognized that it had only one reliable guarantor—hard work. Everybody, friend and foe alike, concedes one quality to the Igbo: they, as a group, are EXCEPTIONALLY HARDWORKING. Accordingly, an Igbo born with mere average natural endowments can harness this vaunted work ethic and become a high-achiever. If, however, she happens to be blessed with substantial aptitude, its admixture with hard work is nothing short of rocket fuel. The gaussian distribution of natural ability is probably similar in all ethnic groups, but I would argue that that of the nurtural, specifically the capacity for hard work, is strongly right-shifted among the Igbo. Although the slothful Igbo laggard is to be found here and there, the group characterization is not vitiated.

The Igbo are also frightfully individualistic and egalitarian, hence the virtual absence of vertical social structures. Yet these intensely private individuals will gladly subsume their individualism to the service of a transcendent imperative when one appears on the scene. Such an imperative usually has to do with the potential and quest for success. A typical example is a hardworking and academically promising young man in the village whose advancement into or through secondary school, for instance, is threatened by fees beyond the means of his parents. The entire village will, without hesitation, pledge the revenue from one or two oil palm harvests to defraying the cost of the young man's education.

The combination of innate talent leveraged by hard work and community support when necessary enabled the Igbo to produce the leading lights in colonial and early independent Nigeria—the first "newspaperman" (Nnamdi Azikiwe, founded the *West African Pilot* in 1937), the first international laureates in sports (Emmanuel Ifeajuna, high jump gold [2.03 meters, record, jumped with one shoe, aged nineteen] at the Vancouver Empire and Commonwealth Games; Dick Ihetu "Tiger," world boxing champion in two weight classes [middle and light heavy]), the first international laureate in literature (Pita

TOWARD UNDERSTANDING THE NIGERIA-BIAFRA WAR AND LINGERING QUESTIONS

Nwanna, the African Language Literature Prize of the International African Institute for *Omenuko),* the first billionaire in West Africa (Sir Louis Odumegwu Ojukwu, father of the Biafran head of state, estimated worth at the time of his death in 1966 was four billion United States dollars), and too many firsts in academia to enumerate here (PhD [MIT] mathematics, Chike Obi; PhD [London] nuclear physics, Cyril Onwumechili, who was vice-chancellor of the University of Ife in the early 1980s when I was on national service at that institution; PhD [History], Kenneth Dike, who became the first Nigerian vice-chancellor of the University of Ibadan). Maj. Gen. Johnson Aguiyi-Ironsi succeeded Maj. Gen. Christian R. Kaldager of Norway as force commander of Opération des Nations Unies au Congo in January 1964. Even though he was not the first African in that role (Lt. Gen. Kebbede Guebre of Ethiopia held that position during April–July 1963), that was some recognition. Unfortunately for the Igbo, these achievements were viewed with green eyes by many of their compatriots, who, rather than be inspired by them to make their own mark, opted to feel existentially threatened. Some of them have claimed that the Igbo did not wear their laurels with humility and never passed up an opportunity to rub the noses of others in it. Kurt Vonnegut, who went on to write the classic *Slaughterhouse Five,* and two friends were among the last foreigners in Biafra in January 1970. The commissioner for information Dr. Ifeagwu Eke gave a party in their honor at the Shell Camp, Owerri. He had a PhD from Harvard. His wife had a PhD from Columbia. There were five other Biafran guests—all had doctorate degrees. Mr. Vonnegut wondered. In his estimation, a good third of all black intellectuals were Biafrans. He was sitting next to Dr. Sylvanus Cookey (PhD [Oxford]), the administrator of Opobo, and admitted to feeling strongly tempted to ask him if there was a chance that there had been a certain arrogance attached to all that brainpower that might have provoked the pogroms. He resisted the temptation and instead continued to sip his brandy as he nibbled away at the antelope meat, listening to the cascading strings of Mantovani from a stereophonic phonograph the size of "a boxcar"!

One final attribute of the Igbo worth drawing attention to is their iconoclasm, and this is well illustrated by their encounter with

Western Christianity. Like all other sentient groups worldwide, the Igbo viewed, interpreted, and tried to understand their universe in religious ways. The following is a precis of the ample literature (Uchendu 1965, Arinze 1970, Ilogu 1974, Echeruo 1979, Iwe 1988) on the interaction between the Igbo and divinity. The Igbo belief in a Supreme Being long predated the advent of the white man, as noted by the Anglo-German missionary, the Reverend James Frederick Schon. The Igbo Supreme Being is a satisfied God. No sacrifices are made directly to Him (He is a male principle), and there is no shrine or priesthood dedicated to Him. Like the Christian God, He is omnibeneficient and does no evil. Yet on an experiential level, the Igbo know all too well that evil exists—harvests fail, wars and pestilence happen, people are inexplicably stricken with disease and death or other misfortune. He has been conceptualized as a "withdrawn God" due to the often parsimonious nature of His intervention in human affairs, with entreaties to Him in times of distress meeting with delayed, little, or no response. Yet through the instrument of *chi*, He is immanent in His creation. He also created beneath Him a demiurge pantheon (*Mmuo, Arusi*) and imbued them with special powers over the material forces of the visible universe. The Supreme Being requires these nature gods (but not humankind) to make sacrifices to Him to justify their continued existence. Now, human beings are the only source of the sacrifices the nature gods need to pay their dues, and to obtain them, they must provide useful services to human beings in return. Igbo nature gods, therefore, have a rather difficult time in their intercalary position between God and humankind, both of whom have expectations of them. Their divine powers notwithstanding, they can thus be manipulated and controlled by human beings to further human interests. They are highly competitive and actively solicit the living for servitors. Each has its own priesthood and cult following.

The nature gods are anthropomorphic and subject to human passions and weaknesses. Some are kind, industrious, and hospitable while others are fraudulent, envious, treacherous, and vengeful. The later cadre of malevolent gods (*mmuo ojoo*) are the ones that are responsible for all the evil in the world. The structure of the Igbo universe is depicted in figure 5.

The relationship between the Igbo and their nature gods is therefore entirely contractual and transactional. The Igbo acknowledge their powers and are appropriately respectful of them. In turn, they are expected to reciprocate that respect in the exercise of their powers for human benefit. Their fate is in human hands as much as that of human beings is in theirs.

The white man's Christianity challenged the authenticity of the nature gods, often in physically violent ways. The Igbo rose valiantly to their defense, and at the turn of the twentieth century, countless battles raged across the length and breadth of Igboland as the Igbo fought to safeguard their belief systems and way of life. Notable among these were the punitive Ahiara Expedition of December 07, 1905 to April 15, 1906, precipitated by the alleged ritual killing of one Dr. Stewart, and the attack on the Ogbunorie Shrine elaborately documented by Professor Felix K. Ekechi. In every case, the resistance was spirited, the inspiration being the expectation that the nature gods would themselves also rise up and defend the Igbo from their assailants. In the event, the British prevailed again and again, through the use of superior forces and rampant brutality. So, it turned out that the nature gods failed to keep their side of the bargain. The pragmatic people they are, the Igbo starved them out of existence and reconciled themselves to the novel spiritual realities and the education that came with them.

The outcome of the experimentation of the Igbo with Western ways has already been alluded to. In her study published in 1939, British anthropologist (as there were then called) Ms. Sylvia Leith-Ross synopsized the perspective of the Igbo on acculturation as follows:

> They want to learn from us but only such things as may be materially productive as soon as possible. They tolerate us because they need us. They do not look upon us resentfully as conquerors, but complacently as stepping stones. (Leith-Ross 1939)

As Mr. Chinua Achebe described in his memoir, citing Mr. Paul Anber, the Igbo advanced furthest in the shortest period of time than all Nigerian ethnic groups. The Yoruba had much earlier contact with the white man and led the nation in educational attainment during the late nineteenth to early twentieth-century period. The Church Missionary Society set up the Mission Station at Onitsha in 1857 with the Reverend J. C. Taylor in charge and Mr. Simon Jonas as catechist, both freed Igbo slaves from Sierra Leone. In overall charge was the Reverend Samuel A. Crowther (PhD [Oxford]), a freed Yoruba slave who was later consecrated bishop of Western Equatorial Africa Beyond the Queen's Dominions on June 29, 1864. Predictably, they were resisted, and penetration beyond Onitsha was initially slow—also because Onitsha was at war with neighboring Ogidi at the time. The Reverend Father Lutz of the Roman Catholic Church arrived in Onitsha in 1885, and both denominations were to compete subsequently in both religious proselytization and the secular education of the Igbo. Enrollment in schools grew exponentially, especially between 1930 and 1950, and by the middle of the twentieth century, the Igbo had become the group with the highest literacy rate, the highest proportion of citizens with postsecondary education, and the highest standard of living. It may come as a surprise to some that the first degree-awarding institution in Nigeria is the University of Nigeria, Nsukka, established in 1960. The University of Ibadan was founded in 1948 but as a college of the University of London, a status that did not change until 1963.

Anti-Igbo resentment grew among other ethnic groups, fueled in no small measure by the British colonial master himself. When he barked "Jump!" in other parts of the country, especially the North, they had meekly asked, "How high?" In Igboland, he was asked "Why?"—the kind of question he was unaccustomed to answering, especially when posed by subject people. He always sought to make sure the Fulani-Hausa were well-rewarded for their fealty. After independence for instance, on October 01, 1960, the governor-general Sir James Robertson did not leave for home immediately as colonial officers were supposed to do when the curtain came down on imperial rule at their deployment. Instead he stayed back in Lagos, and documents published about a decade ago by the Institute of Commonwealth Studies of the University of London revealed that he did so to supervise the rigging of Nigeria's first election in favor of the Fulani-Hausa.

The Igbo had done very well educationally and come to occupy many of the important technocratic positions in the public and private sectors. Innately capitalistic, they had also done well economically. Unfortunately, they were politically weak and either did not know it or were deluded into the belief that their handle on the other levers was good enough compensation. They had seized the canopy but much that was critical still happened on the forest floor.

The political weakness of the Igbo was and remains the price they pay for their individualism and supreme self-confidence. Citing Paul Anber, Chinua Achebe wrote in his memoir that the Igbo have no compelling traditional loyalty beyond town or village. They do not concern themselves with "Pan-Igbo" unity or scheme to gain advantage over non-Igbo Nigerians. Their detractors, however, would never be persuaded and insisted that all that acquisition of wealth and knowledge could just not be innocent. They must, somehow, be wanting to "take over" and "dominate."

And what were the implications of Igbo individualism for their cohesiveness in Biafra? As already mentioned, they gladly accept common challenges collectively, and if there ever was one such challenge, the existential threat posed by the war and the pogrom that preceded it was that. The citizenry turned out in mass demonstrations when Lagos reneged on the Aburi Accords even though many of them were orchestrated by the trades union movement, the student union, and the government itself. As the conflagration approached, they showed up to enlist in numbers far more than the armed forces could handle. Others organized themselves into civil defense units and other community support services.

The outrage was uniformly felt across the board, and although the conviction to resist was unanimous at the outset, individualism asserted itself in the differences of opinion held and expressed as to the modus operandi. It is hard to believe, but dissenting voices were raised in the intoxicating atmosphere of the time. They ranged from those urging gradualism (Dr. Nnamdi Azikiwe and many of the First Republic politicians) to disavowal of secession (Gen. Hilary Njoku) to very blunt opposition (Emeribe Michael Ejimofor [Nigerian ambassador to West Germany]). Not surprisingly, they were in a negligible minority and were easily drowned out.

Secession did eventually happen, but after ninety days of hostilities, the capital fell into enemy hands. The citizenry was incredulous. An ill-prepared leadership blamed the debacle on the treachery of Gen. Victor Banjo et al. A new term, *saboteurs*, which had first been used a few months before by one of the treasonable felons, Maj. Philip Alale, entered the popular lexicon as "sabo." From then on, all military reversals were to be attributed to these shadowy creatures who seemed to lurk everywhere and successfully undermine the best-made plans. As mentioned earlier, the loss of Enugu was a good point in time to stop, take stock, and yes, reshuffle the deck. Unfortunately, that did not happen. Voices of dissent petered out, or the commander in chief became more deaf to them. The accretion of toadies around him progressively thickened, and they sang from a songbook that merely echoed his thoughts. Inevitably, the head of state came to hear less and less from persons outside his cocoon. As the conflict wore on and Biafra steadily shrank territorially, people fled from town to town ahead of federal forces, and these forces could be really savage. On September 16, 1968, the Nigerian Air Force bombed Aguleri market, killing 510. At the individual level, there was resignation to catering primarily to the basic animal instinct of self-preservation. Few had the intellectual energy to ponder the politics of the situation anymore. A strange zeitgeist, captured in the expression "Biafra has survived, what remains is Individual Survival," settled upon the land.

Just after midnight, on January 10, 1970, matters came to a head. General Odumegwu-Ojukwu flew out of Uli airport into exile in Côte d'Ivoire. Gen. Philip Efiong, officer administering the Republic of Biafra, assumed leadership of the government, and at 4:40 p.m. on January 12, 1970, made a broadcast from Radio Biafra, Obodo-Ukwu, instructing "an orderly disengagement of troops."

Epilogue

So, did Nigeria win? I think not. Instead, Biafra lost, and the present exploration has been an effort to understand why that happened. My finding is that a colossal failure of political leadership caused the loss. The people on whom the responsibility fell to take decisions on behalf of the Biafran people exercised very poor judgment and either lacked or chose not to utilize the requisite skills in statecraft. The decision in May 1967 to secede was wrong and inadequately thought through but still not mortal. What proved fatal was the insistence that, against all the evidence, the continued pursuit of the realization of Biafra was viable.

Nevertheless, the Igbo spirit remains indomitable. The loss was indeed deeply felt, but the vast majority were quick to shrug it off. Rather than bemoan the spilled milk, the reaction was "let's go find another cow." They rebounded with a resolve that astonished then frustrated and disappointed their detractors. An entrepreneurial people, they were handed only twenty pounds in exchange for whatever their account was in banks *antebellum*. Then in 1972, the so-called Enterprises Promotion Decree was promulgated, indigenizing the economy in the full knowledge that, with only twenty pounds in their pockets, the Igbo could possibly not participate. In the scheme of their detractors, this would be the coup de grâce that solved "the Igbo Question" for good. To their consternation, unfortunately, there was an explosion of creative energy and resourcefulness which reduced the carefully contrived monumental impediments placed in their recovery path to merely difficult but surmountable obstacles. What had been missing in the calculations of the schemers was the fact that not only were the Igbo "naturals" at striving, they had also been through a crucible in which their finest instincts were refined even further. Slowly but steadily, they clawed and chipped away at the structural strictures imposed on them.

Even as some had misgivings about the Biafra project, the Igbo overwhelmingly trusted their leadership and made every sacrifice demanded of them. They are an infinitely optimistic people and, rightly or wrongly, had believed that their qualitative edge in technical competency was the critical determinative ingredient for success at both individual and collective levels. They had good reason to believe that it was up to the leadership to do their part and deliver victory. Obviously, that never happened, and so what was the reaction? I think the answer to this question inheres in their iconoclasm that has already been described.

Having failed to deliver on its own side of the bargain, leadership has suffered the fate of similar delinquents in Igboland—it has lost cachet. The devaluation of leadership was not difficult anyway, considering that the Igbo set more store on individual enterprise than collective endeavors that require leaders and leadership. I suspect that it is for this reason that the Igbo have, since the return of civil rule, given insufficient, if any, thought to its political leaders, presumably in the subliminal perception that they do not matter anyway. Unfortunately, they, in present-day reality, do. They have power and control over vast resources. Shunning all direct active participation in the political process and hoping instead to be able to influence them positively, using clout gained in other spheres of endeavor is a fraught strategy in which the fungibility of power which it presumes may not have predictable efficacy. With the playing field abandoned by the serious-minded, charlatans and miscreants have flourished. Again and again, the Igbo states, especially Imo and, to a lesser extent, Abia, have seen the emergence of the most improbable characters in the highest political positions, with disastrous consequences for the commonweal.

Gen. Yakubu Gowon should never have been head of state. He might not have been the leader of the coup that brought him to power, but he was anointed by hands that were dripping with too much innocent blood. He remains unrepentant and unreconstructed, apparently not having managed to acquire the capacity or willing-

TOWARD UNDERSTANDING THE NIGERIA-BIAFRA WAR AND LINGERING QUESTIONS

ness to really cogitate the consequences of his actions and inactions. In September 2019, he was at the funeral of his wartime secretary, Mr. Ufot Ekaete, still rhapsodizing about his One Nigeria accomplishment—the same character who, on August 01, 1966, had told the world that there was no basis for Nigerian unity. Unfortunately, not knowing better is never exculpatory. He did have ample educational exposure for useful learning. Before he became head of state, he had participated in more than his fair share of sponsored training courses in British military academies (Sandhurst, Camberley, Latimer), and after he was overthrown on July 29, 1975, he enrolled in the University of Warwick. Sadly, evidence that the experience was of any benefit has been hard to find. General Gowon should come to terms with the fact that he, as head of the Federal Nigerian State during August 1966 to July 1975, has total responsibility for all the atrocities perpetrated in the name and purported interest of the Nigerian State in that time period. Chief among those atrocities was the slow agonizing death of at least one million children. After reconciling himself to the fact of that holocaust and his responsibility for it, vicarious and otherwise, Gen. Yakubu Gowon should, for the sake of decent humanity, offer public atonement.

In his policy of appeasement, General Ironsi had promoted Lt. Col. Gowon far beyond his level of competence and way beyond his coevals of superior ability. As a result, he was out of his depth and perpetually confused. Brig. Gen. Babafemi Ogundipe, chief of staff, Supreme Headquarters, was reported to have been constantly intrigued by Lt. Col. Gowon, at his fecklessness and ineptitude. He seemed to be always carrying files around, some in his hands, some in his armpits, and others he secreted in the trunk of his car. Yet his work output as chief of staff, Army Headquarters, was invisible. Responsibilities assigned to him went unattended to. Most critically, the Supreme Military Council, according to Gen. Hilary Njoku, did reach a decision to court-martial the perpetrators of the January 15, 1966, coup and charged the chief of staff, Army Headquarters with its implementation. That was momentous—a game-changer literally because it met a key demand of many of the restive northern elements of the Nigerian Army. The chief of staff laid it to rest in one of his numerous files, perhaps wittingly because, if he were to act as instructed, a grievance that was to be invoked as justification for the bloodbath of July 29, 1966, and thereafter, which was then in advanced stages of planning, would no longer exist.

The revenge coup of July 29, 1966, quickly degenerated from an intramural payback for January 15, 1966, into a pervasive horrific orgy of mindless and indiscriminate bloodletting. According to Max Siollun, who has so eloquently chronicled the mutinous proclivities of the Nigerian Army and their reverberations during the 1960s and '70s, mobs assisted in many cases by soldiers massacred tens of thousands of Nd'Igbo residing in Northern Nigeria. It is undeniable that a veritable ethnic pogrom was attempted. It is also undeniable that it failed to achieve its ultimate objective—reducing the Igbo to insignificant existence.

In modern times, a mechanism that has been used by nations traumatized by horrendous internecine strife to heal, especially spiritually, is the "truth and reconciliation process." Both perpetrators and victims are invited to openly share their experiences on the same platform. The perpetrators own up to their actions in the past, show contrition, and are absolved by both the victims and the state. Restorative, not retributive, justice is the goal. Dr. Ijeoma Nnodim Opara, a globalist physician, once returned from a trip to Rwanda and remarked upon how favorably impressed she was by the results of "truth and reconciliation" in that country. On analysis, however, it turns out that the outcome tends to depend on the side of the conflict under whose auspices the process is organized. Nigeria had a Human Rights Violations Investigations Commission in 2001 (Chair: Justice Chukwudifu Oputa), which was supposedly inspired by the truth and reconciliation philosophy. And here, according to newspaper reports, is the submission by Maj. Gen. Ibrahim Haruna (who was lieutenant colonel in 1967):

> Igbos constituted only 15% of Nigeria's population. They were dominant and in control of most of the sectors of the country's public and private commercial life. They were everywhere and freely doing anything. This was not necessar-

ily because of their dynamism and adaptability...
but because of their nature of being overbearing, unduly aggressive, ethnocentric and inward looking. They had, after 1960 Nigeria's independence, one ambition left to be realized: federal political power. (Siollun 2009)

As the Commanding Officer and leader of the troops that massacred 500 men in Asaba, I have no apology for those massacred in Asaba, Owerri and Ameke-Item. I acted as a soldier maintaining the peace and unity of Nigeria. (Ojeifo and Ugheghe 2009)

Certainly no redemption there. At the time of the Oputa hearings, Major General Haruna had become a lawyer and was actually participating in the guise of advocate of the Arewa Consultative Forum. It is as perplexing as it is cringe-worthy that a member of the legal profession would bandy around a term like "massacre" seemingly oblivious of its war-crime implications. The general appeared to relish his lack of compunction and sounded blasé about the role he might or might not have played. Some accounts cite him as the commanding officer of the unit that entered Asaba in October 1967, while others state that he never was in that sector of the war until the following year. If the latter is correct, it means he was merely trolling, and such levity underscored the point that the massacre of the Igbo, wherever and by whomsoever, was perfectly in order so long as it was for the peace and unity of Nigeria, as perceived by the perpetrator.

In the event, national territorial boundaries are not immutably sacrosanct after all. They have changed and will continue to do so. The contextual archetype is the Balkans, whence the term balkanization and its imagined evils. The Federal Peoples Republic of Yugoslavia, comprising Serbia, Croatia, Slovenia (former territories of the Austro-Hungarian empire), Bosnia-Herzegovina, Montenegro, and Macedonia, first came together in 1946 under the erstwhile partisan Josip Broz ("Tito"), after the abolition of the monarchy the previous year. It was renamed the Socialist Federal Republic of Yugoslavia in

1963. Twenty-nine years later, the constituent republics went their separate ways. In 2008, even the two provinces of Serbia, Vojvodina and Kosovo, dissociated.

Italians settled the area around Assab in 1882 and, eight years later, created the colony of Italian Eritrea. In 1942, the British defeated the Italian colonial army, took over, and administered the territory until 1952. It was then federated with Ethiopia, which proceeded to annex it in 1962 instead of granting it independence. The Eritrean Liberation Army took up arms and victoriously entered Asmara in 1991.

In 1922, the Republics of Russia, Byelorussia, Ukraine, and the Transcaucasus formed the Union of Soviet Socialist Republics under Vladimir Ilyich Lenin. Sixty-nine years later, the Union fizzled as a hapless Mikhail Gorbachev looked on.

By an act of parliament in 1953, the British government federated its self-governing colony of Southern Rhodesia with its protectorates of Northern Rhodesia and Nyasaland. A decade later, it seemed to have no qualms in dissolving the federation. Northern Rhodesia became Zambia, and Nyasaland gained independence as Malawi. On November 11, 1965, Mr. Ian Smith unilaterally declared the Colony of Southern Rhodesia independent.

To the west and across the ocean, also by an act of parliament, the British Caribbean Act of 1956, the British government created the Federation of the West Indies. It came into existence on January 03, 1958, and comprised all the main islands and island groupings in the Caribbean, the largest of which were Jamaica, Trinidad, and Tobago. In September 1961, Jamaica held a referendum on secession, and it passed on a 54 percent vote. Independence was proclaimed on August 06, 1962. Twenty-five days later, Trinidad and Tobago followed. Britain made no attempt to hold the federation together.

The chicanery of the British government—*divide et impera*, hypocrisy, double standards, and all—was also in full display on the Indian subcontinent. Some background is needed to set the scene. As in Nigeria but about two and half centuries earlier, British mercantile interests began setting up trading posts in the coastal towns and contracted treaties with the Mughal emperors and other local potentates in 1612. By 1757, the East India Company had attained a

TOWARD UNDERSTANDING THE NIGERIA-BIAFRA WAR AND LINGERING QUESTIONS

status similar to that of the Royal Niger Company. Then on May 10, 1957, Indian soldiers in the service of the company's security apparatus mutinied. Civilians joined in, and the insurrection raged for over one year. Thereafter, the British government took over, assuming direct sovereign control and establishing the British Raj, which lasted until independence in 1947.

In September 1939, the British viceroy Victor Hope, second marquess of Linlithgow, declared war on Germany without consulting Indian political leaders. The India National Congress (founded in 1885) took offense and withdrew its ministers from provincial governments. In contrast, the All-India Muslim League (founded in 1906) weighed in strongly behind the raj and was duly rewarded with elevation to parity with Congress. At its convention in Lahore the following year, the League passed the so-called "Pakistan Resolution," calling for parts of India with a Muslim majority to be constituted into independent states.

League leader Muhammad Ali Jinna proclaimed August 16, 1946, "Direct Action Day," and Muslims set upon Hindus in Calcutta, as it was then known. The following day, Hindus retaliated, and the violence rippled across the country. The new viceroy Louis Mountbatten, first marquess of Milford Haven, came to the conclusion that partition was inevitable if Britain was going to be able to leave India by June 1948 as planned. In other words, there was official acknowledgment that sufficient incompatibilities could exist between groups of people to render coexistence within the same national boundaries untenable. On August 14, 1947, the Muslim-dominated areas became the Independent Dominion of Pakistan, with Muhammad Jinna as governor-general. The remainder of British India became the Independent Dominion of India the next day. Mr. Jawaharlal Nehru was its prime minister, and Lord Mountbatten, with whom he had a rather interesting relationship, remained as governor-general. Such it was that British authorities, who would become intemperately exercised about Biafra a couple of decades later, themselves managed and supervised the breakup of India.

Timor-Leste gained independence from Portugal on November 25, 1975. Nine days later it was invaded and annexed by Indonesia.

The Revolutionary Front for the Independence of East Timor fought back. Indonesia was compelled to relinquish control in 1999. Timor-Leste regained its independence on May 20, 2002.

The United Kingdom dodged the bullet in the Scottish Independence Referendum on September 18, 2014. Only 53.3 percent of Scots voted to remain. However, in the Brexit Referendum of June 23, 2016, the Exit-ers won by a slim majority (51.9 percent) while regionally, the Scots voted very strongly to remain—by 62 percent (and so too Northern Ireland—by 55.8 percent). The UK has thus left the European Union, but Scotland would rather stay in it. There's more to come, maybe soon.

The story of the Sudan probably deserves to be told at some length. The Sudan gained its independence from the British-Egyptian Condominium in 1956. The southern Nilotic peoples were Christian and traditional. They were very different from the northern Muslim Arabs, and soon, a civil war erupted. It ended in 1972 with the formation of the South Sudan Autonomous Region. Eleven years later, another civil war broke out and lasted for twenty-two years. The leader of the Sudan People's Liberation Movement (SPLM) Col. Dr. John Garang de Mabior (PhD, economics, Iowa State University) became head of the government, as well as first vice president to Gen. Omar al-Bashir in Khartoum (July 09–30, 2005). He was killed in a helicopter crash while returning from a visit with Gen. Yoweri Museveni in Uganda. His successor was Gen. Salva Kiir Mayardit, commander of the military wing of the SPLM—the Sudan People's Liberation Army (SPLA). It wasn't until January 2011 that a referendum on independence was held and 98.8 percent of South Sudanese voted to leave. The Republic of South Sudan was proclaimed on July 09, 2011.

Of note, the process was sedate and painstaking. Dr. Garang was actually willing to accept an arrangement whereby South Sudan, while fully autonomous, remained structurally integral to the Sudanese state. In this, he differed from one of his more mercurial senior commanders, Gen. Dr. Riek Machar (PhD mechanical engineering, University of Bradford), whose heart seemed set on total independence from the outset. Dr. Machar had joined the SPLM straight out of graduate school in 1984 but left seven years

TOWARD UNDERSTANDING THE NIGERIA-BIAFRA WAR AND LINGERING QUESTIONS

later, forming his own militia, the Sudan Peoples Defense Forces (SPDF). He rejoined the SPLM in January 2002 but never really regained trust at the highest level. After independence in 2011, he was appointed vice president. He, however, made no secret of his opposition to the president, who, on July 23, 2013, fired him and ten others for attempting a coup d'état. This touched off yet another civil war which only ended on February 22, 2020, after the estimated loss of four hundred thousand lives.

Observers of South Sudan comment on Dr. Machar's divisiveness, outsize ego with personal ambition to match, a willingness to exploit ethnic differences (he is Nuer, Dr. Garang and General Kiir are Dinka), and duplicity. His militia, the SPDF, signed a treaty with and received aid from the government in Khartoum in 1997. During the civil war of 2013–2020, he was suspected to have renewed acquaintances with Khartoum because the Chinese-made weapons his forces used could only have come from that source.

Dr. Garang cultivated relationships with neighbors, Uganda and Ethiopia, and even received support from Libya, of all places. Although his people had not been savaged by waves of pogrom, his circumstances were substantially complex economically, politically, and diplomatically (oil was involved). He was accused of treating dissenters very harshly, but overall, he did keep his worst impulses under reasonable check. He continued to exercise good judgment on the big issues and did not proclaim a new republic. That eventually came to pass, and the lines on the map did change.

Among the expatriates in Biafra, who looked on in horror and disbelief at the depth of bestiality some human beings were willing to descend to inflict the most gruesome harm on their fellow human beings, all ostensibly in the defense of lines on a map, was the French-Jewish International Committee of the Red Cross (ICRC) physician Dr. Bernard Kouchner. His grandfather had perished in Auschwitz. On June 05, 1969, the Nigerian Air Force shot down a Swedish Red Cross DC-6 aircraft on a mercy flight to Biafra, killing four crew, to press the point that federal authorities had sovereignty over the skies and that the delivery of sustenance to famished Biafra was undermining their war effort. Recall that Federal Nigeria had made it clear that starvation was a weapon in their arsenal. Dr. Kouchner's harrowing experience in Biafra led him and Dr. Pascal Bosviel, along with eleven other French physicians and journalists, to found Medecins sans Frontières (MSF) on December 22, 1971. The organization has since then operated in conflict zones around the world on the principle that the priority was to serve the needs of the victims, without regard to the politics and lines on the map. In 1999, MSF was awarded the Nobel Peace Prize.

Whenever I drive that stretch of road between Awo-Omama and Ihiala, I am reminded of the history that was made there. It was the runway of Uli Airport (call sign "Annabelle"), designed by Chief Alexander Ekwueme (one of the first Fulbright scholars, first Nigerian architect, PhD, University of Strathclyde, vice president in Alhaji Shehu Shagari's government, 1979–1983, which was overthrown in a coup by Gen. Muhammadu Buhari, who is currently in the office of president of Nigeria) and built by Biafran engineers. The inability to maintain infrastructure had been and remains the badge of shame of Nigerians, but every day during the war, repair crews always had the runway ready by nightfall to receive heavy freight aircraft, no matter the damage inflicted on it by the Nigerian Air Force.

The Biafran Airlift remains the largest civilian airlift on record. It was run entirely by humanitarian effort—Joint Church (Catholic and Protestant) Aid (JCA, nicknamed "Jesus Christ Airlines")—and nongovernmental organizations, unlike the Berlin Airlift of 1948, which was a military operation. At peak, Uli handled nineteen to twenty-four flights each night, delivering an average of 250 tons per night. It was busier than all airports in Africa, except for Johannesburg. The vast majority of the personnel involved were volunteers, who quickly learned to perform tasks for which they had no prior experience with great efficiency and without the benefit of special equipment. Each flight, for instance, was turned around in under thirty mins on average, often under the threat of or actual aerial attack. The pilots of JCA alone flew over 5,300 missions, delivering over 60,000 tons of relief aid. Sadly but inevitably, a heavy price was paid. About thirty pilots and crew were killed, in either accidents or air attacks. The shooting down of an ICRC aircraft by the Nigeria Air Force

TOWARD UNDERSTANDING THE NIGERIA-BIAFRA WAR AND LINGERING QUESTIONS

in June 1969 has already been mentioned. All the losses were tragic and deeply felt, but that of Capt. August Harvey Martins was particularly sad. Capt. Martin was a veteran Tuskegee Airman who flew B-25 aircraft in the 477th Bombardment Group of the US Army Air Force during the Second World War. He subsequently became the first African American commercial airline pilot when he was hired as captain by Seaboard World Airlines in 1955. While on vacation, he volunteered to fly a mercy mission to Biafra with his wife, Gladys, who was an actress. That fateful night of July 01, 1968, his Lockheed L-1049G Super Constellation crashed as he tried to land it in a thunderstorm. He, his wife, and 2 ICRC staff perished.

Not all of the aircraft of the Biafran Airlift departed Uli empty after discharging their cargo. Those of Joint Church Aid took some of the protein-calorie malnourished children too sick to manage in Biafra to Gabon, Sao Tome, and Côte d'Ivoire. Many perished, but a good number survived and were nursed back to health. After the war, the United Nations High Commissioner for Refugees (UNHCR) identified 3,911 of these survivors and repatriated them to the then East Central State to reunite with who, if anyone, was left of their families. Many certainly remain in exile and have made lives for themselves in their host countries. Documentation on the subject is poor or nonexistent, but a little-known organization, the Igbo League, which was based in East Chicago, Indiana, once launched a bold effort, the Echezona Project, to create a database of all the airlifted children, including the use of genetic analysis on forensic material to identify those who did not survive. The Igbo League website sadly appears dormant, but undoubtedly, they were on to something very important. In 2014, the French writer Pierre Pean alleged that the Gabonese president, Monsieur Ali Bongo Ondimba, was actually Igbo, airlifted out of Biafra during the conflict and adopted by then President Albert Bongo Ondimba. Monsieur Ali Bongo presumably beat out fifty-three other declared heirs to assume the presidency on the death of their father in 2009. Surely, the story of the airlifted Biafran children is one that deserves to be told at some point.

After the thirty-month night, dawn did come as the sun rose to dispel the darkness. In the fifty years since that morning, erstwhile

Biafra has been carved up into nine states. The Igbo are native to six of them. They are also indigenous to Delta state across the Niger and are dispersed all across the thirty-six states of Nigeria. Everywhere, their inimitable spirit and ebullient character have revived and endured. In 1975, the name of the body of water hitherto known as Bight of Biafra was changed by a decree of the Nigerian government to Bight of Bonny, obviously an attempt to "disappear" cartographic reference to that country that once was. It was one of numerous other acts of erasure which included the willful destruction by the Nigerian federal government of all Biafran state records it could lay its hands on rather than archiving them for history. Unfortunately, those attempts were foredoomed because after physical Biafra ceased to exist in January 1970, it seemed to have migrated into the metaphysical realm and has remained "a thing," as the millennial generation would say. In the words of Chukwuemeka Vincent Ike, the spirit of Biafra "ascended into the heavens in full military regalia"! In some mystical fashion, the lore of Biafra is distinct and separate yet intermingled with that of Nigeria. As a result, for as long as there is a Nigeria, the story of Biafra will continue to be told. In homes and schools, at places of work and at play, generations yet unborn will talk about Biafra. They will ponder what happened and wonder about what might have happened but didn't. Was it because of mistakes made? Or was it because it just couldn't happen? Any suggestion that Biafra would have been a utopia is childish reverie. It would have had its challenges and growing pains as it struggled to tame its inner demons as well as find and take its place in the comity of nations. What is incontrovertible is that Biafra would have been unprecedented on the African continent—and dangerously so from the perspective of the imperial hegemons—the first country whose conception and accouchement departed radically from the colonial master's script. Only such a country could justifiably lay claim to autonomy and self-determination. Future generations, as they contend with the challenges of their day and age, not least of which will inevitably be an equitable modus vivendi in the reconstituted Nigeria, will nevertheless wistfully wonder.

TOWARD UNDERSTANDING THE NIGERIA-BIAFRA WAR AND LINGERING QUESTIONS

I sometimes wonder whether I did the right thing in keeping Nigeria together.

—Francis Edward Hovell-Thurlow-Cumming-Bruce 8th Baron Thurlow (March 09, 1912–March 24, 2013) British High Commissioner to Nigeria (1963–1966)

Appendix

Biosketches of Principal Characters

Benjamin Nnamdi Azikiwe
November 16, 1904–May 11, 1996
First indigenous Governor General of Nigeria (1960–1963); first President of the Republic of Nigeria (1963–1966)

Nnamdi "Zik" Azikiwe was born in Zungeru, Northern Protectorate and received his early education in Calabar (Hope Waddell Training Institute) and Lagos (Methodist Boys' High School). He then proceeded to the United States of America where, during the 1920s and 1930s, he studied at various institutions, including Lincoln, Howard, and Columbia universities and the University of Pennsylvania, earning degrees in political science, religion, and anthropology. He was briefly on the faculty of Lincoln University, Oxford, Pennsylvania, where he taught history and political science. He was also a regular contributor to the black press, and it was during this period that his political philosophy crystallized and his writing skills were honed.

Nnamdi Azikiwe returned to Africa in 1934, and his first job was as editor of the *African Morning Post* in Accra, Gold Coast. Three years later, he relocated to Lagos, Nigeria, where he founded the *West African Pilot* group of newspapers and became the charismatic master spirit in the struggle for Nigerian independence. Although the Republic of Biafra benefitted from his colossal international reputation early in the struggle and in many other ways (he composed the Biafran national anthem), he apparently never earned the full confidence of the head of state and was often excluded from key decision-making. On August 17, 1969, an airplane in which he was traveling from London to Monrovia made a brief "unscheduled" refueling stop at Ikeja airport, Lagos. The Nigerian head of state, General Yakubu Gowon, hastened to meet with him and mend fences. The following month, his Nigerian-ness rediscovered, Dr. Nnamdi Azikiwe accompanied General Yakubu Gowon to the Organization of African Unity summit at Addis-Ababa, Ethiopia.

Dr. Azikiwe reentered the political scene in the second republic and ran unsuccessfully for his former office as flag-bearer of the Nigerian Peoples' Party in 1979. He retired from public life after the military coup on December 31, 1983, led by General Muhammadu Buhari. His contributions to Nigerian independence earned him the honorific "Father of the Nation." Many will also continue to remember his role in the Biafra misadventure.

Johnson Thomas Umunnakwe Aguiyi-Ironsi
March 3, 1924–July 29, 1966
Head of the National Military Government and Supreme Commander of the Nigerian Armed Forces, January 17–July 29, 1966

Johnson "Ironside" Aguiyi-Ironsi enlisted in the Royal West African Frontier Force in 1942 and, after officer training at Camberley, England, was commissioned second lieutenant in 1949. During the visit of the British monarch to Nigeria in 1956, he served as equerry. In 1960, he led the contingent contributed by Nigeria to the United Nations peace-keeping effort during the Congo crisis (ONUC—Opération des Nations Unies au Congo), and in January 1964, he succeeded Maj. Gen. Christian Kaldager of Norway as overall force commander. With the departure of Major General Welby-Everard, he became the first indigenous general officer commanding the Nigerian Army (GOC) on May 23, 1965.

He narrowly escaped death in the coup of January 15, 1966, which he proceeded to suppress. The civilian government handed power over to the armed forces, and he became the head of state. In the revenge coup of July 29, 1966, he and Lieutenant Colonel Adekunle Fajuyi were abducted from the government house, Ibadan, and killed. During his 193-day tenure as head of state, General Aguiyi-Ironsi correctly identified "rigid adherence to regionalism" as a crucial ailment from which the country was suffering. Unfortunately, the remedial steps he proposed gave his enemies all the excuses they needed and cost him his life.

Chukwuemeka Odumegwu-Ojukwu
November 3, 1933–November 26, 2011
Head of State of the Republic of Biafra and Commander-in-Chief of the Armed Forces May 30, 1967–January 10, 1970

Chukwuemeka "Emeka" Odumegwu-Ojukwu was born in Zungeru, Northern Nigeria. He attended King's College, Lagos, and Epsom College, Surrey, and graduated in modern history from Oxford University (Lincoln College) in 1956. After a brief stint in the colonial civil service as assistant divisional officer, Udi division, he enlisted as a noncommissioned officer in the queen's own Nigeria regiment of the Royal West African Frontier Force in 1957, to the intense displeasure of his very wealthy father, Sir Louis Odumegwu-Ojukwu, who had prevailed on the governor-general, Sir James Robertson, to deny him a cadetship. In due course, he was sent to Eaton Hall, Cheshire, for officer training and became the first university graduate to receive a combatant commission in the Nigerian Army. In 1962, he taught tactics and military law at the West African Frontier Force Training School, Teshie, Ghana, and, after a tour of duty in the Congo, proceeded to the Joint Services Staff College, Camberley.

Upon his return in 1963, he was promoted lieutenant colonel and appointed quartermaster-general of the Nigerian Army, the first indigenous officer to hold that position. He became the military governor of the Eastern region after the January 1966 coup. Lieutenant Colonel Yakubu Gowon emerged as leader after the revenge-coup on July 1966 but Lieutenant Colonel Ojukwu, while agreeing to work with him as head of the federal government in Lagos to defuse the crisis, refused to recognize him in the role of supreme commander since there were over half a dozen officers superior to him in rank.

When the Gowon administration reneged on the implementation of accords reached at Aburi, Ghana, in January 1967, declared a state of emergency and restructured the country, Lieutenant Colonel Odumegwu-Ojukwu proclaimed the Eastern region the sovereign and independent Republic of Biafra on May 30, 1967.

War broke out and raged for thirty months. Biafra lost and General Odumegwu-Ojukwu flew out to exile in Cote d'Ivoire. On May 18, 1982, he was amnestied by the government of Alhaji Shehu Usman Aliyu Shagari. He returned to a rapturous welcome on June 18, 1982, but soon—ill-advisedly many would argue—became embroiled in party politics. It was a vastly different terrain and climate, and so his impact in the decades that followed was both relatively limited and controversial.

Philip Asuquo Efiong
November 18, 1925–November 6, 2003
Officer Administering the Government (*de facto* Head of State) of the Republic of Biafra January 10–15, 1970.

Philip Efiong enlisted in the Royal West African Frontier Force in 1945 and rose through the ranks, becoming sergeant major in 1955. The following year, he proceeded to Britain for officer training (Eaton Hall). After post-commission tours of duty in West Germany with units of the British Army on the Rhine, he returned to Nigeria in 1959 in the rank of captain. He was promoted major in 1960 and served as company commander with the United Nations Forces in the Congo. He subsequently transferred to the ordinance corps and became its first indigenous director of services in 1963. After the January 15, 1966, coup, then-Lieutenant Colonel Efiong was appointed principal staff officer to the head of state. At the time of the July 29, 1966, counter-coup, he was deputy commander, 1 Brigade, Kaduna and narrowly escaped with his life to Lagos and then the East.

In the Biafran Army, he was at various times chief of logistics, commandant of the militia, and chief of general staff. On January 9, 1970, the reins of government of the Republic of Biafra were formally handed over to him. He met with civilian and military leaders on January 11, 1970, and the decision was taken to abandon the armed struggle. He made a broadcast to the nation the following day and, on January 15, 1970, traveled to Lagos to meet with the Nigerian head of state, General Yakubu Gowon, for the formal declaration of the cessation of the existence of the Republic of Biafra.

General Efiong was a rare breed. He was a paragon of probity, and he exuded a reassuring calmness and confidence. All who knew him agreed he did his duty as he saw it and rightfully earned the sobriquet "People's General."

Hilary Mbilitem Njoku
March 31, 1928–(?)
Commander, Biafran Army, June 19, 1967–September 18, 1967

Hilary Njoku enlisted in the Royal West African Frontier Force and was one of the foundation members of the indigenous Nigerian Army officer corps, receiving his commission in the mid-1950s. In 1960, he commanded A company of the Fifth Battalion in the Congo, distinguishing himself in the rescue of Austrian missionaries taken hostage by dissidents. He and nine others (including his commanding officer, Lieutenant Colonel J. T. U. Aguiyi-Ironsi) were decorated with the "Sign of Honor" by the Austrian government for their heroism. He served as acting chief of staff, Nigerian Army, under the last expatriate general officer commanding. When he attained the rank of lieutenant colonel, he was given command of Second Battalion, Ikeja. He was about to hand over to Lt. Col. Yakubu Gowon and then transfer to the Nigerian Military Training College as commandant when the January 15, 1966, coup happened. Instead, he remained in Lagos and replaced the slain Brig. Gen. Zakaria Maimalari as commander, 2 Brigade. He was in General Aguiyi-Ironsi's entourage when the countercoup of July 29, 1966, took place, and he narrowly escaped with his life.

After the Aburi Meetings in January 1967, he was appointed commander, Eastern Command of the Nigerian Army, which became the Biafran Army on May 30, 1967. Unfortunately, perhaps understandably, the commander-in-chief could not bring himself to fully trust the senior officers, like General Njoku, who were his superiors in the Nigerian Army and also skeptical about the Biafra project. General Njoku was as disenchanted with the Nigeria of 1967 as anyone else and very keen to fight to defend the East but did not think secession was a viable proposition at the time. Unlike the other senior officers, though, he left the commander-in-chief in no doubt regarding his sentiments, and as a result, their relationship was very fraught.

General Njoku was very highly respected for both his professional competence and strength of character. Even the plotters of the coup to overthrow the government of Biafra knew he would not brook indiscipline from any quarter for whatever reason and so needed to be taken off the scene. They cleverly arranged for a trusted aide of the commander-in-chief to bring him the misinformation that the general was going to move against him on September 18, 1967. The commander-in-chief promptly ordered his arrest. General Njoku remained in detention until the end of the war.

Yakubu Dan-Yumma Gowon
October 19, 1934–
Head of the Federal Military Government of Nigeria August 1, 1966–July 29, 1975

Yakubu "Jack" Gowon attended Government (now Barewa) College, Zaria, and enlisted in the Royal West African Frontier Force in 1954. He was commissioned second lieutenant on his twenty-first birthday the following year. He proceeded to Teshie, Ghana, for officer training, and later to Eaton Hall, Chester, and the Royal Military Academy, Sandhurst. During the crisis in the Congo in the early 1960s, he served two tours of duty with the Nigerian contingent to the ONUC (Opération des Nations Unies au Congo). He subsequently became the first indigenous adjutant general of the Nigerian Army and was about to assume command of the Second Battalion when the coup on January 15, 1966, took place. He was instead appointed chief of staff of the Nigerian Army by General J. T. U. Aguiyi-Ironsi who became head of state and supreme commander of the armed forces. It was his responsibility as chief of staff to bring to book the perpetrators of the January 1966 coup and was duly authorized by the supreme mil-

TOWARD UNDERSTANDING THE NIGERIA-BIAFRA WAR AND LINGERING QUESTIONS

itary council to do so. Unfortunately, that task was never carried out, and no explanation for that failure is traceable. On July 29, 1969, there was a revenge countercoup in which the head of state was assassinated. One of the coup plotters, then-Captain Joseph Garba, later wrote that all Northern officers of the Nigerian Army in the south of the country were involved in one way or another, but many other chroniclers of the events averred that Lieutenant Colonel Gowon did not participate. Nevertheless, he was anointed leader of the mutineers and, on August 1, 1967, proclaimed himself head of the federal military government after the abscondence of Gen. Babafemi Ogundipe, the next in line to the slain head of state.

Waves of pogrom victimizing Easterners swept the Northern parts of the country, and Lieutenant Colonel Gowon was helpless to stop them. In January 1967, he and regional military governors met at Aburi, Ghana, and agreements were reached on measures to defuse the festering crisis. When he returned to Lagos, he refused to implement them, opting instead for reinterpretations by ulteriorly motivated career civil servants. On May 27, 1967, he structurally reconfigured the country, dividing the Eastern region into three states and declared a state of emergency. The governor of the Eastern region responded by proclaiming the region the sovereign and independent Republic of Biafra three days later. On the slogan "to keep Nigeria one is a task that must be done," Lieutenant Colonel Gowon launched a so-called police action to quell the insurrection on July 6, 1967. Three months later, federal forces entered the Biafran capital, Enugu. Biafra soon became encircled and was only accessible by air. Efforts at a negotiated settlement of the conflict were made, but Nigeria kept insisting on the renunciation of secession by Biafra as a precondition. With the support of Britain and the Soviet Union and his very name as acronym for his policy (go on with one Nigeria), now-General Gowon and his government relentlessly waged a very savage, no-holds-barred war against the people of Biafra. The most ignoble of their stratagems was the deliberate use of starvation as a weapon. At least one million children died. It was an unspeakable atrocity, for which the least General Gowon should do—on behalf of the government he headed—is make a public and unreserved atonement.

The same officers who elevated him to headship of the Nigerian state in 1966, humiliated him in the eyes of the world by deposing him on July 29, 1975, while he was attending the Organization of African Union summit meeting at Kampala, Uganda. He was granted exile in Britain and, the following year, was implicated in a coup attempt which claimed the life to his successor, General Murtala Mohammed. He was declared *volebant persona* by his erstwhile colleagues and stripped of his military rank and pension. In 1981, he was granted pardon by President Shehu Usman Aliyu Shagari, the Turakin Sokoto.

One subsequent military head of state, Gen. Ibrahim Badamasi Babangida, declared himself president and tried unsuccessfully to swap his fatigues for the flowing robes favored by politicians. Nevertheless, retired military brass proceeded to flood and dominate the political scene. General Gowon himself tried his hand in 1992 but was seen off by Dr. Dalhatu Tafida in the party primaries. Thereafter, he faded into relative obscurity.

Figure 1. Colony and Protectorate of Nigeria. On January 1, 1914, the Northern (NP) and Southern (SP) Protectorates and the Colony of Lagos (*) were amalgamated to create the Colony and Protectorate of Nigeria, with Sir Frederick Lugard as governor-general.

TOWARD UNDERSTANDING THE NIGERIA-BIAFRA WAR AND LINGERING QUESTIONS

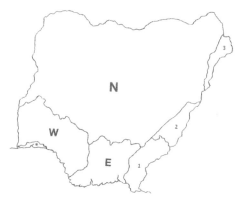

Figure 2. Nigeria, 1939–1960. In 1939, the governor-general Sir Bernard Bourdillon divided Southern Nigeria into two regions: East (E) and West (W). Under his administration also were parts of Cameroon that had been transferred from Germany to Britain after the First World War by the League of Nations; (1), (2), and (3) were governed as parts of the Southern, Adamawa, and Borno Provinces respectively (N = Northern Region; * = Lagos colony).

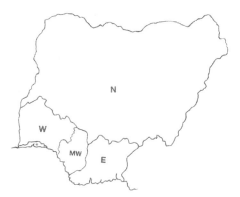

Figure 3. Nigeria, 1963–1967. On February 11, 1961, the mandated territories of British Cameroon adjoining Northern Nigeria voted to amalgamate with Nigeria while their counterparts to the south opted to join La République de Cameroun. The Mid-West Region (MW) was created by referendum on August 09, 1963 (N = Northern Region; E = Eastern Region; W = Western Region; * = Lagos, Federal Capital Territory).

Figure 4. Nigeria, May 27–30, 1967 and January 15, 1970–February 3, 1976. On May 27, 1967, Lt. Col. Yakubu Gowon, head of the Federal Military Government, announced the transformation of the country into twelve states. The Northern Region was carved up into six states, and the Eastern Region, into three (B1 = East-Central; B2 = Rivers; B3 = South-Eastern). The Western and Mid-West Regions as well as Lagos (*) were structurally unaltered. Three days later, the Military Governor of the Eastern Region proclaimed the region the Sovereign and Independent Republic of Biafra. A civil war ensued and raged until January 1970. Seven more states were created in February 1976. The numbers continued to grow under subsequent military regimes in the years that followed, reaching thirty-six as of October 01, 1996.

TOWARD UNDERSTANDING THE NIGERIA-BIAFRA WAR AND LINGERING QUESTIONS

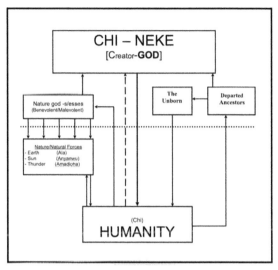

Figure 5. Igbo cosmology. In the Igbo traditional belief system, the universe exists in two realms: an invisible domain inhabited by divine beings, spirits, departed ancestors, and the unborn and a visible material domain. In this depiction, the two realms are separated by a boundary represented by the horizontal broken line. The two realms are in constant interaction across the boundary. For instance, the living, the dead, and the unborn exist in a continuum mediated through reincarnation and immortality. Each living being carries within him-/herself a "particle of the divine" (*chi*), and the relationship between an individual and his *chi* is a key determinant of the Igbo worldview. The living may petition the creator God through prayer. More commonly, though, they transact with the nature gods who have direct control over the forces of nature, making sacrifices to them in the expectation that, in reciprocation, these gods will exercise their powers for human benefit.

The creator God is omnibeneficent, but the nature gods share the proclivities of human beings, ranging from benevolent to malevolent.

BIBLIOGRAPHY

Achebe, C. *There Was a Country: A Memoir*. New York: Penguin Books, 2012.

Afigbo, A. E. "The Political Systems of the Igbo." Tarikh IV(2): 13–23, 1973.

Alao, A. "The Republican Constitution of 1963: The Supreme Court and Federalism in Nigeria." Univ. Miami Int'l and Comp. Law Rev. 10: 91–107, 2001.

Anekwe, S. O. "The Tragedy of Professor Diamond," *Africa Today* 11: 8–10, 1964.

Anene, J. C. *Southern Nigeria in Transition, 1885–1906*. Cambridge University Press, Cambridge.

Anglin, D. G. "Brinkmanship in Nigeria: The Federal Elections of 1964–1965." *International Journal* 20 (1965): 173–188.

Arinze, F. A. *Sacrifice in Igbo Religion*. Ibadan: Ibadan University Press, 1965.

Baxter, P. Biafra: *The Nigerian Civil War, 1967–1970*. Solihull, 2014.

Carland, J. M. *The Colonial Office and Nigeria, 1898–1914*. Hoover Institution Press, 1985.

Chukwukere, B. I. "Individualism in an Aspect of Igbo Religion," in *Igbo Traditional Life, Culture and Literature, vol. III,* edited by M. J. C. Echeruo, Obiechina, E. N. Owerri: Conch Magazine Ltd., 1971.

Conley B., and A. de Waal. "The Purposes of Starvation. Historical and Contemporary Uses." *Journal of International Criminal Justice* 17 (2019): 699–722.

Crowder, M. *The Story of Nigeria*. London: Faber, 1962.

Daly, S. F. C. *A History of the Republic of Biafra: Law, Crime and the Nigerian Civil War*. Cambridge: Cambridge University Press, 2020.

de St. Jorre, J. *Nigerian Civil War*. London: Hodder and Stoughton, Ltd., 1972.

de Waal, A. *Famine Crimes: Politics and the Disaster Relief Industry in Africa*. London: Villiers Publications, London, 1997.

Dike, O. K. *Trade and Politics in the Niger Delta 1830–1885: An Introduction to the Economic and Political History of Nigeria*. Oxford: Oxford University Press, 1956.

Directorate of Intelligence. "Intelligence Memorandum: Impact of Civil War on the Nigerian Economy." Central Intelligence Agency; 1968; approved for release 2001.

Echeruo, M. J. C. "A Matter of Identity." Ahiajoku Lecture Series, Imo State Ministry of Arts and Culture, Owerri, 1979.

Editorial. "Times of London." June 28, 1969.

Efiong, P. *Nigeria & Biafra: My Story*. New York: African Tree Press, 2007.

Ejiogu, E. C. "The Roots of Political Instability amongst Indigenous Nationalities and in the "Nigerian" Supra-national State, 1884–1990: A Longitudinal and Comparative Historical Study." Dissertation submitted to the faculty of the Graduate School of the University of Maryland at College Park in partial fulfillment of the requirements for the degree of doctor of philosophy, 2004.

Ekechi, F. K. *Tradition and Transformation in Eastern Nigeria: A Sociopolitical History of Owerri and its Hinterland 1902–1947*. Kent: Kent State University Press, 1989.

Forsyth, F. *The Biafra Story: The Making of an African Legend*. Barnsley: Pen & Sword, 2017.

Geary, W. N. M. *Nigeria Under British Rule*. London: Frank Cass and Co. Ltd., 1989.

Hansard. Nigeria (Kano Riots), 20 May, 1953; 515: cc 2082–5.

Hansard. Eastern Region, Nigeria (Commission of Inquiry) 24 July, 1956; 557: cc215–21.

Heerten L., and A. D. Moses. "The Nigeria-Biafra War: Postcolonial Conflict and the Question of Genocide," *Journal of Genocide Research* 16, no. 2–3 (1989): 169–203.

Howe, P., and S. Devereux. "Famine Scales: Towards an Instrumental Definition of famine," in S. Devereux (Ed.) *The New Famines* (27–49). Abingdon: Routledge, 2007.

Hutter, S. "Starvation as a Weapon—Domestic Policies of Deliberate Starvation as a Means to an End under International Law," *International Humanitarian Law Series* 46 (2015), Brill/Nijhoff.

Ignatieff, M. *The Warrior's Honor: Ethnic War and the Modern Conscience*. New York: Henry Holt, 1997.

Ike, V. C. *Sunset at Dawn*. London: Collins and Harvill Press, 1976.

Ilogu, E. C. *Christianity and Igbo Culture*. New York: NOK Publishers, 1974.

Isichei, E. H. "Ibo and Christian Beliefs: Some Aspects of a Theological Encounter," *African Affairs* 68 (1969): 121–134

Isichei, E. H. *History of the Igbo People*. London: Macmillan Press, 1970.

Isichei, E. H. *The Igbo People and Europeans: The Genesis of a Revolution to 1906*. New York: St. Martins Press, 1973.

Iwe, N. N. S. "Igbo Deities," Ahiajoku Lecture Series, Imo State Ministry of Arts and Culture, Owerri, 1988.

Izuagie, L. "The Willink Minority Commission and Minority Rights in Nigeria," *Ekpoma Journal of Theater and Media Arts* 5i (1–2) 16 (2016): 206–223.

Kigali Genocide Memorial. Jenoside—in memory of those we loved and lost. Aegis Trust, Kigali, 2016.

Kirk-Greene, A.H.M. "The Genesis of the Nigerian Civil War and the Theory of Fear," Research Report No. 27. The Scandinavian Institute of African Studies, Uppsala, 1975.

L. P. M. "Nigeria under the Macpherson Constitution," *The World Today* 9, no. 1 (1953): 12–21. Retrieved January 13, 2021, from http://www.jstor.org/stable/40392558.

Leith-Ross, S. *African Women: A Study of the Ibo of Nigeria*. London: Faber and Faber, 1939.

Macintosh, J. P. *Nigerian Government and Politics*. Evanston: Northwestern University Press, 1966.

Mayer J. "Time to Ban the Use of Starvation as a Weapon of War," The Christian Science Monitor, December 24, 1984.

Mbiti, J. S. *Introduction to African Religion*. London: Heinemann Press, 1975.

Metu E. I. *God and Man in African Religion: A Case Study of the Igbo of Nigeria*. London: Geoffrey Chapman Press, 1981.

Mulligan, M. Nigeria, the British Presence in West Africa, and International Law in the 19th century," *Journal of the History of International Law* 11, no. 2 (2009): 273–301.

Nafziger, E. W. "The Economic Impact the Nigerian Civil War," *J Modern Afr Studies* 10 (1972): 223–45.

Newbury, C. "Accounting for Power in Northern Nigeria," *J Afr History* 45, no. 2 (2004): 257–77.

Njoku, H.M. *A Tragedy without Heroes: The Nigeria-Biafra War*. Enugu: Fourth Dimension Publishing, 1987.

Nohlen, D. et al. (eds.) *Elections in Africa—A Data Handbook*. Oxford: Oxford University Press, 1999.

Nwala, T. U., editor-in-chief. *The Nigerian January 1966 Coup and Biafra: Myths and Realities*. Enugu: Fourth Dimension Publishing, 2018.

Nwankwo, A. A. *Nigeria: The Challenge of Biafra* (3rd ed.) Enugu: Fourth Dimension Publishing, 1980.

Nwankwo, A. A. *Nigeria and Her Path to Doom*. Enugu: Fourth Dimension Publishing, 2018.

Nzimiro, I. *Studies in Igbo Political Systems: Chieftaincy and Politics in Four Niger States*. London: Frank Cass, 1972.

Obi-Ani, N. A., and P. Obi-Ani P. "Zikist movement 1946–1950: A Reappraisal," *Nsukka Journal of the Humanities* 23, no. 2 (2015): 31–41.

Odogwu, B. *No Place to Hide*. Enugu: Fourth Dimension Publishers, 1985.

Ojeifo, S. and Ugheghe, L. "No regrets for the Asaba massacre of Igbo-Haruna," *Vanguard*, October 10, 2001.

Okolo, A. "The Nigerian Census: Problems and Prospects," *The American Statistician* 53 (1999): 321–325.

Okpe, A. *The Last Flight*. Lago: Aeromax International, 1999.

Osakwe, C. C. C., and L. Udeagbala. "Naval Military Operations in Bonny during the Nigerian Civil War 1967–1970," *Advances in Historical Studies* 4 (2015): 232–238.

Phillips, J. F. "Biafra at 50 and the Birth of Emergency Public Health," *American Journal of Public Health* 108, no. 6 (2018): 731–733.

Power, C. *The Igbo Women's War.* 1992; 10.13140/RG.2.2.11576.14083.

Riaz, M. R. "Sovereignty ltd.: Sir George Goldie and the Rise of the Royal Niger Company," undergraduate senior thesis, Department of History, Columbia University, New York, 2019.

Robinson, R., J. Gallagher, and A. Denny. *Africa and the Victorians: The Official Mind of Imperialism.* London: MacMillan, 1981.

Schon, J. F. *Journal of the First Niger Expedition.* University of Birmingham Information Archives. 1841 (GB 0150 CMS/ACC728).

Siollun, M. *Oil, Politics, and Violence: Nigeria's Military Coup Culture (1966–1977).* New York: Algora Publishing, 2009.

Soyinka, W. *You Must Set Forth at Dawn.* New York: Random House, 2009.

Stafford, M. R. "Quick Kill in Slow Motion: The Nigerian Civil War," in War Since 1945 Seminar. United States Marine Corps Command and Staff College, Quantico, 1984.

Stokke, O. Nigeria. *An Introduction to the Politics, Economy and Social Setting of Modern Nigeria.* Uppsala: The Scandinavian Institute of African Studies, 1970.

Thomas, N. W. *Anthropological Report on the Ibo-Speaking Peoples of Nigeria.* New York: Negro Universities Press, 1970.

Uchendu, V. C. *The Igbo of Southeast Nigeria.* New York: Rinehart and Winston, 1965.

Uwechue, R. *Reflections on the Nigerian Civil War: Facing the Future.* New York: Africana Publishing, 1971.

Venter, A. J. *Biafra's War 1967–1970: A Tribal Conflict in Nigeria that Left a Million Dead.* Solihull: Helion & Company, 2015.

Walzer, M. *Just and Unjust Wars.* New York: Basic Books, 1977.

Whiteman, K. Lord Thurlow obituary, https://amp.theguardian.com/world/2013/apr/16/lord-thurlow.

Wilson, H. *The Labour Government, 1964–1970: A Personal Record.* London: Weidenfeld and Nicholson, 1971.

INDEX

A

Aba, 70, 83, 107, 123, 130, 202, 228, 230–231, 233
Aba Women's Uprising ("Aba Riots"), 123
Abacha, Sani, 79
Abayomi, Kofoworola Adekunle, 40
Abdallah, Raji, 224
Abdulrazaq, Abdul GaniyuFolorunsho, 69
Abeokuta Garrison Organization, 58, 67, 81, 95
Abubakar, D. S., 82, 86
Aburi, 103–109, 119, 121, 131, 138, 151, 191, 200, 225, 227, 239, 258–261
Achebe, Chinualumogu, 171
Achukwu, William O., 159
Achuzia, Joseph, 168, 196, 221
Action Group, 26–34, 36, 38–42, 46, 123
Adamu, Martin, 68, 79, 82, 91, 144
Addis Ababa Peace Conference, 130
Adebayo, Robert Adeyinka, 51
Adebayo, Waidi, 136
Adebo, Simeon Olaosebikan, 75
Adedoyin, Adeleke, 24
Adegbenro, Dauda Soroye, 36
Adekunle, Benjamin, 120, 167, 181, 196
Adelabu, Adegoke, 27
Adeleke, Ganiyu, 72
Ademola, Adetokunbo Adegboyega, 37, 39, 44, 91, 110
Ademoyega, Adewale, 52, 63, 72, 166, 170
Ademulegun, Samuel Adesujo, 51
Adeola, Joseph, 83
Aderemi, Adesoji Ooni, 36–37
Aduwo, Akintunde, 155
Afonja, Kakanfo, 14
Africa and the World, 146
Africa Concern, 205
African Continental Bank (ACB), 30, 118
Agbamuche, Samuel Ironka, 180
Agbor, 165, 167, 185
Aghanya, Ebenezer Ejike, 119
Aguiyi-Ironsi, Johnson ThomasUmunnakwe, 51, 256
Aguiyi-Ironsi, Thomas, 86
Aguleri market, 240

Agunwa, Osita, 224
Ahia Attack, 120
Ahiara Expedition, 237
Ahidjo, Ahmadou, 35
Ahmadu Bello University, 79
Ajuluchukwu, Michael C. K., 136, 224
Akagha, Festus, 65, 164, 216
Akahan, Joseph, 73, 83, 98, 137, 147
Akenzua, Solomon, 104
Akilu, Ali, 75, 104
Akingbade, Tunji, 147
Akinjide, Richard Osuolale Abimbola, 69
Akinloye, Augustus, 27
Akinrele, Abiodun, 67
Akintola, Samuel Ladoke, 23, 29, 35
Akpan, Ntieyong, 104
Akpaukwa Barracks, 190
Akpuaka, Aloysius, 59
al-Kaneimi, Shaykh, 14
Alafin, Oyo Empire, 10, 14
Alale, Philip Maya, 173
Alaribe, Anthony, 161
Alaribe, Njoku, 231
Allwell-Brown, Ibikare, 110, 218
Aloba, Abiodun, 224
Alooma, Mai Idris, 14
Ama, 228
American Colonization Society, 126
Anazonwu, Obi, 7
Anber, Paul, 238–239
Anglo-Boer War, 198
Anglo-Ethiopian Treaty, 126
Anglo-French Convention, 12, 17

Ankrah, Joseph, 103
Anna Pepple Trading House, 7–8
Anti-Color Bar Movement, 224
Anuforo, Christian, 60, 63, 71
Anuforo, Cyril, 196
Anuku, Wilfred, 155
Anwunah, Patrick, 66, 68, 79, 141, 169
Apapa Naval Shipyard, 154
Apollo, Sule, 144
Arab-Israeli War, 207
Archibong, William, 168, 218
Arewa Consultative Forum, 245
Arikpo, Okoi, 113, 201, 218
Army Council, 44
Arugo, Ekwem, 228
Arusi, 236
Asaba, 7, 165–168, 184, 196, 245
Asama, Major, 165
Asen, Jonathan, 65
Asiodu, Phillip C., 106, 109
Attahiru II, Muhammadu, 18
Atua, Operation, 115
Atumaka, Theodore, 168
Auna, H. A., 100
AURE, Operation, 81
Awolowo, Jeremiah Oyeniyi Obafemi, 26
Ayida, Allison Akene, 121, 129, 202, 209
Azikiwe, Benjamin Nnamdi, 17, 255

B

Badagry, 15
Baez, Joan Chandos, 219
Baikie, William, 16
Bairamian, Vahe Robert, 37

Bakassi Peninsula, 134, 201
Bako I., 86
Balewa, Abubakar Tafawa, 25, 42
Balkanization, 245
Ball Rule of Power, 180
Balogun, Kola, 27, 224
Bamali, Nuhu, 67
Bamum, Kingdom, 35
Banjo, Victor Adebukunola, 52, 164
Barbarossa, Operation, 134–135
Barewa College, 25, 52, 260
Bassey, Wellington Umoh ("Duke"), 51
Bathurst, Lord, 14
Bayero, Ado, 77, 101
Beecroft, John, 3
Bello, Ahmadu, 25, 29, 41, 52, 54, 58, 79, 89
Bello, Mohammed, 88
Bello, Muhammad, 14
Bello, Sani, 79
Benin City, 11, 59, 65, 78, 165–167, 174, 176, 181–185
Benson, Theophilus Owolabi Shobowale, 34
Berlin Agreement, 8
Berlin Airlift, 121, 250
Berlin Conference, 5
Bill of Rights, 32
Bismarck, Otto von, 5
Boers, 197
Bonaparte, Napoleon, 127, 132
Bongo, Albert-Bernard, 223
Bongo Ondimba, Ali, 251
Bonny, 8, 10, 155–160, 181, 252
Boro, Isaac Jasper Adaka, 47
Bourdillon, Bernard, 23, 263
Bourguiba, Habib, 131
Brett, Lionel, 37, 39, 44, 77
Brexit Referendum, 248
British Caribbean Act, 246
British deputy high commissioner, Benin City, 182, 190
British-Egyptian Condominium, 248
British Raj, 247
Brockway, Fenner, 29, 31
Brown, George, 203–204, 206
Broz, Josip ("Tito"), 245
Buhari, Muhammadu, 250, 256
Burkina-Faso, 14

C

Cable Point, 168
Calabar, 8, 11–12, 28, 31, 46, 180, 196, 230–231, 255
Calabar-Ogoja-Rivers state, 46
Camberley, Joint Services Staff College, 62, 257
Cameroons, 6, 14, 23, 30, 34, 43, 120–121, 143, 148, 201
Caritas, 201–202, 205, 207
Census, 24, 40, 43, 120, 200, 229–230
Central African Trading (CAT) company, 6
Central Intelligence Agency, 103, 118
Chamberlain, Joseph, 12, 17
Checkmate, Exercise, 146
Chi, 236, 265
Chukwu, John Ikeokwu, 122
Chukwueke, John, 86
Chukwuka, Humphrey Iwuchukwu, 61

Chukwumerije, Uche, 180, 184, 186, 192
Church Missionary Society (CMS), 4, 7, 16, 238
Churchill, Winston Leonard, 153
Clapperton, Hugh, 14
Clifford constitution, 22
Coastal Patrol Craft (CPC), 155–158
Cocoa House, 35
Coker, George Baptist, 38
Cold War, 123–124, 134, 218–219
ColonialHotel, Kano, 29
Command Workshop, Yaba, 67
Commission on Minority Groups in Nigeria (Willink Commission), 31–32, 41, 226
Commonwealth of Nations (CoN), 61, 128–129
Compagnie Francaise de l'Afrique Equatoriale (CFAE), 16
Congo Crisis, 126, 256
Consultative Assembly, 113–114, 142, 182, 216, 220, 223–226
Cote d'Ivoire, 258
Cotonou, Dahomey, 204
Council of Northern States, 114
Court of Appeal Edicts, 110
Crocker, Walter R., 20
Crowther, Samuel Ajayi, 22
Cumming-Bruce, Francis, 67

D

Dada, Garba "Paiko", 83
Dambo, S., 72
Dambo, Yakubu, 79, 89
Damcida, Ibrahim, 106
Damisa, Exercise, 57
dan Fodio, Abdullah, 14
dan Fodio, Usman Shaykh, 13, 18, 25
Dan juma, Theophilus Yakubu, 79
David-Osuagwu, Christopher, 180, 192
Davies, Hezekiah, 23, 67
Davis Jr., Sammy, 219
De Gaulle, Joseph-Marie Charles, 125
Decree No. 8, 108–109
Decree No. 14, 114–116, 218, 220
Decree No. 34, 75–77, 97, 131
Decree No. 33, 75
Degel, 13
Dickson, Paul, 101
Dike, Kenneth Onwuka, 131
Dimka, Buka Suka, 89
Dinka, 249
Diori, Hamani, 130
Dipcharima, Zana Bukar, 24, 67
Directorate of Military Intelligence, 97, 110
Disembodied head, 101
Divide et impera, 246
do Po, Fernao, 35. *See also Po, Fernando*
Dodan Barracks, 61, 63, 71, 87, 162
Dolus specialis, 210
Durang, Phillipe, 161

Dutch disease, 117
Duvalier, Francois, 132

E

East African Community Conciliation Commission, 128
East India Company, 246
Eastern Command, 138–139, 141, 143, 150, 259
Eastern Nigeria Broadcasting Corporation, 46
Easton, S. F., 5
Ebubedike, E., 37
Echezona Project, 251
Edet, Louis Orok, 44
Efiong, Philip Asuquo, 258
Egbe Omo Oduduwa, 23, 26–27, 33, 40
Eghagha, Harris, 72
Egonu, Winifred Kaine, 152
Eha-Amufu, 160
Ejimofor, Emeribe Michael, 240
Ejindu, Dennis, 146
Ejoor, David Akpode, 59
Eke Akpara, 231
Eke, Ifeagwu, 219, 235
Ekechi, Felix K., 237
Ekpo, Eyo O., 137
Ekwensi, Cyprian, 141
Ekwueme, Alexander, 250
Elias, Taslim Olawale, 44, 75
Emembolu, Joseph, 182
Emeruwa, Mark, 229
Emezie, Jude, 47
Emordi, John, 163
Enahoro, Anthony Eronsele, 39, 209
Eneli, T. C. M., 91

Enterprises Promotion Decree, 241
Enugu, 28, 115–116, 118, 120, 150, 153, 158, 162, 164–167
Equatorial Guinea, 205, 207
Erefamote, Leading Seaman, 156–157
Eritrea, 246
Eso, Kayode, 171
Essien, Nyang, 24
Ethiopia, 126–127, 129, 205, 235, 246, 249, 256
Exham, Robert, 53
Extraordinary Orders of the Day, 64
Eyo, Effiong, Okon, 30
Eze, Anthony, 137, 146, 148, 163
Eze, Nduka, 224
Ezedigbo, Godfrey, 61
Ezeilo, Godwin, 163
Ezenwugo, Lucius, 191
Ezi, 228

F

Factory Road, 231
Fadahunsi, Joseph Odeleye, 34, 46
Fajuyi, Francis Adekunle, 67, 86
Fani-Kayode, Victor Remilekun, 41
Federal Electoral Commission, 43, 47
Federal Executive Council, 106, 108, 178, 209
Federal Guards, 59–63, 71, 73, 78–79, 87, 98

Federation of the West Indies, 246
Fegge, Useni, 86
Ferguson, Clarence, 208
Ferguson, James, 9
Feudalism, 42, 140
Finucane, Aengus, 205
Foot, Hugh, 225
Forster, Norman, 53
Forsyth, Frederick, 105, 130, 168, 177, 208, 216
Foster-Sutton, Stafford, 44
The Four "Imperatives", 215
France, 5, 34, 119, 124–125, 132, 134, 219, 221, 233
Fraser, Louis, 3
Fulani-Hausa, 29, 31, 94, 99, 170, 228, 238–239
Futa-Toro, 13

G

Gabon, 115, 129, 134, 205, 223, 251
Galadima, Ibrahim Tanko, 66
Gang of Four, 187, 189, 192–193, 196
Garang de Mabior, John, 248–249
Garba, Joseph Nanven, 73, 79
Gascoyne-Cecil, Robert, 9
Geneva Conventions, 200
Mr. Genocide, 205
Ghana, 3, 28, 38–39, 151, 257–258, 260–261
Gladstone, John, 3
Gladstone, William, 3
Gobir, Yusuf, 106
Gold Coast, 3, 10, 23, 28, 255
Goldie-Taubman, George, 6

Goshawk, H.M.S., 10
Gower, Laurence, 44
Gowon, Yakubu Dan-Yumma, 52, 260
Grant, Ulysses S., 135
Great famine, 197
In-Group, 180–185, 191–192, 194, 217
Groups of Provinces, 75, 77, 91
Gudu, 13
Guebre, Kebbede, 235
Gwandu, 14, 16

H

Haiti, 132
Haitian Revolution, 132
Hamman, Ted, 196
Hammarskjold, Dag H. A. Carl, 126
Hannaniya, Haladu, 79
Harcourt, Lewis, 19
Harrison Factory, 10
Haruna, Ibrahim, 244
Headless body, 101
Hendrix, Jimi, 219
Herero, 198
Hewitt, Edward H., 7
Hillenbrand, Martin, 136
Hope, Victor, 247
Hopkinson, Henry, 29
House of Assembly, 24–26, 28, 30, 33, 36–37, 39
House of Chiefs, 25, 32
HouseofRepresentatives, 24, 27–28, 30, 33, 35, 38, 41
House of Senate, 32–33
Human Rights Violations Investigations Commission, 244

Human wave assault, 151
Hunt, David, 177, 214
Hunt-Grubbe, Walter, 10
Hutu, 217

I

Ibadan, 26–28, 36–37, 58–59, 71, 73, 77–79, 82–83, 174–175
Ibadan, NNS; BNS, 154–156
Ibadan People's Party (IPP), 27
Ibiam, Francis Akanu, 142, 189
Ibibio, 4, 230, 233
Ibrahim, Kashim, 58
Ifeajuna, Emmanuel Arinze, 52, 164
Igbo, 98–102, 233–239
The Igbo Question, 241
Igboba, Henry, 70, 83, 86
Ignatieff, Michael, 197
Iheanacho, Felix, 182
Ihedigbo, Joseph, 59, 73, 99
Ihenacho, Lambert, 168, 196
Ihetu, Dick "Tiger", 234
Ike, Chukwuemeka Vincent, 252
Ikeja Cantonment, 62, 66, 86, 88–89, 91
Ikejiani, Okechukwu, 124, 132
Ikenne, 46, 171
Ikenze, Michael, 180
Ikoku, Alvan, 142, 182, 188
Ikoku, Samuel Gomnso, 39
Ikoli, Ernest, 22
Ilorin, 14
Ilyasu, Alhaji, 78
Imo, Ogere Umo, 71
Impuzamugambi militia, 217
Independence Constitution, 32–33, 41

India, Independent Dominion, 247
India National Congress, 247
Indirect rule, 22–23, 233
Interahamwe militia, 217
International Committee of the Red Cross(ICRC), 201–208, 249–251
Inyagha, Sam, 110
Ireland, Republic of, 205
Isichei, Jonathan, 168
Israel, 71, 89, 95, 102, 124, 134, 157, 161
Ita, Eyo, 22–23, 28, 46, 124
Ivenso, Michael C. O., 137

J

Jaja, King, 7–10
Jaja, Milan, 84
Jalo, Gibson, 72
Jamaica, 246
James, Captain, 231
James VI, King of Scotland, 127
Jamiyya Mutanem Arewa, 25
Jebba, 66, 165
Jefta, Operation, 163
"Jesus Christ Airlines", 250
Jibowu, Samuel Olumuyiwa, 44
Jihad, 13–14, 17, 34
Jinna, Muhammad Ali, 247
Joda, Ahmed, 106
Johannesburg, 250
Johnson, Femi, 172
Johnson, Lyndon Baines, 125
Johnson, Mobolaji, 91, 104, 172
Johnston, Henry, 8, 10
Joint Church Aid (JCA), 205–208, 250–251
Jonas, Simon, 238

Jones, Alfred, 6
Jones, Arthur Creech, 24
Jones, M.V., 66
Jubogha, Jubo, 7

K

Kale, Peter M., 24
Kalu, Ogbugo, 138
Kamerun, 35
Kampala Peace Talks, 129
Kanem-Borno Empire, 13
Kano, 14–15, 18, 27–29, 64–65, 99–101, 149, 161, 224
Kano, Animu, 101
Kano-Sokoto Expedition, 18
Kanu, Godwin Ndubisi, 157
Katsina, Hassan Usman, 133
Katsina, T., 72
Katsina Training College, 26
Kebbi, 13
Kelly, Patrick, 166
Kennedy, Raymond, 205
Kiir Mayardit, Salva, 248
Kindu, 55
Kirk, John, 11
Kirkley, Leslie, 203
Kissinger, Henry Alfred, 126
Kosoko, Oba, 3
Kouchner, Bernard, 249
Kpera, John Atom, 72
Kriller, Jean, 206
Kuka, 14–15
Kure, Yohanna Yarima, 60
Kurubo, George Tamuno, 67, 158
Kwale, Sabo, 81
Kwashiorkor, 203
Kyari, Abba, 90, 100

L

Lafayette, Guy de, 125
Lagos, 3, 11–12, 22–23, 59–60, 63–67, 70–71, 78–79, 169, 172–174, 201–204
Lagos Crown Colony, 11
Lagos Garrison Organization, 67, 71, 87
Lagos Town Council, 22–23
Laird, MacGregor, 4, 8, 15
Lake Ladoga, 198–199
Lander, John, 15
Lander, Richard, 15
Largema, Abogo, 58, 69, 71, 95
Lawani, Daniel, 104
Lawrence, William F., 11
Lawson, Rex Jim, 227
Leaders of Thought, 103, 215
Leclerc, Rene, 162
Lee, Robert Edward, 135
Legislative council, 20, 22, 26
Legum, Colin, 102
Lenin, Vladimir Ilyich, 246
Lennon, John, 219
Lennox-Boyd, Alan, 30
Letmauck Barracks, 85
Leventis, A. G., 177
Liberation Army, 164, 167, 175–176, 181, 190, 192, 246, 248
Liberia, 126, 129–130
Lindt, August, 206
Lion Building, 66, 88, 90
Lokoja, 11, 15, 17, 155
Lokoja, NNS, 155
Lugard, Frederick Dealtry, 17
Lumumba, Patrice Emery, 126
Lutz, Rev. Fr., 238
Lyttleton Constitution, 30

M

Macaulay, Herbert Olayinka Badmus, 22
Macpherson Constitution, 24–28, 46
Madiebo, Alexander, 65, 79, 89, 137–138, 186, 188, 191, 194
Maimalari, Abubakar Zakaria, 51
Maje, Maisamari, 81
Majekodunmi, Moses Adekoyejo, 38
Major Seminary of Ss Peter and Paul, Bodija, 84
Makarios III, Archbishop, 59
Makurdi, 65, 100–101, 160
The Man Died, 175
Maratta (Gobir Sultanate), 13
Margery Perham Report, 231
Mark Press, 219
Maroua Declaration, 201
Marsden, Leslie, 66
Martins, August Harvey, 251
Mass Starvation, 122, 197, 200, 209–210
Matthews, Elbert, 91
Mayer, Jean, 199
Mayrock, Bruce, 219
Mbabie, Godson, 86
Mbadiwe, Kingsley Ozurumba, 67, 95, 111, 124
Mbanefo, Louis Nwachukwu, 44, 129
Mbu, Matthew, 111
Mbuembue, Mfon, 35
McCoskry, William, 3
Medecins sans Frontieres (MSF), 250
Meek, Charles K., 233
Megwa, Kevin, 148
Memorandum to the Strategic Committee, 152
MFI-9B (Minicoin), 145, 158
Mid-West, 40–41, 43, 59–60, 99, 164–169, 172–176, 179–182, 263–264
Middle Belt, 31, 42, 93, 120
Midwest State Movement (MSM), 41
Mirza, Iskandar, 139
Mmuo, 236
Modebe, Anthony, 141
Mohammed, Kur, 60, 95
Mojekwu, Christopher, 116, 188, 223
Monrovia Peace Talks, 130
Montgomery, Bernard, 132, 153
Moore and Company, 11
Morgan, J. P., 19
Morland, Thomas, 18
Moscow, 134, 136, 159, 173, 206
Mountbatten, Louis, 247
Mughal emperors, 246
Muhammed, Murtala, 67, 70, 78–79, 82, 91, 98, 128, 137, 167–168, 181, 196
Mumuni, Dauda, 100
Mungono, Ali, 69
Mwadkon, Pam, 82

N

Naguib, Muhamed, 139
Nama, 198
Namibia (German Southwest Africa), 198
Nassarawa, Malami, 86
Nathan, Nuhu, 86

National African Company, 6–7
National Council of Nigeria and the Cameroons (NCNC), 23–30, 41–42, 46–47, 53–54, 224
National Council of Nigerian Citizens(NCNC), 23–30, 32–34, 41–42, 46–47, 53–54
National Independence Party (NIP), 28, 30
National (Re) Conciliation Committee, 110, 215
Native Authorities, 19
Navy Act, 45
Navy Board, 44
Nchi, 228
Ndem, Okokon, 227
Nd'Igbo, 102, 233, 244
Necklacing, 46
Nehru, Jawaharlal, 247
Nembe, 7, 11
New York Times, 121
News Talk, 227
Ngwube, Douglas, 180, 184–185, 192
Niamey Peace Talks, 121
Niger Delta Republic, 115
Nigeria Army Training Depot, 64
Nigeria Military Training College (NMTC), 56–58, 89
Nigeria, NNS, 122, 154–155, 157–159
Nigerian National Alliance (NNA), 42–43, 45–46, 56–57

Nigerian National Democratic Party (NNDP), 22–23, 42, 46
Nigerian Union of Teachers, 23
Nigerian Youth Movement, 22, 224
9 Mile Corner, 194
Nixon, Richard Milhous, 126
Njemanze, Osuji, 229
Njoku, Eni, 129, 189, 223
Njoku, Hilary Mbilitem, 259
Nkemena, George, 190
Nkrumah, Francis Kwame, 103
Nobel Prize, 45, 171, 250
Nogbaisi, Ovonranmwen Oba, 11
Nord Church Aid, 205
Northern Elements Progressive Union, 33
Northern People's Congress (NPC), 25–33, 36, 41–42, 46, 52–54, 67, 69
Nowell Commission, 23
Nsudoh, Assam, 168, 196
Nsukka Front, 145–146, 148, 152, 218
Numan, Titus, 85–86
Nupe, Emir of, 16
Nwachukwu, Ike, 65
Nwachukwu, Ogbede, 84
Nwajei, Sylvanus B., 137
Nwankwo, Andrew, 85
Nwanna, Pita, 235
Nwanya, Onuora, 110
Nwanyieruwa, Madam, 229–230
Nwawo, Conrad, 70, 163, 165–166, 188
Nwobosi, Emmanuel, 58

Nwokedi, Francis, 75, 131, 222–223
Nwokolo, Jacob, 152
Nyasaland (Malawi), 246
Nzefili, Macaulay, 71, 73
Nzegwu, Theophilus E., 57, 101
Nzeogwu, Patrick Chukwuma Kaduna, 57

O

Obalende Police Headquarters, 66, 88
Obasanjo, Matthew Olusegun Okikiola Aremu, 65
Obi, Chike, 195, 235
Obi-Rapu, Lieutenant, 157
Obiaruku-Warri-Sapele Axis, 165
Obienu, John Ikechukwu, 63
Obilagu, 121, 206
Obioha, Clement, 85
Obioha, Frank, 195
Obodo-Ukwu, 240
Observer, 102, 105, 208, 249
Ochei, Ben Okechkwu, 78, 124, 132
Odogwu, Bernard, 97, 107, 113, 143, 146, 180, 182, 192, 195
Odu, Mark Anamelechi, 110
Odu, Paschal, 154–156
Odumegwu-Ojukwu, Chukwuemeka, 17, 52, 70–71, 104, 111, 177–178, 186–187, 200, 216, 225, 257
Odumosu, Peter, 104
Ofo, 228
Ogbe Osowa, 168
Ogbeke Square, 168

Ogbemudia, Samuel Osaigbovo, 89
Ogbonna, Rowland, 82
Ogbunigwe (Mine System), 145
Ogbunorie Shrine, 237
Ogoja, NNS, 155
Ogoni, 115
Oguchi, Jerome, 59
Ogundipe, Babafemi Olatunde, 51
Ogunewe, David, 82, 98, 136–138, 194
Ogunsanya, Adeniran, 34
Oguta, 149, 202
Oha, 228
Ohafia, 145
Ohaya, J., 119
Ojukwu, Juventus Chijioke, 66
Ojukwu, Louis Odumegwu, 235
Okafor, Donatus, 60, 63, 71, 98
Okafor, P. C., 101
Okagbue, B.A., 91
Okeke, Patrick I., 141
Okigbo, Christopher, 152
Okigbo, Pius Nwabufo, 75
Okitipupa, 128, 166, 175, 177
Okogwu, Leonard, 168
Okonkwo, Albert, 166
Okonweze, Gabriel, 59, 81, 95
Okoro, Israel, 71, 89, 95
Okotie-Eboh, Festus, 41, 61
Okoye, Godfrey, 142, 182
Okpa, Ebony, 191
Okpara, Michael Iheonukara, 124, 189
Okpe, August, 158, 160
Okugo, 229–230
Okunnu, Lateef Olufemi, 130
Olafimihan, Festus, 72

Olaniyan, A. O., 81
Oloibiri, 117
Oloko, 229–231
Olorun-Nimbe, Abubakar, 24
Olubadan of Ibadan, 11
Olufunwa, Emmanuel, 110, 171, 216
Oluleye, James, 73
Olutoye, Olufemi, 52, 137–138, 170
Oluwa Bridge, 167
Omo-Bare, Timothy, 104
Ondo Improvement League, 27
Onitsha, 4–5, 7, 28, 120, 128, 168, 196, 221, 229, 238
Onuaguluchi, Obed, 195
Onukogu, Andrew, 84
Onwuatuegwu, Timothy, 58, 71, 147, 152, 196
Onwubiko, Israel, 157
Onwumechili, Cyril, 235
Onyiuke, Gabriel, 76, 87, 102
Opara, Ephraim, 87
Opara, Ijeoma Nnodim, 244
Operation "Wet-ie", 46
Opi Junction, 181
Opobo, 7–10, 231–232, 235
Oputa, Chukwudifu, 244
Order of the Holy Ghost of Ireland, 207
Order of the Holy Rosary of Ireland, 207
Ore, 128, 166–167
Organization of African Unity(OAU), 126–131, 202, 226, 256
Orizu, Nwafor, 67, 69, 124
Orkar coup, 74
Orok, E. B., 81

Osadebay, Dennis Chukude, 59
Osoba, Segun, 95
O'Sullivan, John, 40
Otu Edo, 27
O'tuathail, Eamon, 147
Oudney, Walter, 14
Owerri, 123, 138, 142, 148, 189, 230–231, 235, 245
Owerrinta, 230
Oxford Committee for Famine Relief (OXFAM), 203, 207
Oxford University, 52, 106, 233, 257
Oyewole, Fola, 72
Oyo Empire, 14
Ozurumba, Mbanaso, 7

P

Paiko's Wedding, 81
Pakistan, Independent Dominion, 247
Pakistan Resolution, 247
Palm produce, 4, 8, 229
Pam, Elizabeth, 61
Pam, James Yakubu, 61, 95
Paris, 125, 198–199
Patani, 7
Pean, Pierre, 251
Peterside, Shoe, 9
Philips, James F., 208
Phillips, James R., 11
Pioneer, H.M.S., 5, 7
Pleiad, The, 16
Po, Fernando, 8, 15, 35, 205, 207. See also do Po, Fernao
Police Action, 133, 261
"Pool" arrangements, 23

Port Harcourt, 121, 128–129, 142, 155–156, 159, 162, 168, 182, 202–203
Portugal, 5, 134, 187, 202, 247
Promised Land, 221
Protectorate, Niger Coast, 11–12
Protectorate, Northern, 17–19, 51, 255
Protectorate, Oil Rivers, 8, 11
Protectorate, Southern, 1, 12, 18–19

Q

Quarshie-Idun, Samuel, 36
Quinine, 15

R

Radio Biafra, 240
Ransome-Kuti, Frances Fumilayo, 24, 34
Rape at Choba, 115
Rawson, Harry, 11
Red Devils, 144, 148
Registration of Companies Edict, 110
Regular Officers Special Training School, 151
Remawa, Mohammed, 81–82
Renascent Africa, 28
Republic of Benin, 167
Republic of South Sudan, 248
Research and Production (RaP), 119, 145, 156, 159, 221
Revenue Collection Edict, 110
Revere, Paul, 82
Rhodesia, Northern (Zambia), 126, 129, 246
Rhodesia, Southern, 246

Ribadu, Muhammadu, 41
Richards Constitution, 23–25
River Benue, 15–16, 35, 101, 144, 160
River Cross, 3, 128, 201
River Niger, 1, 3–4, 15, 120, 128, 165, 167, 196, 201–202
River Nile, 1
Robertson, James, 54, 238
Romanov, Alexandr, 136
Rome Statute, 200
Roosevelt, Franklin Delano, 153
Roosevelt, Theodore, 133
Rotimi, Oluwole, 52, 170
Royal Charter, 9, 16
Rwanda, 244

S

Sabon Gari, 100
Sack of Odi, 115
Sanda, Emirof, 16
Sandhurst, Royal Military Academy, 52, 54, 169
Santa Cruz, 10
Sao Tome, 134, 204–205, 251
Schon, James Frederick, 236
Science Group, 119
Scottish Independence Referendum, 248
Sea Jack, Operation, 156
Seaboard World Airlines, 251
Selassie, Haile, 131
Sclcm, Kam, 69, 104
Shagari, Shehu, 67, 69, 95, 250
Shaw, Flora, 1
Shell-BP, 118
Shell D'arcy, 117
Shelleng, Abdullahi, 79

Shokanlu, Titus, 95
Shuwa, Muhammed, 73, 99, 144
Siege of Leningrad, 198
Siollun, Max, 52–54, 60, 82, 88, 91, 98, 244
Sitting on a man, 230
Slavery Abolition Act, 3
Smith, Arnold, 128
Socialists, 152
Sodeinde, Ralph, 51
Sokei, Louis Chude, 110, 116, 159, 221
Sokoto Caliphate, 13–14, 17–18, 25
Soroh, Nelson, 155
South Sudan Autonomous Region, 248
Southern lady of means, 19
Soviet Union (USSR), 124–125, 134–136, 161, 191, 203, 205, 219, 261
Sowemimo, George Sodeinde, 38
Soyinka, Akinwande Oluwole Babatunde, 45
St. Vincent, West Indies, 10
Stalin, Joseph, 153
State of Emergency, 29, 38, 40, 108–109, 114, 201, 258, 261
Strategic Committee, 139–140, 152, 189
Stratofreighter C-97, 208
Stuart and Davis, 11
Sudan People's Liberation Movement (SPLM), 248–249
Supreme Council of the Revolution, 64
Supreme Military Council (SMC), 73, 76, 88, 92–94, 108–110, 120, 137–138, 243
Survival Edicts, 110–111
Swanton, John, 72

T

Tait, Henry C., 7
Taiwo, Ibrahim, 168
Talakawa, 13
Tanzania, 129
Taxation without representation, 233
Taylor, J. C., 238
Taylor, John Idowu, 37
Telli, Boubacar Diallo, 130
Tenerife, 10
Teshie, 151, 257, 260
Thant, U., 126, 132, 219
Things fall Apart, 102
Third Force, 172, 174–176
Tijani, Sergeant, 86
Timor-Leste, 247
Tiv, 59, 140
Toronkawa Clan, 13
Trimnell, Rudolf, 87
Trinidad and Tobago, 246
Tripoli, 15, 153
Truth and Reconciliation, 244
Tubman, William, 130
Tunisia, 131
Tutsi, 217

U

Ude, Chris, 160, 194
Ude, Goddy, 65
Udeaja, Emmanuel, 52, 57, 170

Uganda, 129, 248–249, 262
Ugboaja, William, 190
Ugboka, Patrick, 85
Ugboma, Louis Victor, 51, 65
Ugokwe, Chukwuma, 225
Ukam, 231
Ukehe, 146, 184, 187
Ukeje, Elendu, 66, 160
Ukiwe, Ebitu, 157
Ukonu, Anyaogu Elekwachi, 46
Uli Airport ("Annabelle'), 205, 240, 250
Umar, Lieutenant, 84
Umuduru, Amaigbo, 7
Umunede-Uromi-Auchi Axis, 165
Umunna, 228
Unegbe, Arthur Chinyelu, 60
United African Company, 6
United Middle Belt Congress (UMBC), 42
United Nations, 32–33, 35, 43, 53, 208–209, 218–219, 251, 256, 258
United Nations High Commissionerfor Refugees, 251
United Nations International Children's Emergency Fund (UNICEF), 199
United NationsUniversal Declaration of Human Rights, 32
United Peoples Grand Alliance(UPGA), 42–46
United People's Party (UPP), 41–42
United States of America, 5, 182, 203, 208, 255
University of Ibadan, 37, 131, 141, 171, 175, 235, 238
University of Lagos, 44, 129
University of London, 26, 238–239
University of Nigeria, Nsukka, 77, 143, 238
University College Hospital (UCH), Ibadan, 84–85
Usman, Baba, 83
Utu-Etim-Ekpo, 231
Utuk, Edet, 196, 218
Uwechue, Raph, 125, 131–133, 226

V

Vatican, 128
Viceroy of British India, 178
Victoria, Queen, 8
von Braun, Werner, 222
von Manstein, Erich, 135
von Rundstedt, Carl Gerd, 135
Vonnegut, Kurt, 235

W

Wada, Inua, 54, 72
Walbe, William, 79, 86
Wallace, William, 16
Waribor, Dag, 72
Warrant Chief, 229–231
Warri, 12, 31, 41, 165–167
Wehrmacht, 134–135, 198
Welby-Everard, Christopher, 44
Wesley College, 26
West African Frontier Force (WAFF), 17–18, 51, 65, 256–260
West African Pilot, 28, 234, 255

West Indies, 4, 10, 246
Western Area Command, 173–175, 177
Wey, Joseph Edet Akinwale, 44, 68
Wey, S. O., 72
Wharton, Henry "Hank", 202
Wild, Wild West, 46
Williams, Rotimi, 75
Willink, Henry, 31
Wilson, James Harold, 177
Winter War (Russo-Finnish), 135
World Council of Churches (WCC), 201–202, 205, 207
World Health Organization (WHO), 199
World War I, 35, 198–199, 210, 263
World War II, 51, 128, 251

Y

Yam, 229
Yar-Adua, Shehu Musa, 59, 83
Yisa-Doko, John, 66
Yola, 16
Yoruba, 14, 26, 29–34, 51–54, 68, 178, 213, 228, 238
Yugoslavia, 245
Yusuf, Muhammad Dikko, 78

Z

Zambia, 129, 246
Zero-Four, Operation, 164
Zhukov, Georgy, 135, 153
Zikist Movement, 223–225

About the Author

Joseph Ogbonna Nnodim is a native of Owerri, Imo State of Nigeria. He was born in Aba, and his early education was in that city, Degema and Owerri. After medical school in Lagos, he pursued doctoral studies in the United Kingdom and also received certification in Switzerland. For over a decade, he was on the faculty of the medical school at Benin City. In the midnineties, he expatriated to the United States of America to take up a position at the University of Michigan. He is a Fellow of the American College of Physicians and the American Geriatrics Society. He and his wife live in the outskirts of Ann Arbor, Michigan. They have many children and grandchildren.

Printed in the USA
CPSIA information can be obtained
at www.ICGtesting.com
JSHW080437290723
45530JS00003B/6